WALKS AROU Buxton

10 WALKS UNDER 6 MILES

DALESMAN

Dalesman Publishing Company Ltd
Stable Courtyard, Broughton Hall,
Skipton, North Yorkshire BD23 3AE

First Edition 1998

Text © Andrew McCloy

Illustrations © Christine Isherwood:
p4 woodcock; p11 knapweed, harebells and ladies' mantle; p14 alder
catkins; p17 pied flycatcher; p22 long tailed tit; p25 bluebells, white
deadnettle and ground ivy; p29 small pearl bordered fritillary; p32
willow warbler.

Cover: Buxton from Solomon's Temple by Karen Frenkel

A British Library Cataloguing in Publication record
is available for this book

ISBN 1 85568 147 1

Printed by Amadeus Press, Huddersfield

Contents

Introduction

Ever since the Romans discovered Buxton's thermal springs in the first century people have been coming to stay in this attractive town high up in the Derbyshire hills. For a long time they came mainly to 'take the waters', and wander sedately around the ornamental gardens. But despite the town's architectural lure and events like the Buxton Festival most of today's visitors have become more adventurous, and if you choose to walk a little further than the Pavilion Gardens there is a wealth of fine scenery waiting to be discovered on Buxton's doorstep.

Although Buxton is not within the Peak National Park the breathtaking hills, moors and valleys are all around, and it is a handy place from which to explore. At around 1,000 feet Buxton is one of the highest towns in England, but you don't have to climb Kinder Scout or embark on a 20-mile hike in order to enjoy the Peak's charms. There are many different

types of walks within easy reach of Buxton, and you may find that some in this book tempt you to return and explore in more detail. If that's the case then make sure to buy an Ordnance Survey Outdoor Leisure map to the White Peak and get walking!

The book begins with two easy walks from the town centre to great local viewpoints and back, then for the next couple we hop over to the Goyt Valley in the west, where there is a variety of valley and moorland walking around two remote reservoirs where motor traffic is often restricted.

To the south of Buxton we switch from gritstone to limestone scenery, from dark moorland to light drystone walls and angular peaks and valleys. The Longnor and Earl Sterndale walks work their way among a stunning landscape that confirms that this is most definitely a 'peak' district.

There are more limestone dales to the east, as the River Wye carves its way from its Buxton source through the plunging hillside. This is also the place for old railway trails and nature reserves, and it is quite simply a naturalist's delight during the spring and summer months. The final walk takes you to a hidden valley north of Buxton, ringed with high moors and edges, and with great views over the High Peak.

Corbar Hill

Short and varied walk from Buxton to a local viewpoint and back.
Length of walk: 2¹/₂ miles.
Start/finish: Pavilion Gardens, Buxton.
Terrain: Easy, surfaced paths, plus some rougher woodland tracks.

Whether your approach is from the town centre shops, car park or railway station, make sure to admire Buxton's architectural splendour before you set off. The Crescent, designed by John Carr of York in the 1780s, includes the Natural Mineral Baths (now home to the tourist information centre), and although it is not open for public use the source of the famous spa waters is on display. As far back as the first century the Romans stayed at Buxton and enjoyed the restorative thermal springs, naming it *Aquae Arnemetiae*, or the Spa of the Goddess of the Grove. The natural springs rise from nearly a mile underground, and maintain a constant 27.5°C all year round.

The walk starts with a gentle amble through the Pavilion Gardens, whose ornamental lakes and gardens, playgrounds, crazy golf, bandstand, miniature railway, etc could keep you occupied for most of the day! Follow the obvious path upstream alongside the River Wye and cross Burlington Road to continue into Serpentine Walks. This leafy, landscaped stretch is particularly pretty, and although there are paths on either bank the right-hand one is probably the nicer. Rejoin the path on the left bank in order to cross St John's Road for the surfaced path diagonally opposite. At the end of the tree-lined green turn right into Gadley Lane, a rough track that crosses the Wye by a footbridge and gently climbs until it joins the driveway of Cavendish Golf Club. Walk past the clubhouse and car park and up the wide track beyond, with the fairways to your left. The track becomes a narrow path alongside the perimeter wall, and watch for mis-driven shots aiming at the nearby green!

The path emerges on Manchester Road (A5004) from where there are terrific views back across the golf course to Burbage Edge. Cross this busy road carefully and turn right, following the pavement for 300 yards until, by a bus stop, a clear path climbs into Corbar Woods on your left. Making sure to keep left at a fork, this easy track climbs the hillside in a series of wriggles to reach a sort of clearing where several paths appear to cross. Although not obvious at first, there is a path straight on through the trees that reaches the top of the woods by a series of steps. But an easier way is to turn left and, keeping the

caravan park below on your left, follow what is soon a distinctive track around the far edge of the woods. After swinging around to the top, with open fields above, you reach a stile in the wall, and a short linking path across fields to the windy pinnacle of Corbar Hill. At 1,433 feet it may not be particularly high, but the views are wide-reaching. The cross fixed on the bare gritstone summit was erected in 1950 by local Roman Catholics.

There is no public access beyond the summit, nor into the fields surrounding, so retrace your steps to the track along the top of the woods and turn left. Follow it to the far corner of the woods, and then down a rather steep slope with wide steps which emerges on a small side road by red railings. In sight at the far end of this is Corbar Road. Turn right, then left into Marlborough Road, then second left into Devonshire Road to end up outside the imposing Palace Hotel and Devonshire Royal Hospital.

For a slightly longer return via Buxton's wide, quiet back streets turn left into Corbar Road, right into Lightwood Road, then immediately after St Ann's School take the alleyway on your right to emerge into Palace Road next to the railway station.

6

Buxton Country Park

**Circular walk from the town centre out to Buxton Country Park, with
a visit to a fascinating natural cave and a hilltop folly.
Length of walk: 3 miles.
Start/finish: Pavilion Gardens, Buxton.
Terrain: Easy, surfaced paths, and more bumpy grass
and woodland tracks.**

Begin your walk by the fabulous glass and iron structures of the Pavilion
and Concert Hall that overlook the Pavilion Gardens in the centre of Buxton.
Nearby is the famous Opera House, which hosts the Buxton Festival (a
series of arts' events) each summer. Go across the River Wye and ahead of
you to join the Broad Walk along the far side of the Gardens. This
thoroughfare was built in the 1850s for the wealthy gentry to enjoy gentle
relaxation, and today it still provides a pleasant lakeside stroll. At the far end
leave the Gardens and go across a multiple road junction for Temple Road
on the opposite side (it is clearly signed). Follow it as it eventually turns left
and cross Green Lane for the entrance to Poole's Cavern.

Poole's Cavern is a natural limestone cave inhabited in the Stone Age, and
is said to be named after an outlaw who lived in the area during the reign of
Henry IV. It is also the source of the River Wye, which flows eastwards from
Buxton to Bakewell until it joins the River Derwent at Rowsley. The cave is
usually open for visitors from Easter to early November. You are now
entering the small but pleasant confines of Buxton Country Park. Take the
stepped path that leads from the car park up into Grinlow Woods, and turn
left on to another path signposted Solomon's Temple. This wide, easy track
makes its way gradually up through the woods. Ignore a smaller path off to
the left, then nearing the top of the woods go right at a fork and emerge on
to the open hilltop. Go over a stile and turn left for the short distance to
Solomon's Temple (also known as Grinlow Tower).

The panoramic view over Buxton and the surrounding countryside is superb
and full of interest. Note the contrast between the darker gritstone moors to
the north and west, typified by the moorland of Axe Edge and Combs Moss,
and the lighter limestone that lies mainly to the south and east – hence the
'Dark' Peak and 'White' Peak. The hilltop features evidence of prehistoric

activity, but more recently was the site of a local lime-burning industry in the 17th and 18th centuries. At that time the hillside was dotted with limekilns, and the outine of an old kiln is still visible on the slope between the tower and the woods. Indeed, the elms, beech and sycamore of Grinlow Woods were planted by the Duke of Devonshire in 1820 in an effort to disguise the unsightly ash tips produced from the lime-burning. At one time the heaps of ash were so great that after rain they would turn into solid masses, and it is reported that some of the very poorest workers at the kilns even cut caves in the solid ash heaps in which they lived for a while. As for the curious little tower on the summit, it is not an ancient Greek temple but a Victorian folly, built by a Buxton man called Solomon Mycock to provide work for the local unemployed.

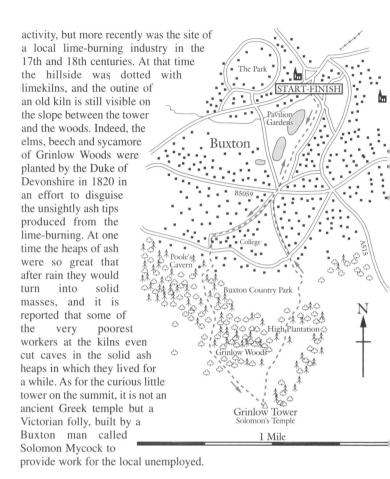

From Solomon's Temple head down the bumpy hillside towards Buxton. Initially make for the white sign which indicates a path into Grinlow Woods, but since this returns to Poole's Cavern ignore it and continue down the open slope to the woods at the very bottom of the hill. Here another path descends through the trees, and on the far side take the narrow, well-walked path directly across the middle of some school playing fields (*not* a public play area). At the far side turn left on to another path which soon comes out at the junction of College Road and Green Lane. Go down the former to return to the Pavilion Gardens, or turn right along Green Lane to finish via the High Street.

Walk 3

Fernilee Reservoir

**Pleasant and easy circuit around this quiet reservoir in the
lovely Goyt Valley.
Length of walk: 4¹/₂ miles.
Start/finish: The Street car park, north west shore of Errwood
Reservoir. Note: there is no entry to the Goyt Valley for cars from the
A537 – approach via the Buxton/Whaley Bridge road (A5004) or via
Lamaload to the west.
Terrain: Mostly gentle forest tracks and easy field paths.**

On most weekends and during the summer the Street car park has the advantage of a resident ice cream van, although Bunsal Cob car park on the far shore has a WC (open in season). So take your pick depending on your needs. From either, make your way down to the dam between the two reservoirs and join the clear path on the western edge that heads gently down to a break in the wall, and beyond towards the part-forested waterside. There is a steeper, alternative path that drops down to the foot of the dam, but this can be quite slippery.

Go over a high stile (or through the gate) and then for more than half a mile follow the easy and attractive path above the shore. There are lovely views across the water towards Long Hill, while the forest around you displays some broadleaf trees such as ash and oak and not just the regimented dark green conifers of the plantation, so that there is a variety of wildlife to be seen. Look out for tiny birds such as great tits and goldcrests that flit about the branches, or treecreepers and nuthatches that run up and down the trunks. In summer you may also see the redstart, with its distinctive black face and throat and bright red and chestnut breast.

At one point a lower path forks off to run above the shore, which you can take if you like since it rejoins the main route as you approach a small ravine that bites into the shoreline. This is known as Deep Clough, and the path is forced uphill where you turn right on to a broad woodland ride that takes you to the far end of the forest. Go over a stile and turn right on to a lane that leads to the dam at the northern end of Fernilee Reservoir. After a pause to admire the views back up the reservoir turn left, for a farm track along the

9

edge of the Goyt Valley. (If you want to shorten the walk by more than a mile and avoid the descent to the valley bottom continue across the dam on the reservoir road and rejoin the walk on the far shore.)

Now that the flooded head of the Goyt Valley is behind you there are much more revealing views of the landscape as it used to look before the reservoirs were built. Fernilee was constructed in 1938 and has a capacity of 935 million gallons. Errwood Reservoir was built in 1967, and together they supply an average of 7-8 million gallons of water for the thirsty residents of Stockport and south-east Manchester every day. Incidentally, the River Goyt flows into the Mersey near Stockport.

A few minutes' walking will bring you to a farm overlooking the valley, and when it appears leave the track and drop down to the gate on your right (it has a dash of yellow paint on it). Go through this and turn left, and keeping what turns out to be Knipe Farm on your left descend diagonally across the field towards a small post in the ground displaying a yellow public footpath arrow. Proceed ahead, with a ditch on your right, and walk towards another helpful little post. This points you through a gate (again with a dab of yellow paint) and down a wide, sunken track that snakes it way down to the bottom of the valley.

Here a number of different paths converge on a footbridge over the tree-lined River Goyt. Further down the bank is a nature reserve managed by Derbyshire

Wildlife Trust, and access is via a stile which leads to a very inviting bench. Altogether this a charming and relaxing place for a spot of lunch!

Go over the footbridge and turn right for an easy and obvious path back to Fernilee Reservoir. It hops over a few stiles, and soon joins the surfaced access road through the reservoir works' buildings and back up by the edge of the massive dam (note the huge overspill channel that runs off below you). Alternatively, you could leave the footbridge over the Goyt for a track across the pasture that heads half-left behind the footpath sign then curves around and up to the right (keep the wall on your left). This climbs to the hamlet of Fernilee, where there is a pub, and a little further along the A5004 the reservoir road will lead you back down to the water's edge.

The return is along the eastern shore of Fernilee Reservoir and is entirely straightforward. The walking could not be easier since the direct and flat route belongs to a former railway line. The Cromford and High Peak Railway was built around 1830 to connect the Cromford Canal near Matlock with the Peak Forest Canal at Whaley Bridge, so providing a link between the coalfields of Derbyshire and Nottinghamshire with the rapidly expanding industrial North West.

The railway was built only because the prospect of constructing a continuous canal across the high and exposed limestone upland of the central Peak District was too difficult and expensive. And because of the peculiar problems of gradient the Cromford and High Peak Railway employed the unusual technique of hauling wagons up and down the most severe inclines by ropes pulled by fixed steam-powered beam engines. No wonder the 33-mile journey took as long as 16 hours. Although passenger services ceased fewer than 40 years later, the line remained open and saw new life transporting limestone from quarries opened alongside the track. It finally closed in 1967, but since then small sections of the former trackbed, such as that along the shore of Fernilee Reservoir, have been opened up for public recreation, most notably the continuous stretch of $17^{1}/_{2}$ miles between Dowlow (south east of Buxton) and High Peak Junction near Cromford. This has been re-opened as the High Peak Trail, a traffic-free route for walkers, cyclists and horse riders.

Walk 4

Errwood Hall

A short circular walk that explores the former Errwood estate.
Length of walk: 2¹/₂ miles.
Start/finish: Errwood Hall car park or, due to road closure, The Street
car park on Sundays, May-Sep, adding an extra 1¹/₄ miles.
Terrain: Easy paths among the trees lower down, but up to Foxlow
Edge and back the ground is much steeper and rougher.

There is an informative noticeboard at Errwood Hall car park giving some
background details on the area, as well as showing the route of some
waymarked woodland walks. Your walk begins by following the path
beyond the notice and aiming for the white-marked post by the gap in the
wall. Turn right on to the main track into the woodland, and immediately
you will notice the lush undergrowth that seems rather out of place in a
remote Derbyshire valley. But more of that in a minute.

The firm track makes its way down the side of the heavily-wooded hillside,
with the valley narrowing all the time. As the ground rises bend sharply right
at a hairpin to emerge by the ruins of Errwood Hall.

Errwood Hall was built in 1830 by the Grimshawe family who lived here
for nearly a century. They seem to have been quite well-off, since the estate
included a school and workers' cottages, and they even developed a small
coal mine in the valley which was worked until 1929. The Grimshawes were
also devout Catholics, with their own chapel and resident priest. Surviving
photos (see the nearby noticeboard) show an impressive main building. But
sadly most of the family died out or moved away, and the hall was
eventually demolished, with some of the stone being used in the
construction of Fernilee Reservoir dam.

A lasting legacy, however, is the thriving foliage of the Grimshawes' former
estate. The pine, rhododendron and azalea plantations were all grown from
seeds brought back as ballast in the family yacht from their many overseas
voyages. It certainly makes the narrow valleys feel luxuriant, and provides
a stark contrast with the bare moors and hillsides above. However, well
before the the Grimshawes imported shrubs and Stockport Corporation
introduced concrete reservoirs the Goyt Valley was a wild, semi-forested

12

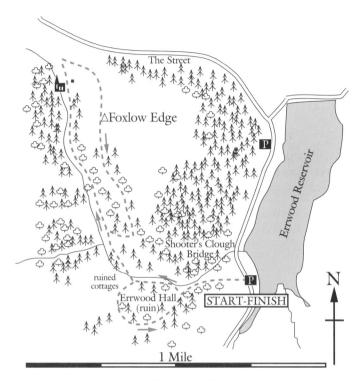

place that in the centuries following the Norman Conquest marked the divide between the Macclesfield Forest in the west and the Royal Forest of the Peak to the east. Across these rough, untamed valleys, wolves and even bears would roam, and noblemen on horseback would hunt wild boar.

From the ruined hall continue up the track until it drops to cross a small stream by (quite easy) stepping stones, then climbs up the opposite bank to reach a junction of paths. Go straight across and up a clear path indicated '2' (all the paths around here are usefully numbered). Initially, it's a steep pull, but before long it levels out and for almost ¾ mile you walk at the foot of the lower slopes of Foxlow Edge on your right, and dense swathes of conifers on your left. Then all of a sudden you come across a most unexpected sight just off the path below you.

The tiny, circular stone building nestling on its own in the hillside is a shrine built by the Grimshawes in 1889 in memory of the family governess, Miss

Delores de Bergrin. Miss Delores, who came from a Spanish aristoratic family and was evidently much loved, died on a trip to Lourdes. The shrine is still tended to this day, and if you venture inside the cool, dark interior you will see an altar, pictures and various other relics distributed around this miniature place of remembrance.

Continue up the main track until the point where it swings left towards the surfaced lane that crosses the moor from Pym Chair down to the reservoirs. Leave the main path by turning right on to a fairly faint grassy path indicated by a low post inscribed '2a', which then continues to swing to the right in order to reach the top of Foxlow Edge. From this high, airy position there are fabulous views towards the High Peak, and closer to home, over Fernilee and Errwood Reservoirs to Combs Moss, Wild Moor and Axe Edge Moor. To your right across the valley plantation the whalebone ridge of Cats Tor and Shining Tor dominates the scene, and with a continuous path joining the tops of both hills perhaps you should pencil that one in for a more adventurous expedition on another day.

Continue along the crest for about half a mile on a fairly well-walked path, which at one point switches to the left of the tumble-down wall. After a while it drops down the bracken covered hillside, hemmed in between the wall and a fence, and after no more than 100 yards turn right through a clear gap in the wall (look for another '2a' post). Follow the short but fairly steep route that cuts back through the trees down to rejoin the main track to the shrine that you took earlier (there are several marker posts to aid direction).

Turn left, back down to the junction of paths above the stepping stones. Here turn right, for a series of wooden steps down to a footbridge then up the other side, and on past the remains of the servants' cottages. (The Grimshawes had a staff of 20.)

At a crossroads of tracks turn left to descend the side of an increasingly wooded valley back towards the old hall. The family cemetery can be visited on the hill to your left; and a set of forlorn but rather stately gateposts testify to the former splendour of this grand but short-lived country residence. Soon you reach the hairpin turn that you took much earlier, but this time continue straight down the track and retrace your steps to the car park.

Shutlingsloe

Circular walk up to a great mini peak, with extensive views over the
surrounding countryside.
Length of walk: 3½ miles.
Start/finish: Clough House car park, near Wildboarclough, about 5
miles south-west of Buxton.
Terrain: Bumpy grass tracks give way to steeper rocky ground towards
the summit, with a small patch of potentially boggy
moorland on the return.

Go out of the car park and picnic site and turn left to walk down the lane
towards the hamlet of Wildboarclough, with the angular shape of
Shutlingsloe above. Branch off to the right for the public footpath
signposted 'Langley via Shutlingsloe'. This attractive and easy grassy track
contours the hillside above a strip of woodland, with open fields above. Go
past Bank Top cottage and join its short drive to the gate at the far end. Here
turn sharply right on to an unfenced track that leads to Shutlingsloe Farm.
In less than 300 yards a sign indicates that the footpath departs to the left
and heads directly up the eastern slopes of Shutlingsloe towards the summit.

After a couple of stiles the path leaves the walled pasture behind and enters
the high, open hillside. Continue uphill on the main path, ignoring a turning
to the right. As the top approaches the ground steepens, and you should
watch your footing among the boulders since erosion has rendered some
sections a little tricky after bad weather. Anyway, there's no need to rush –
pause a moment to get your breath back and enjoy the ever-widening view
down to Wildboarclough, with Crag Hall noticeable on the far side.

Despite its appearance from below, the summit of Shutlingsloe is quite flat
and benign, but at 1,659 feet the panorama is fantastic. (Do bear in mind that
your ascent from what is already a high valley is well under half that figure.)
Near the Ordnance Survey trig point is a view indicator in the rock that
points out some of the main sights visible in clear conditions: Shining Tor
and Axe Edge to the north, with Macclesfield Forest and Tegg's Nose to the
north-west; Croker Hill, with its distinctive transmitter mast, and beyond
that the Cheshire Plains and even the Clwydian Range in Wales (low cloud

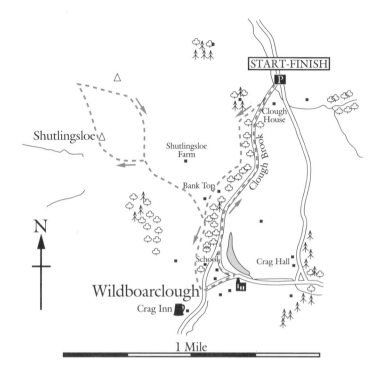

permitting). Southwards lies Staffordshire, with the Roaches, Mow Cop and Tittesworth Reservoir near Leek all in sight in favourable weather.

Once you have had your fill of the views, and possibly your packed lunch, you have two options. Either retrace your steps down Shutlingsloe's eastern face to the fields below (which will take about ³/₄ mile off the distance of the overall walk) or proceed down the far side of the hill for a path back around the northern slopes. This is quite easy at first, since the route follows rough, stone steps down the hillside and then a line of flagstones across the moor by the wall, placed there deliberately to counter the problem of erosion.

At the stile at the far end the path to the left heads across the open moor to Langley via Macclesfield Forest. You should turn sharply right (signposted Wildboarclough), and cross what can be rather wet ground in the direction of a tiny wooden enclosure. Continue straight on, then keeping the summit of Shutlingsloe on your right, the path descends to the bottom of a short gully, with its distinctive bare slopes of dark shale. At the foot of the hillside go half-right to cross a wall by a high stile, and from here the clear path skirts the lower eastern slopes of Shutlingsloe to rejoin the main path down from the summit.

Turn left and follow the path back down to rejoin the farm drive, and instead of turning left by the gate towards the car park keep going straight down the farm track alongside woodland. At the bottom it emerges on a surfaced lane, and if you want to visit the pub (200 yards) or Brookside tea rooms ($^1/_3$ mile) turn right.

Otherwise turn left, then right across a bridge which was rebuilt after it was washed away in 1989 when Clough Brook flooded following heavy rain. In the early 19th century this same stream powered a 30-foot water wheel as Clough Brook was harnessed to provide power for local textile mills. A calico-printing factory called Crag Works was established here, and a small reservoir, Stanley Pool, was also built. This is still behind the church, which is built on the site of the former dyehouse. For several decades Crag Works produced this printed patterned fabric, and especially popular at this time was chintz, involving elaborate Indian and exotic designs. After a while the works switched to printing carpets, but as the Industrial Revolution progressed steam power began to make the old, remote water-based operations obsolete, and in 1860 Crag Works closed.

Walk up the lane as far as St Saviour's Church. The stately building off the road behind the phone box was part of the mill works and later housed the village post office! Further up the lane is Crag Hall, home of the Earl of Derby, and it was his predecessor who ordered the building of the church at the beginning of the 20th century "as a memorial for the safe return of his sons from the South African War", the dedication in the building explains.

Leave the metalled lane by turning left at the church for a track around the edge of the churchyard, and past the old school house and some former mill cottages to rejoin the lane alongside Clough Brook. Follow this all the way back up to the car park.

Longnor

Easy circular walk visiting the upper Dove and Manifold valleys.
Length of walk: 4¹/₂ miles.
Start/finish: Longnor, 6 miles south-east of Buxton.
**Terrain: Gentle and uncomplicated paths, but may be wet and muddy
near the river and farms**

Start the walk at the lovely cobbled main square in Longnor. It is surrounded
by a pleasing number of pubs (all of which welcome walkers), plus a craft
centre/coffee shop in the former Market Hall. Look for the old sign above
the entrance which records the dues once payable by stallholders and buyers
at Longnor Market. The reason for Longnor's prominence and relatively
prosperous appearance is down to its position on the crossroads of local
turnpikes in the 18th century.

Go past the fish and chip shop and out along the Crowdecote road, before
turning left into Dove Ridge at the edge of the village. Where it ends there
are breathtaking views across the Dove valley, and your route is straight on
and down a rough track to the barn below. Leave the track as it bends right
and walk around the left side of the barn to the opposite side, in order to join
the bridleway across wide, valley bottom meadows.

Approaching the river the ground can be a little soft after wet weather, but
the river is safely negotiated by a footbridge known as Beggar's Bridge.
Once across you will have switched from Staffordshire to Derbyshire, since
the River Dove forms the border between the two, although you will soon
change back. At the end of a long, grassy lane on the Derbyshire bank don't
join the surfaced farm drive but instead go over a stile in the wall on the
right for a series of field paths. Keep the wall close on your left, and after a
while you join a farm track via Meadow Farm that emerges on a minor road.
Turn right to enter the small village of Crowdecote, named after the Saxon
Cruda who built a farm on this site. Carry on down the hill past the Pack
Horse Inn and almost immediately turn off left by Toll Bar Cottage for a
short lane to Bridge End Farm.

Before reaching the farm take the track that forks right below the buildings,

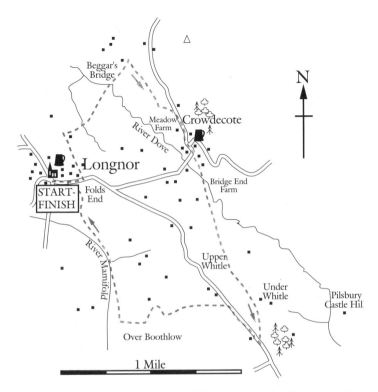

and then at a junction of tracks turn right to re-cross the river by another footbridge (follow the signs for Sheen). On the far side turn half-left, heading, in effect, down the valley, and cross the field, signposted Sheen. There now follows a number of stiles, small footbridges and footpath signs that all guide you through successive fields and up the slowly rising hillside. Initially the infant Dove is quite close by, having carved itself quite a deep and meandering tree-lined course through the valley, but gradually you leave it below and gain height.

At the very far side, below the farm, cross a wall stile to walk along the bottom edge of a field and then turn left into a short but sometimes very muddy farm track between fields towards two barns. Before you reach them take the clearly indicated path over a stile on your right, and follow this past the upper of the two handsome buildings and diagonally up the hillside. Don't be tempted to join a farm track coming up from the valley below, but continue above this before finally crossing the track where it hairpins right. Go over another stile and take the clear path above a wall with fine views up and down the valley. The path stays above the attractive farmhouse of Under Whitle, before joining its drive that leads up to the road that runs along the hilltop.

The young River Dove still wriggles across the narrow valley floor far below, and at the foot of the steep, bare hillside almost opposite you now are Pilsbury Castle Hills. No ruined medieval battlements here, rather something much older. On a small spur of the hill there once stood motte and bailey earthworks, although it is generally agreed that long before the Normans arrived this was probably the site of an Iron Age hillfort. The ground has never been properly excavated, so the mystery of this remote location continues.

Turn right and walk along the wide road that runs along the top of the ridge from Longnor to Sheen. The distinctive bump to the south is Sheen Hill, but far more arresting are the expansive views across the Manifold valley, now spread out before you. Contrast this wide, gentle scene with the more rugged, cramped Dove valley behind. The reason for this difference is, not surprisingly, the underlying rock, since the Manifold flows over soft, clay-based shale, while the Dove carves its way through the far tougher limestone.

After a few minutes of the wind-in-the-hair hilltop sensation you might appreciate turning off to the left through a gate and down a wide, well-used farm track. At the far end go through another gate and straight ahead down the hillside on the rutted track to the *right* of the wall. This soon curves right, above a clump of trees, and once through the gate at the bottom turn left as the signpost directs and down to Over Boothlow Farm. Go through the middle of the farmyard and out along the drive opposite, which leads down to the river (not the other path past the actual farmhouse).

As you approach the River Manifold there are two curiously isolated old stiles either side of the drive. Turn right at these and walk across the open pasture to the gap in the wall at the far side – it is shown by a yellow footpath mark. Then continue in roughly the same direction on a well-walked route through a succession of fields, getting ever nearer to the banks of the river. When the buildings of Longnor loom on the hilltop before you, swing right, through more gaps in walls and more fields, and head for Folds End Farm. The public footpath goes over a stone stile and straight through the middle of the farmyard, returning to the village up the short farm drive.

Earl Sterndale

Circular walk around the upper Dove Valley among fascinating limestone scenery, including a dry valley and two spectacular mini peaks.
Length of walk: 5 miles.
Start/finish: Earl Sterndale, 5 miles south-east of Buxton.
Terrain: Rough field paths and tracks, with the potential for mud after wet weather, and including several steep slopes.

Earl Sterndale is a village literally rooted in the ground: 'Sterndale' means stony ground in Old English, and not only is it surrounded by some small but dramatic limestone peaks but many of its inhabitants also work at the quarries across the ridge to the north. The village pub is called the Quiet Woman, and below its sign is the message 'Soft words turneth away wrath', but why the sign should depict her as headless points perhaps to a more gruesome origin.

Walk around the front of the pub to the right, and turn right again for the path signposted Hollinsclough (not the one to Crowdecote leading off from the rear). Go through some small pens and out over fields. In the first aim half-left for the end of the wall, then maintain this direction through one more, before dropping diagonally across a steep slope to reach the crossing in the wall below, and then on to the road at the far side of the bottom field. Pause as you make your descent into Glutton Dale to appreciate your first views of Parkhouse Hill, a miniature Matterhorn, and the more bulky Chrome Hill beyond. In the course of this walk you will encircle these two fine peaks, formed from the hard and highly resistant reef limestone. The reason for the term 'reef', plus the fact that many of these reef limestone knolls are rich in fossils, indicates that they originated as particular coral-type deposits in the Carboniferous sea around 330 million years ago.

Cross the road carefully, then go over a stile and through the next field on a fairly well-walked path, and around the lower slopes of Parkhouse Hill. After another stile drop down to join an unfenced lane. (Do remember to stick to the path as this is private land – there is no public access to the summit above.) Continue ahead, and as the surfaced lane swings away to the

21

right turn off left for an unmade track through the gateposts of Stannery Farm. Here turn round and have a closer look at the western end of Parkhouse Hill, which culminates in an odd series of jagged rock towers.

Where the farm drive peels off continue on a grassier track straight ahead and stick with this for $^3/_4$ mile until it emerges on the lane into Hollinsclough. The track includes a footbridge crossing of a stream, and an abrupt left-hand turn where another track comes in from the direction of Chrome Hill, sitting impressively above.

Turn right to walk the lane into Hollinsclough, a quiet and unspoiled hamlet which once supported a small silk weaving cottage industry. Turn right by the Methodist Chapel and up the rising lane past some well-restored barns until a public bridleway is signposted off to the right. With great views across the valley, follow this down the grassy hillside, making for the footbridge across the River Dove tucked away at the foot of the slope. Go across and through a curious white metal stile/gate on the far side, then immediately left up the hillside and left again on to a firm track along the northern rim of the valley opposite a high, green ridge called Moor Side. Follow this unmistakable route for about a mile via Fough until you come to a surfaced lane above Booth Farm.

As the fenced lane gently climbs the hillside away from the farm it passes a couple of dew ponds. Typical of limestone and chalk uplands, where surface water drains away quickly, these simple, centuries-old constructions trap the dew and rain and provide a useful source of drinking water for cattle and sheep.

Half-way up the hill a track to Stoop Farm branches off to the right, with glorious views towards Chrome Hill once more. Follow this for 200 yards before a signpost directs you over a stile by the left of two gates and across open fields above the farm. Stay alongside the broken wall and keep the farm buildings and plantation below to your right. Once over the brow of the hill, veer left to the gate in the wall with a public footpath sign. Go through and ahead to turn right on to the mostly unfenced and deserted lane that threads its lonely way across the high upland pasture.

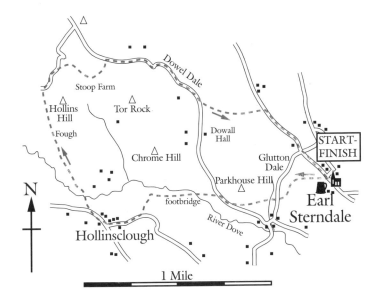

Don't worry about route finding for the next ¾ mile or so, but simply walk down the lane into Dowel Dale. This is a classic dry limestone valley, reminiscent of the Three Peaks area of the Yorkshire Dales. Beyond the cattle grid, on the right, are several sink or swallow holes, where the surface water disappears into the soluble limestone only to reappear further down the valley near Dowall Hall. As you descend you will also notice that the narrowing valley is hemmed in by large, rocky outcrops known in limestone terminology as scars.

Where the lane bends right go over a stile on the left and take the short but steep path up the grassy hillside above. If you fancy a break for refreshments before this exertion then continue down the lane for another 400 yards to the the tearooms at Dowall Hall.

At the top of the steep bank go over stone steps in the wall by a solitary post, and then head through a wide field in the direction of the far left corner. Cross another wall by more stone steps and go down the hillside next to the wall on your right, until at the bottom climb over another stile for the farm track to the road up ahead. Turn right on to this, and head back into Earl Sterndale, going straight over the crossroads at the bottom of Glutton Dale.

Miller's Dale & Monk's Dale

A circular walk incorporating an old railway, a quiet village with a
famous son, and some spectacular limestone dales.
Length of walk: 4 miles.
Start/finish: Miller's Dale station, off B6049, 4 miles east of Buxton.
**Terrain: Variety of paths and tracks, including some steep slopes and
in upper Monk's Dale a very rocky section (but see alternative route).**

Miller's Dale Station was once a thriving station on Midland Railway's
London-Manchester line that crossed the Peak District via Bakewell, and
since the main line did not connect directly with Buxton there was a branch
line connection to the spa town from Miller's Dale, which necessitated the
station having four platforms. In addition, Miller's Dale was one of the few
stations in the country to have a post office on the platform!

The line closed in 1968, but thanks to the efforts of the Peak National Park
part of the former railway line was purchased for the future enjoyment of
walkers and cyclists. Today what's known as the Monsal Trail stretches for
8^{1}/$_{2}$ miles between Blackwell Mill Junction, three miles east of Buxton, and
Combs viaduct, near Bakewell. Four tunnels have had to be closed, but there
are alternative paths. Full details from the Peak National Park Office at
Bakewell or Buxton Tourist Information Centre.

Many of the original station buildings at Miller's Dale have been kept intact,
as have the platforms and two high bridges across the River Wye. There are
picnic tables and toilets (and although there is no tearoom any more the
Wriggly Tin Café opposite the station entrance is generally open weekends,
Feb-Nov). It is worth wandering about for a few moments trying to imagine
what this now quiet place must have been like with all the smoke and noise
of the steam engines. Head west along the former line, signposted Buxton
and Chee Dale, to reach the former East Buxton Lime Kilns. Here limestone
that had been dug out of the huge quarries that scar the upper Wye valley
east of Buxton was burned with coal to produce lime for use in agriculture
and the chemical industry.

The Monsal Trail continues until it reaches a small but impressive viaduct
over the River Wye, and although it's worth admiring the view from the top
do not proceed any further since the tunnel on the far side is closed to the

public. Instead go down the stone steps on the right, and at the bottom turn right to walk along the riverside path towards Chee Dale and Buxton. Make sure to look out for river birds such as grey wagtails (despite its name it has a yellow underside) and the distinctive dipper, often to be found bobbing on a rock amid the fast-flowing water.

The deep limestone valley soon broadens out, and at a footbridge there is a junction of tracks. Ignore the river crossing, and also the tempting footpath ahead to Chee Dale (which becomes very rough and rocky) but instead take the right-hand path uphill signposted Wormhill. As you climb the hillside there are excellent views over the Wye to Blackwell Dale; then at the top the path swings into a small wooded defile and emerges on the road by Chee-Tor Cottage. Turn left and walk into Wormhill. On your left is the Farmhouse Tearoom, offering excellent light refreshments for most of the year (a sign reads: 'Boots welcome - provided your feet are in them'). A few yards ahead across the road is a curious and rather grand stone well, which turns out to be a monument to the great canal engineer James Brindley who was born in nearby Tunstead in 1716.

From the Brindley memorial leave the main street for the lane to St Margaret's Church, and continue past Holly House before going left at an old footpath sign into a short walled passage. At the end go over a stile, and keeping clear of the farmyard on the left cross the field to the gap in the wall and ahead to the far side of the next. Turn right and with the wall on your left walk along this long field to the far end, then half-left across another field to join a grassy, walled track. This is joined by another from the left, and continue along this easy thoroughfare until eventually a gate leads to an open descent down the hillside to the road at the head of Monk's Dale.

Here you have two choices. There is a continuous, walkable path along the whole of Monk's Dale back to Miller's Dale, and in the lower stages the grassy, winding hillside provides easy and pleasurable walking. But for the first half mile it is very different, as the densely-wooded valley floor is strewn with rocks and tree roots, and can be very slippery and very arduous after wet weather. If you're in no hurry and keen to explore then this route is fine, since this is also a National Nature Reserve and there is plenty to see. When the trees eventually end the solitary path climbs the hillside high

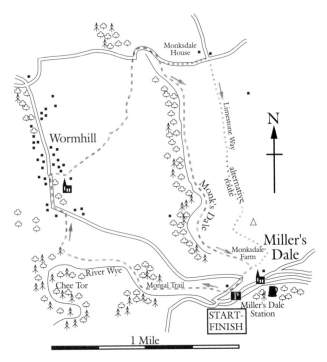

above the stream for a while, and there are great views of what is a real gem of a dale (no coach parties here!). Towards the end of the dale the path switches banks via a footbridge and climbs the far slope, turning right by a National Nature Reserve sign in the wall to reach a row of cottages above. Turn left for the road back down to Miller's Dale Station.

The alternative to Monk's Dale is more straightforward, and for those that enjoy the high limestone plateau and not the cool shade of the valley, then instead of turning right into Monk's Dale go through the gap in the wall and take the road up the far hillside and turn right opposite Monksdale House on to a walled farm lane that heads south for almost a mile (follow signs for the Limestone Way). This easy, airy route finally drops down to pass Monksdale Farm, then little more than 100 yards later turn off right for a steep winding path down to stepping stones below (if the slope or stepping stones present problems simply carry on down the lane from Monksdale Farm to the main road at the bottom and turn right). On the far side of the stream turn left to join the track issuing out of Monk's Dale.

Hay Dale and Peter Dale

Short and very easy circular walk around two dry limestone valleys west of Tideswell.
Length of walk: 4 miles.
Start/finish: Wheston, 4 miles north-east of Buxton.
Terrain: Quiet lanes and straightforward paths, occasionally muddy.

Wheston is a small and unassuming farming village out on the high limestone plateau, and although there is some farm produce for sale locally, if it's teashops and pubs you're after look to Tideswell, 1½ miles to the east. From the centre of Wheston, where there is a small lay-by, walk down the lane as it curves gently left down towards Hay Dale. Just before a gate on the right it bends more acutely, and a few yards after the gate go over a step stile in the wall on your right and join the rough track across the field ahead of you. This gravelly track sticks close to the wall on your left, and affords good views beyond Hay Dale (for the moment tucked away in a cleft of the land at your feet) to Wormhill Moor.

The track finishes at the left-hand end of a line of trees that come marching down the hillside. Go over a wall step-stile by the last tree, not through the gate, and drop gradually down through the field in front of you, making for the lower left corner, and in the next simply walk along the bottom of the pasture with the fence on your left. There are now dramatic views into Hay Dale for the first time. To reach it cross over a wooden stile in the fence at the end of the second field and continuing your general direction descend over the grassy hillside and through a small, thin patch of woodland. After this a faint, grassy path leads you safely and relatively easily down a small rocky chink in the valley side until you finally reach the tree-lined floor. Turn left and walk the obvious path back along the bottom of Hay Dale.

If it was windy on the top it will be calm and still down here, or if it was baking hot across the earlier fields you can now find shade and cool. Hay Dale, and Peter Dale further on, are miniature oases. Two short, narrow dry limestone valleys, they are hidden away and accessible only to walkers, and the more curious and adventurous ones at that. Yet they are both fascinating and peaceful places, rich in wildlife and lime-tolerant plants, and full of fascinating limestone scenery. This will be obvious already, as the absence

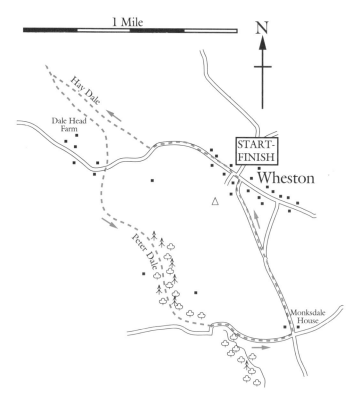

of any surface stream means that it has probably eroded its way between the limestone blocks long ago and even now is trickling along far below. The sides of the dale are dotted with crags, small cliffs and rock scars, where the thin covering of soil has been torn away. Ahead you will also see the remains of a long-abandoned mine cut in the hillside (and if you ventured along Hay Dale in the other direction you would be following the line of the former mine railway). The entrance to the mine is still visible, but don't be tempted to stray too close to the dark opening as these Peak District workings claimed enough casualties when they were active!

As Hay Dale draws to a close you cross a couple of stiles before turning right into a narrow lane, then almost immediately left for a wide dale bottom path that continues all the way through Peter Dale. As you leave the lane by the signpost to Miller's Dale you may notice a waymark disc depicting a ram's head and horns attached to the post. This refers to the Limestone Way, which you are following all the way through Hay Dale and Peter Dale (and which can also be sampled in Walk 8). The Limestone Way began as a 28-mile long distance footpath from Matlock to Castleton, but in 1994 was extended to almost twice that distance by an extension south to Rocester in Staffordshire, plus an additional spur to Ashbourne. A guidebook to the route is available from local bookshops.

The most striking first impression of Peter Dale is the wooded cliffs that guard the northerly entrance, with another tier further up the hillside. Soon both sides of the dale are lined with intermittent rock and cliff, and there is evidence of previous rock falls with boulders lying about the path. If you look up at some of the rocky faces you will see small trees and saplings that are clinging on desperately to what soil is left, and growing at some curious angles. Lower down, in both Hay Dale and Peter Dale, there are plenty of flowers and plants to be seen during spring and summer. It's a good idea to take a simple identification book, because you may find the likes of cranesbill, herb robert, cow parsley, foxglove and red campion, plus various vetches and orchids. In summer, these attract a host of colourful butterflies.

The dale opens out a little where another tributary valley enters from the right, and at the far side of this continue through the gateposts of a semi-ruined wall on what soon becomes a much more rocky path that swings left through a narrow gap towards Monk's Dale. A noticeboard explains that you are now entering Monk's Dale National Nature Reserve, and that long ago a secret tunnel supposedly linked this hidden valley with the church in nearby Tideswell, possibly to provide a hideaway or a means of escape in times of trouble.

Across an area of open pasture you reach the lane that separates Peter Dale and Monk's Dale. Turn left on to this road, which climbs sharply out of the dale back on to the limestone upland. At Monksdale House turn left by the isolated building for a single-track, walled lane across fields which include a couple of dew ponds. There are particularly good views west towards Hargatewall and Wormhill. After about $^1/_3$ mile, where the lane bends to the right, go straight ahead on a wide, unsurfaced farm track that takes you back to the centre of Wheston.

Combs

Circular tour of a quiet valley north of Buxton, with fine views
towards the High Peak of Kinder Scout.
Length of walk: 4 miles.
Start/finish: Beehive Inn in Combs, 3 miles north of Buxton.
Terrain: Undulating tracks and lanes, plus several steep, grassy
ascents through fields which may be boggy in places.

Combs is a quiet, rather hidden-away village near Whaley Bridge, north of
Buxton. It is locally pronounced 'Coombs', rather than the toothed device
you use on your hair. The area does not attract walkers and other visitors in
quite the same number as the likes of the Goyt Valley and Kinder Scout,
which is fine since you won't be disturbed too much and they are all missing
out on a most delectable spot for walking.

With the Beehive Inn behind you leave the centre of the village for the
gently climbing lane to Dove Holes. After several rows of cottages, and a
partially hidden pond in trees, turn off the road to the right for Rye Flatt
Farm, and keeping to the left of the farmhouse and its large barn take a semi-
sunken fenced lane through fields. In the distance, above as much as ahead,
is the high and dominating ridge of Combs Moss. Up to your left is Combs
Edge, whose rocky shelves and crags are popular with climbers. At the far
end, remains of an Iron Age hillfort have been discovered (what a great
lookout spot!). The easy track from Rye Flatt Farm strides out confidently
for $^1/_3$ mile until it bears left into Allstone Lee Farm. At this point carry
straight on, over a stile and a plank footbridge by a signpost to White Hall,
and with the ditch and field edge on your right walk down the open pasture.

Where the fence on your right falls away, by a solitary old stone gatepost,
carry straight on through the wide but sometimes boggy field to the stream at
the bottom, and cross this by a plank footbridge. Cross the bottom of another
field and another stream. On the far side go straight on and up a short bank
to a stile in the wall above. Keep going straight on, with the wall on your right
and over the field falling away to the stream on your left. Go through an old
gate entrance in the wall and across an open field, aiming for the left-hand
end of another dark stone wall. Then, with the wall on your right for a few
yards, go through a gateway and up the field towards the telephone posts.

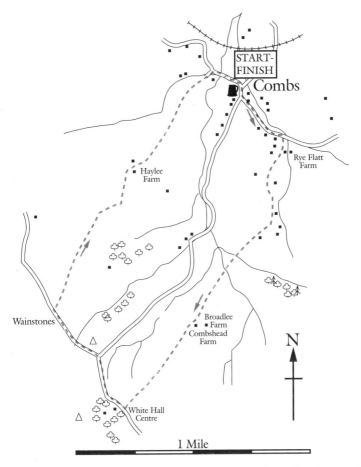

START-FINISH

Combs

Rye Flatt
Farm

Haylee
Farm

Wainstones

Broadlee
Farm

Combshead
Farm

N

White Hall
Centre

1 Mile

Across the fence on your left are Combshead Farm and Broadlee Farm, and cross over the end of their driveway for a steep pull up a grassy bank ahead.

For large parts of this walk – like here – there is no defined path, but the route remains obvious, with stiles and gates as well as signposts all the way along. From the farm drive pull steadily up the hillside, drifting gradually left over to the fence above a gully on the left. Eventually go over a wooden stile in the fence and continue uphill with the wall on your right. Once through an old wooden gate White Hall comes into sight among trees, and the ascent is almost over. Now the wall switches to your left, and the ground can be a little boggy in a couple of places where the water drains off the bulk of Combs Moss. At the far side go over a stile and into the hilltop lane. Before you go any further take a look over the wall opposite at the splendid views south westwards to the Upper Goyt Valley and Shining Tor.

Now head down the lane past White Hall, an outdoor pursuits centre run by Derbyshire County Council. Near its gateway a bridleway is indicated off to the left, and if you have the time or energy you may choose to walk this as far as the top of the ridge for the views down to the Goyt reservoirs (see Walks 3 and 4). You may also notice on the signpost that this is the route of the recently-created Midshires Way, a 225-mile bridleway route that runs

from Bledlow in the Chilterns all the way north to Stockport.

From opposite the entrance to White Hall carry on along the quiet lane, which was formerly the Romans' route from Buxton to Manchester. Ignore a tempting turning back down to Combs and walk for half a mile as far as a stile on the right opposite Wainstones. Go over this and past some fallen-down

buildings and take the clear, grassy track beyond that heads through a gate and out along the hillside. The views from this lofty position are wonderful. Combs Moss and Combs Edge dominate the skyline across the valley, while immediately below is Combs and its nearby reservoir, and beyond the village is the much larger settlement of Whaley Bridge. But astride the horizon like a colossus is Kinder Scout, that barren plateau that dominates the Dark Peak and is, at more than 2,000 feet, the high point of the Peak National Park. The Pennine Way struggles up and over the huge barrier from Edale, amid weird formations of rock and deep trenches or 'cloughs' in the featureless expanses of peat that makes walking on Kinder Scout such a fascination and a challenge.

Meanwhile, on much safer ground, the grassy track drifts down towards a wall, with improved pasture beyond. Don't enter this, but follow the rutted track downhill with the field on your left, and at its foot turn left and walk below the line of a long-fallen-down wall. Soon you join a narrowing walled passage that comes out at Haylee Farm. Go through the gate, and simply follow the pleasant lane as it winds its way down past several groups of buildings. It then becomes a lovely tree-lined affair, accompanied by a gurgling brook, and takes you all the way back to the road at the bottom, where you should turn right to return to Combs.

TREATISE ON AWAKENING MAHĀYĀNA FAITH

OXFORD CHINESE THOUGHT

Series Editors
Eric L. Hutton and Justin Tiwald

Zhu Xi: Selected Writings
Edited and translated by Philip J. Ivanhoe

Treatise on Awakening Mahāyāna Faith
Edited and translated by John Jorgensen, Dan Lusthaus,
John Makeham, and Mark Strange

TREATISE ON AWAKENING
MAHĀYĀNA FAITH

Edited and translated by John Jorgensen,

Dan Lusthaus, John Makeham

AND

Mark Strange

OXFORD
UNIVERSITY PRESS

OXFORD
UNIVERSITY PRESS

Oxford University Press is a department of the University of Oxford. It furthers
the University's objective of excellence in research, scholarship, and education
by publishing worldwide. Oxford is a registered trade mark of Oxford University
Press in the UK and certain other countries.

Published in the United States of America by Oxford University Press
198 Madison Avenue, New York, NY 10016, United States of America.

Library of Congress Cataloging-in-Publication Data
Names: Jorgensen, John, 1952– translator.
Title: Treatise on Awakening Mahāyāna Faith /
translated by John Jorgensen, Dan Lusthaus, John Makeham and Mark Strange.
Other titles: Dasheng qixin lun. English
Description: New York, NY, United States of America :
Oxford University Press, [2019] | Series: Oxford Chinese thought |
Includes bibliographical references and index.
Identifiers: LCCN 2018052190 (print) | LCCN 2019013667 (ebook) |
ISBN 9780190297725 (updf) | ISBN 9780190297732 (epub) |
ISBN 9780190297701 (cloth : alk. paper) | ISBN 9780190297718 (pbk. : alk. paper)
Subjects: LCSH: Mahayana Buddhism. | Dasheng qixin lun.
Classification: LCC BQ7374 (ebook) | LCC BQ7374.D3713 2019 (print) |
DDC 294.3/42042—dc23
LC record available at https://lccn.loc.gov/2018052190

1 3 5 7 9 8 6 4 2

Paperback printed by Marquis, Canada
Hardback printed by Bridgeport National Bindery, Inc., United States of America

CONTENTS

MAPS

SERIES EDITORS' PREFACE

ERIC L. HUTTON AND JUSTIN TIWALD

Chinese writings from premodern times constitute a vast body of texts stretching back over 2,500 years, and while Western studies of China have been growing, many riches from the Chinese tradition have remained untranslated or have been given only partial translations, sometimes scattered across multiple publication venues. This situation obviously poses a problem for those who want to learn about Chinese thought but lack the ability to read Chinese. However, it also poses a problem even for scholars who specialize in Chinese thought and can read Chinese, because it is not easy to read across all the time periods and genres in the Chinese corpus. Not only did the Chinese language change over time, but in some genres particular vocabularies are developed and familiarity with certain earlier texts—sometimes quite a large number of texts—is presumed. For this reason, scholars who focus on one tradition of Chinese thought from a given era cannot simply pick up and immediately understand texts from a different tradition of thought in another era. The lack of translations is thus an impediment even to specialists who can read Chinese but wish to learn about aspects of Chinese thought outside their normal purview. Furthermore, scholars are often hampered in their teaching by the lack of translations that they can assign to students, which then becomes a barrier to promoting greater understanding of Chinese history and culture among the general public.

By offering English translations of Chinese texts with philosophical and religious significance, Oxford Chinese Thought aims to remedy these problems and make available to the general public, university students, and scholars a treasure trove of materials that has previously been largely inaccessible. The series focuses on works that are historically important or stand to make significant contributions to contemporary discussions, and the translations seek to strike a reasonable balance between the interests of specialists and the needs of general readers and students with no skills in Chinese. Translators for the series are leading scholars and experts in the traditions and texts that they render, and the volumes are meant to be suitable for classroom use while meeting the highest standards of scholarship.

The present volume, *Treatise on Awakening Mahāyāna Faith*, is itself a treasure trove of historical, philosophical, and religious insight. The avowed aim and purpose of the *Treatise* is to establish faith in the soundness and efficacy of the Mahāyāna Buddhist path, which it accomplishes in part by setting forth a framework for much of Buddhist metaphysics and psychology, reconciling what had largely been competing views about the nature of mind, consciousness, the buddha-nature, the phenomenal world of arising and ceasing, and the sources of ignorance and falsehood. The *Treatise* is without question one of East Asia's most influential philosophical and religious texts. From the late sixth century CE to the present day, it has been the subject of over three hundred commentaries and has been invoked by countless Buddhist thinkers as an authority on doctrine and practice. It is often credited with shaping the schools and lineages of Buddhism that are most distinctively East Asian, including Huayan and Chan (in Japanese, Zen). This translation was conducted by a team of leading Buddhologists and specialists in Chinese thought, and is accompanied by a substantial introduction as well as several other supporting tools, including glossaries, that should be of use both to novice learners and established scholars of Buddhism alike. We hope and expect that students and scholars and even non-academic Buddhist practitioners will find it an indispensable window into some of the most stimulating and important developments in the history of Buddhism.

ACKNOWLEDGMENTS

This translation began as an ANU Literary Chinese Reading Group exercise in 2012. Since then, the project has grown considerably in scope and complexity. We would like to thank John Powers for his contributions to the Reading Group; Jason Clower for his input at the workshops; and the Chiang Ching-kuo Foundation for International Scholarly Exchange for funding our research on the doctrinal and exegetical strategies employed in key commentaries on the *Treatise*. We extend a particular note of gratitude to Keng Ching for his generous contributions to the introduction and his valuable constructive feedback on the draft translation.

EDITORS AND TRANSLATORS

John Jorgensen is a senior research associate in the China Studies Research Centre at La Trobe University. A specialist in Chinese, Japanese, and Korean Chan Buddhism, he taught at Griffith University in Queensland and was a researcher at The Australian National University before taking up his current role at La Trobe University.

Dan Lusthaus, a leading scholar of Yogācāra Buddhism, has published extensively on Indian, Chinese, and Japanese philosophy. He has taught at UCLA, University of Illinois Champaign-Urbana, and Boston University, and has been a research associate at Harvard University since 2005.

John Makeham is chair and director of the China Studies Research Centre at La Trobe University. He is a specialist in the intellectual history of Chinese philosophy. Educated in Australia, China, Taiwan, and Japan, he has held academic positions at Victoria University of Wellington, University of Adelaide, National Taiwan University, Chinese University of Hong Kong, and The Australian National University.

Mark Strange is a senior lecturer at The Australian National University. Before moving to Australia, he taught at the University of Warwick, University of Oxford, and University of Cambridge. His research focuses on the intellectual and political history of medieval China.

ABBREVIATIONS

T   *Taishō shinshū Daizōkyō* 大正新修大藏經 (*Taishō* Revised *Tripiṭaka*), edited by Takakusu Junjirō 高楠順次郎 and Watanabe Kaigyoku 渡邊海旭 et al. (Tokyo: Taishō issaikyō Kankōkai, 1924–1934)

X   *Dai Nihon zokuzōkyō* 大日本續藏經 (Kyoto Supplement to the Canon), CBETA Chinese Electronic Tripiṭaka Collection edition, Taipei, www.cbeta.org

ABOUT THE COMPANION WEBSITE

http://global.oup.com/us/companion.websites/9780190297718

Oxford has created a website to accompany the *Treatise on Awakening Mahāyāna Faith*, where the full Chinese text is provided. The reader is encouraged to consult this resource in conjunction with the English translation.

Introduction

Appearing in sixth-century China, the *Dasheng qixin lun* 大乘起信論, *Treatise on Awakening Mahāyāna Faith,* has been one of the most important texts of East Asian Buddhism between the late sixth century—soon after it started to circulate—and the present. Conceptual structures derived from the *Treatise* became a shared resource for East Asian philosophers and religious theorists over centuries. Over three hundred commentaries were written on it in East Asia before 1900. It was crucial in the development of the Sinitic Buddhist schools of Huayan and Chan (Japanese Zen), and had some importance in Tiantai and Pure Land. The text was attractive because it was concise and relatively comprehensive. It seemed to resolve tensions and disparities between competing forms of Buddhist doctrine and practice, providing a model for later schools to harmonize teachings and sustain the idea that, despite different approaches, there was only one doctrine, or Dharma. It provided a theoretical basis for practice and stressed the importance of faith for beginners or those not yet committed to Mahāyāna Buddhism.[1]

---

1. For a convenient, introductory overview of such topics as traditional and modern commentaries, Western-language translations, and modern philological and historical studies on the *Treatise*, see Jason Clower, "The Awakening of Faith," in Richard K. Payne, ed., *Oxford Bibliographies in Buddhism* (New York: Oxford University Press, 2013).

1. THE TITLE OF THE TEXT

As indicated by the title, *Treatise on Awakening Mahāyāna Faith*, this text is about the first steps a Mahāyāna Buddhist needs to take, namely an initiation of faith, a conviction that Mahāyāna teachings are correct and effective and therefore should be practiced. Without this faith, there would be no grounds for practice. The *Treatise* outlines a theoretical framework of the psychological mechanisms that enable a deluded person to become enlightened.

The title *Dasheng qixin lun* comprises three components: *Dasheng* 大乘 (Great Vehicle); *qixin* 起信 (giving rise to faith or trust); and *lun* 論 (treatise). *Dasheng* is the Chinese translation of *Mahāyāna*, a Sanskrit term designating the schools of Buddhism that center their concerns on becoming a bodhisattva, with the possibility of eventually becoming a buddha in some future life. Mahāyāna texts speak of the practitioners of three different vehicles, or methods of practice: (1) *Śrāvaka*s (hearers) who, according to Mahāyāna understanding, follow the teachings of disciples of the Buddha who heard his earlier, simplified, low-level teaching. Their goal is to become arhats, awakened beings who attain nirvana but are not buddhas. (2) *Pratyekabuddha*s (solitary buddhas), who become fully awakened on their own, outside any Buddhist lineage. (3) Bodhisattvas (beings pursuing awakening).

The Mahāyāna claim was that the enlightened people of the Lesser Vehicle,[2] such as arhats, worked only for their own salvation,

---

2. *Xiaosheng* 小乘 (Lesser Vehicle), signifying Hīnayāna, was the pejorative label with which Mahāyānists branded non-Mahāyāna Buddhists. In India, Mahāyāna believers were a minority. In China, however, Mahāyāna was introduced by the translator Lokakṣema between 166 and 188 CE and was confirmed as the dominant form of Buddhism in China by the translations of Kumārajīva (344–413) between 401 and 409. It was almost unheard of for anyone other than visiting Indian monks in East Asia to claim to be a follower of the Lesser Vehicle from this time on, even though many of the meditative practices and monastic regulations (*vinaya*) used were in fact those of the mainstream Lesser Vehicle in

while enlightened people of the Greater Vehicle, bodhisattvas, worked for the salvation of others. Bodhisattvas reached their goal by practicing the *pāramitās* (perfections, or in a Chinese understanding, those practices that deliver one to the other shore of enlightenment or buddhahood). The *Treatise* explains that Mahāyāna is the comprehensive teaching that provides a practical pathway to enlightenment. Those capable of becoming buddhas first need to arouse the aspiration for awakening, and the author claims to target beginners who have not yet aroused that basic aspiration.

The implication of the term *qixin*, awakening or giving rise to faith, is key to understanding the project that the text lays out for itself. To become a bodhisattva, in pursuit of full awakening, one must embark upon the Mahāyāna bodhisattva path. In sixth-century China, this was mapped onto ten levels of practice, or *bhūmis* (see the discussion of Ten *Bhūmis* below). At various points the *Treatise* directly alludes to these levels and indicates which practices and achievements occur at which levels.

Qixin is an invitation to enter the early bodhisattva levels. According to the *Treatise*, to enter the first level of the bodhisattva path one must aspire to proper faith. From that moment on, practice replaces faith with knowledge, as one confirms what had been merely hypothetical at the faith level. One aspires to enlighten oneself and to enlighten all sentient beings, and that remains one's primary concern. This aspiration is first articulated in the *Treatise* in its Prayer of Homage:

I wish to have sentient beings
Eliminate doubts and abandon wrongly-held views

India. On the introduction of Mahāyāna in the second century CE, see Erik Zürcher, *The Buddhist Conquest of China: The Spread and Adaption of Buddhism in Early Medieval China* (Leiden: Brill, 1959), p. 35. The term Hīnayāna does not appear in the *Treatise* and we use it only to clarify the standard doxography.

And give rise to correct Mahāyāna faith,
Leaving the buddha-lineage uninterrupted.

The author's main purpose is to instill faith, *xin* 信 (a common translation of the Sanskrit term *śraddhā*), in the minds of neophytes. Modern scholars have debated the meaning of "faith" in Buddhism, and in particular how best to understand the significance and role of the term *śraddhā*. Two basic ideas have predominated. One is that Buddhism, since its inception, was an *ehipaśyika*— "come and test it"—tradition. *Śraddhā* was the initial attitude needed to test it earnestly. It is a hypothetical stance with which one tests claims in order to confirm or to deny them. Once confirmed, the hypothetical stance is replaced with the knowledge that what was previously believed to be a probability is now certain. A Buddhist practitioner might believe that Buddhist tenets are true and effective; a buddha knows that they are so because he has confirmed their veracity. The other interpretation of *śraddhā* is that, like the Chinese term *xin* 信 with which it is rendered, its meaning is closer to "trust" than to western religious ideas of faith as something other than knowledge of matters intrinsically immune from rational proof. The *Treatise* explicitly states that it is addressing those who are currently undecided, attempting to instill in them the desire to pursue the path. In sum, giving rise to, or awakening, Mahāyāna faith refers to having the initial faith or trust that the methods and practices of the Mahāyāna Buddhist path will work and are worth pursuing.

A *lun* 論 is a "treatise." Any text that did not purport to be a sutra or a record of a discourse given by the Buddha could be called a *lun*. Although the term *lun* roughly overlaps with the Sanskrit *śāstra*, which also means "treatise," many Indian texts that did not include *śāstra* in their title still received the label *lun* in their Chinese translations.

Finally, we return to the term *dasheng,* Mahāyāna, in the title. The titles of many texts in the Chinese Buddhist canon begin with *dasheng* as a classifier, even when that was not part of an actual Sanskrit title. It informs a reader of the affiliations that a particular text holds, and it indicates to archivists where in the library they should store that text. Similarly, there are titles that begin with *xiaosheng* 小乘, which no non-Mahāyāna Buddhists would attach to the titles of their own texts. When Mahāyāna does appear in a Sanskrit title, translators took care to distinguish this actual appearance of Mahāyāna in the title from other titles in which *dasheng* was merely added as a classifier. So the Chinese title for Asaṅga's (fourth century CE) *Mahāyānasaṃgraha-śāstra* is *She dasheng lun* 攝大乘論 (Compendium of Mahāyāna), sandwiching the *dasheng* between *she* (= *saṃgraha,* "compendium") and *lun,* "treatise."

The author of the *Treatise* appears to have been unaware that *dasheng* was used as a classifier. Instead, he explicitly treats it in the body of his treatise as an intrinsic part of the text's title and program. This is one of many strong hints that the *Treatise* was not a translation of an Indian original, but a Chinese creation pretending to be a translation by a prominent translator of an Indian text by an Indian figure who had assumed major importance at the time.

2. THE AUTHENTICITY AND AUTHORSHIP OF THE TEXT

The authorship of the *Treatise* was attributed to Aśvaghoṣa (ca. first century CE).[3] It was supposedly translated by Paramārtha, an Indian

---

3. In China, Aśvaghoṣa was widely thought of as a bodhisattva—an epithet closely associated with Mahāyāna in the Chinese tradition—who could bridge the chronological chasm between the historical Buddha and sixth-century China. See, for example, Stuart H. Young, *Conceiving the Indian Buddhist Patriarchs in China* (Honolulu: University of Hawaii Press,

translator-monk who arrived in south China in 546 and stayed south of the Yangzi River until his death in 569.[4] An early skeptic was the Baekje monk, Hyegyun 慧均 (fl. 570s), who claimed that the work had been forged by Dilun masters (on the Dilun school see "Debates between Shelun and Dilun Schools" below), in North China, probably at Ye 鄴 (modern Anyang, northern Henan Province).[5] In 594, a cataloguer questioned whether the *Treatise* had been translated by Paramārtha.[6] After 594, however, the attributions to Aśvaghoṣa and Paramārtha remained largely unchallenged. It was not until the first decade of the twentieth century that the attributions were again seriously questioned and there began a sustained debate over the provenance of the text.

There is now wide consensus that the author of the *Treatise* was strongly influenced by the terminology and language of Bodhiruci (d. ca. 535), a translator-monk who came to north China in 508.[7] Where Bodhiruci and Paramārtha use different Chinese equivalents for a Sanskrit term or phrase, the *Treatise* tends to follow Bodhiruci. Between 508 and around 535, Bodhiruci and Ratnamati (fl. early

2015), pp. 130–134, 221, *passim.* The historical Aśvaghoṣa, however, seems to have been unaware of even the existence of Mahāyāna. Indeed, Aśvaghoṣa has no Mahāyāna tendencies in his attested writings.

4. Diana Y. Paul, *Philosophy of Mind in Sixth-Century China: Paramārtha's "Evolution of Consciousness"* (Stanford, CA: Stanford University Press, 1984), pp. 22–37. A thorough study can be found in Funayama Tōru 船山徹, "Shintai sanzō no katsudō to chosaku no kihonteki tokuchō" 真諦三蔵の活動と著作の基本的特徴 (Fundamental Characteristics of the Activities and Works of Paramārtha), in Funayama Tōru, ed., *Shintai sanzō kenkyū ronshū* 真諦三蔵研究論集 (Studies of the Works and Influence of Paramārtha) (Kyoto: Kyōto daigaku jinbunkagaku kenkyūsho, 2012), pp. 1–86.

5. Hyegyun, *Daseung saron hyeonui gi* 大乘四論玄義記 (Record of the Profound Meanings of the Four Treatises of Mahāyāna), cited in Chinkai 珍海 (1092–1152), *Sanron genso bungi yō* 三論玄疏文義要 (Essentials of the Meaning of the *Profound Commentary on the Three Treatises*). T70.2299, 228c18–24.

6. Fajing 法經 (fl. 594) et al., *Zhongjing mulu* 衆經目錄 (Catalogue of Scriptures). T55.2146, 142a16.

7. Our annotations to the translation identify specific examples.

sixth century), another monk from India, translated Yogācāra and Tathāgatagarbha texts from Sanskrit into Chinese under an imperially sponsored project.[8] Bodhiruci translated the *Laṅkāvatāra-sūtra* (*Ru Lengqie jing* 入楞伽經), a fluid and evolving text that mixed Yogācāra and Tathāgatagarbha themes; and Vasubandhu's *Daśabhūmi-vyākhyāna/Daśabhūmika-sūtra-śāstra* (*Shidi jing lun* 十地經論; Commentary on the Discourse on the Ten Levels [of the Bodhisattva Path]),[9] or *Dilun* 地論 for short. Both translations contributed to the teachings found in the *Treatise*.

One theory is that the *Treatise* was written by someone in Bodhiruci's circle. Some contemporary Japanese scholars maintain that the author of the *Treatise* used ideas and terms from the *Jin'gangxian lun* 金剛仙論 (Treatise of *Vajrarṣi), a lecture series probably composed by Bodhiruci around 534.[10] One scholar argues that Huiyuan quoted the *Treatise* around 549.[11] If so, that would

8. Yogācāra (*Yuqie xing pai* 瑜珈行派; yogic practice) is one of the two most influential philosophical systems of Indian Buddhism, along with Madhyamaka. Other names for the Yogācāra school include the Way of Consciousness (Vijñānavāda), and Nothing but Consciousness (Vijñapti-mātra). *Tathāgatagarbha* means the repository of a buddha, the potential to achieve buddhahood; and the *tathāgatagarbha* doctrine is the idea that buddha-nature exists in all sentient beings. The doctrine had a profound influence on the development of East Asian Buddhism but its origins lie in India. The Tathāgatagarbha tradition in Mahāyāna Buddhism is associated with a cluster of texts, central to which is the *tathāgatagarbha* doctrine. For an overview of these texts, see Michael Radich, "Tathāgatagarbha Sūtras," in Jonathan Silk, Oskar von Hinüber, and Vincent Eltschinger, eds., *Brill's Encyclopedia of Buddhism*, Volume One: Literature and Languages (Leiden: Brill, 2015), pp. 261–273.

9. The ten levels through which a bodhisattva proceeds on the way to buddhahood. This work, translated by Bodhiruci and Ratnamati, is a commentary on the "Shidi pin" 十地品 (Ten Levels) chapter of the *Huayan jing* 華嚴經.

10. Ōtake Susumu 大竹晋, "Yugagyōha bunken to *Daijō kishin ron*" 瑜伽行派文献と大乗起信論 (Yogācāra Documents and the *Treatise on Awakening Mahāyāna Faith*), *Tetsugaku shisō ronsō* 哲学・思想論叢 (Chikuba daigaku tetsugaku shisō gakkai), 20 (2002): pp. 49–62, esp. p. 49. This lecture series recorded in *Jin'gangxian lun* is on verses attributed to Vasubandhu concerning the *Diamond Sutra* (*Jin'gang bore boluomi jing* 金剛般若波羅蜜經; *Vajracchedikā-prajñāpāramitā-sūtra*).

11. Okamoto Ippei 岡本一平, "Jōyō ji Eon ni okeru shoki no shikiron" 淨影寺慧遠における初期の識論 (Early Theories of the Consciousnesses by Huiyuan

date the composition of *Treatise* to between approximately 535 and 549, place its origins in Ye, and identify its author as a member of Bodhiruci's translation team. One candidate for authorship under this theory is Tanlin 曇林 (d.u.), an amanuensis of Bodhiruci and a scholar of Tathāgatagarbha material.

Debates continue over the provenance of the *Treatise*, and even over whether it was a translated Indian text or a Chinese composition. It is, however, now clear that the text was strongly influenced by the works of Bodhiruci and was in existence by the 580s in north China.

3. HISTORICAL AND INTELLECTUAL CONTEXTS

In the first third of the sixth century, China was divided into the states of Northern Wei in the north, and Liang in the south (see Map 1). The Buddhism of the north is frequently characterized as focused on meditation and devotion, and that of the south as scholastic. The main texts studied in the south were the *Mahāparinirvāṇa-sūtra* (*Da banniepan jing* 大般涅槃經; Nirvana Sutra), which introduces the buddha-nature and Tathāgatagarbha doctrines, and Harivarman's (c. fourth century CE), **Tattvasiddhi-śāstra* or *Satyasiddhi-śāstra* (*Chengshi lun* 成實論; Treatise on the Demonstration of the Truth), a work amenable to Madhyamaka and especially Yogācāra concepts. In the north, from the early 500s, the main texts studied were the *Avataṃsaka-sūtra* (*Huayan jing* 華嚴經; Flower Garland Sutra)—a foundational text of the Huayan school of Mahāyāna Buddhism—and from 508, the *Dilun*.

of Jingying Monastery) in Geumgang Daehak bulgyo munhwa yeon'guso 金剛大学佛教文化研究所, comp., *Jironshū no kenkyū* 地論宗の研究 (Studies of the Dilun School) (Tokyo: Kokusho kankōkai, 2017), pp. 533–535, 541, 547.

Map 1 States of Northern Wei and Liang in the first third of the sixth-century. *Credit: CartoGIS Services, ANU College of Asia and the Pacific, The Australian National University*

By the 530s, the political situation had deteriorated. North China had split into the rival states of Western and Eastern Wei, followed several decades later by Northern Zhou and Northern Qi (see Map 2). In the southern state of Liang, civil war erupted in the late 540s and was followed by the founding of the state of Chen. Conflict was frequent and widespread in both the north and the south. The monastery site of the massive translation project headed by Bodhiruci in Luoyang, the former capital of Northern Wei, was repeatedly

Map 2 States of Chen, Northern Zhou, and Northern Qi in the mid-sixth-century. *Credit: CartoGIS Services, ANU College of Asia and the Pacific, The Australian National University*

occupied by troops. This led to the project being forced to move from Luoyang to Ye, the capital of Northern Qi.

In 574, in order to strengthen his military and his budget, the emperor of Northern Zhou outlawed Buddhism and Daoism. The following year, the Northern Zhou emperor launched a conquest of Northern Qi, during which many monks were killed, conscripted into the army, or laicized. Those who escaped hid in the mountains or fled south to Chen, where some encountered the works and pupils of Paramārtha. Among the earliest commentators on the *Treatise*, for example, Tanyan 曇延 (516–588) lived in the mountains near Chang'an (modern Xi'an), the capital of Northern Zhou. Another monk, Tanqian 曇遷 (542–607), lived in Northern Qi and fled south in 574, later bringing the ideas of Paramārtha to Chang'an when China was united by Yang Jian 楊堅 (541–604), who made the capital of his Sui dynasty at Chang'an. This Sui emperor, later known as Emperor Wen 文帝, established major Buddhist centers of scholarship under Tanqian and other eminent monks. Tanyan attended lectures by Tanqian on the *Mahāyānasaṃgraha*, one of the signature texts translated by Paramārtha. Huiyuan 慧遠 (523–592), another commentator on the *Treatise*, also attended these lectures.

Debates between Shelun and Dilun Schools

In the sixth century, two major doctrinal approaches were developed on the basis of ideas about the *tathāgatagarbha* (*rulaizang* 如來藏), on the one hand, and the system of Yogācāra enunciated principally by Vasubandhu, on the other. These approaches were identified with the Dilun and Shelun "schools." Each was named after one of its core texts, the *Daśabhūmika-vyākhyāna* (as noted above, abbreviated in Chinese as *Dilun*) and the *Mahāyānasaṃgraha* (abbreviated in Chinese as *Shelun* 攝論).[12]

---

12. The names Shelun and Dilun were not used by contemporaries. They were used with mostly derogatory overtones by later critics of these approaches, such as members of the Sanlun, Tiantai, and Faxiang schools of the seventh and eighth centuries. Ishii Kōsei 石井公成, "Jironshū kenkyū no genjō to kadai" 地論宗研究の現状と課題 (The Present Situation and Issues of Dilun School Studies) in Geumgang Daehak bulgyo munhwa yeon'guso, comp., *Jironshisō no keisei to hen'yō* 地論思想の形成と変容 (The Formation and Transformation of Dilun Thought) (Tokyo: Kokusho kankōkai, 2010), p. 41; Ishii Kōsei, *Kegon shisō no kenkyū* 華厳思想の研究 (Studies on Huayan Thought) (Tokyo: Shunjūsha, 1996), p. 71.

After the Dilun masters had become active, others distinguished two branches (*dao* 道), Northern and Southern. Sui and Tang authors identified these as "lineages" (*zong* 宗) headed by the Indian monk-translators Bodhiruci (Northern) and Ratnamati (Southern). The two men had disagreed over doctrine when they started to translate the *Dilun* in Luoyang in 508.[13] Due to a paucity of information, especially about Northern Dilun, scholarly opinion had been divided about whether the divisions between the Southern and Northern Dilun first emerged in Luoyang between 508 and 534, or only after Bodhiruci's death in about 534.[14] Research from the 1990s, however, suggested that the differences did not emerge until after Bodhiruci's death.[15]

Core disagreements between the Northern and Southern Dilun branches concerned the relationship of the *tathāgatagarbha* and the *ālayavijñāna* (store consciousness; see the discussion below).[16] As Robert Gimello has argued, students of the day would have found the *Dilun* (Bodhiruci's translation) "equivocal to the point of seeming self-contradictory" on the question of whether the store consciousness is identical to the *tathāgatagarbha* or whether it is "a mere reservoir of illusion and thus impure."[17] Another disagreement concerned

---

13. Daoxuan 道宣 (596–667), *Xu Gaoseng zhuan* 續高僧傳 (Supplementary *Biographies of Eminent Monks*). T50.2060, 482c1–4. For a variant story, see T50.2060, 429a12–16. The most comprehensive description of the two lineages is in Yang Weizhong 楊維中, *Zhongguo Weishizong tongshi* 中國唯識宗通史 (General History of the Chinese Vijñānavāda School) (Nanjing: Fenghuang chubanshe, 2008), vol. 1, pp. 64–168.

14. See Yang Weizhong, *Zhongguo Weishizong tongshi*, pp. 58–64; Lü Cheng 呂澂, *Zhongguo Foxue yuanliu lüejiang* 中國佛學源流略講 (Brief Lectures on the Origin and Development of Chinese Buddhism) (Beijing: Zhonghua shuju, rpt. 1979), pp. 140–141.

15. Ōtake Susumu 大竹晋, "Jironshū no busshinsetsu" 地論宗の佛身説 (The Dilun Theory of the Buddha Bodies), in Geumgang Daehak bulgyo munhwa yeon'guso, comp., *Jironshū no kenkyū*, p. 125.

16. Robert Michael Gimello, "Chih-yen and the Foundation of Hua-yen Buddhism" (Ph.D. diss., Columbia University, 1976), pp. 284–307. This consciousness, one of eight or nine identified by Buddhists, retains the impressions of past experiences and permeates or "perfumes" new experiences on the basis of that previous conditioning.

17. Gimello, "Chih-yen and the Foundation of Hua-yen Buddhism," pp. 289–292.

the number and roles of the different consciousnesses. The crucial questions in these debates were: What is the origin of ignorance and what is the basis for enlightenment? And is the basis for awakening a disclosure model (one that is already present) or a development model (the mechanism for awakening must be produced by practice)?[18]

It was at the height of these debates that Paramārtha arrived in south China in 546 and remained there until his death in 569. He translated many texts, among them the *Shelun*, translated in about 563.[19] The *Shelun* taught that there are eight consciousnesses: five sense-consciousnesses;[20] a sixth consciousness (*manovijñāna*), which coordinates sensory data; a seventh continuity- and ego-positing consciousness (*manas*); and the eighth, store consciousness (*ālayavijñāna*), which exists only as the sum of transient seeds that arise from previous deeds and influence future deeds.[21] Paramārtha, however, identified what he refers to as the mind (*xin* 心) with the *manas* (*yi* 意) or *kliṣṭa-manas* (stained mind; *ranwu shi* 染污識) and

---

18. For these two models, see Michael Zimmermann, "The Process of Awakening in Early Texts on Buddha-Nature in India," in Chen-kuo Lin and Michael Radich, eds., *A Distant Mirror: Articulating Indic Ideas in Sixth and Seventh Century Chinese Buddhism* (Hamburg: Hamburg University Press, 2014), pp. 515–517.

19. Diana Y. Paul, *Philosophy of Mind in Sixth-Century China*, p. 32.

20. The visual, auditory, olfactory, gustatory, and tactile consciousnesses.

21. "Seeds" is used as a metaphor. In standard Yogācāra doctrine, the store consciousness is understood to store both pure and impure seeds (*bīja*), just as the memory stores good and bad memories. These seeds are due to past actions or experiences from time without beginning. They influence sentient beings in the same way that perfume pervades a cloth, infusing it with a scent while its basic fabric remains essentially unchanged. As John Powers explains, seeds "are the latent residua of a person's actions. Every volitional action deposits a predisposition within one's mental continuum, which represents a propensity to perpetuate that sort of action and also guarantees the karmic repercussions of one's moral choices. As the metaphor of seeds implies, they lie dormant until the proper conditions for their manifestation are present and then give rise to mental states that resemble the original impulses that led to their creation." See his "Yogācāra: Indian Buddhist Origins," in John Makeham, ed., *Transforming Consciousness Yogācāra Thought in Modern China* (New York: Oxford University Press, 2014), p. 46.

also with the store consciousness. He thus presented mind as having two referents. He also introduced the term *ādānavijñāna* (grasping consciousness; *atuona shi* 阿陀那識), which he identified both with the *kliṣṭa-manas* and with the store consciousness. This use of the same term for different mental processes in different contexts would also have led to some confusion.[22]

The *Shelun* maintains that the store consciousness is the basis (*āśraya*) only for the dependent arising of imaginative constructions (*abhūta-parikalpa*) of the delusory world.[23] Northern Dilun is held to have adopted a similar view, and therefore claimed that the buddha-nature comes to exist only as result of practice; it must be developed.[24] Moreover, the *Shelun* itself is quite explicit that the supramundane mind (*chushi xin* 出世心), the mind of enlightenment, is not internal to the store consciousness; rather, the transformation of the store consciousness into the mind of enlightenment requires that it is "perfumed" externally by "the most pure dharma realm."[25] Southern Dilun is said to have championed the idea that the dependent arising of purity and impurity was based on the dharma nature (or suchness, pure consciousness), a view that in turn was related to the assertion that the buddha-nature exists innately.[26] Whereas Northern Dilun

---

22. *She dasheng lun shi*. T31.1595, 157b21–159b20. For more detailed discussion, see Ōtake Susumu, "Yugagyōha bunken to *Daijō kishin ron*," pp. 49–62, esp. p. 49.

23. Gimello, "Chih-yen and the Foundation of Hua-yen Buddhism," pp. 232–235. Dependent arising (*pratītya-samutpāda; yuanqi* 緣起) is the fundamental Buddhist doctrine that everything arises from causes and conditions and has no inherent self-nature. According to the *Shelun*, the store consciousness is the basis for the imaginative construction of the delusory world through a continuing chain of causes and conditions.

24. Lü Cheng, *Zhongguo Foxue yuanliu lüejiang*, pp. 142–143. Yang Weizhong, *Zhongguo Weishizong tongshi*, pp. 169–173 traces this contrast back to earlier debates in China about whether the buddha-nature "innately exists" (*benyou* 本有) or "exists for a first time" (*shiyou* 始有).

25. T31.1593, 117a8–9. See Robert Gimello's discussion of this point, "Chih-yen and the Foundation of Hua-yen Buddhism," pp. 262–265.

26. Ibuki Atsushi 伊吹敦, "Jironshū Hokudōha no shinshikisetsu ni tsuite" 地論宗北道派の心識説について (On the Mind and Consciousness Theory of the Northern Faction of the Dilun School), *Bukkyōgaku* 佛教学 40 (1999): pp.

seems to have been in accord with mainstream Yogācāra theory, of which the *Shelun* was the most representative text at that time in China, Southern Dilun was closer to Tathāgatagarbha doctrine.[27]

At the time of the composition of the *Treatise*, the relationship between the *tathāgatagarbha* and the store consciousness remained a core topic to debate. If the *tathāgatagarbha* were to be taken as something that existed innately, it would contradict the Yogācāra doctrine of "nothing but consciousness," which claimed that everything that can be perceived is a product of mental processes and is substantially unreal. For the *Treatise*, the *tathāgatagarbha* is functionally equivalent to suchness (*zhenru* 真如; *tathatā*). The *tathāgatagarbha* is therefore taken to provide the ontological grounding for the store consciousness. The store consciousness represents external defilements, which cover or obscure realization of the *tathāgatagarbha*.[28]

47–50; Aoki Takashi 青木隆, "Tonkō shahon ni miru Jiron kyōgaku no keisei" 敦煌写本にみる地論教学の形成 (The Formation of the Doctrines of the Dilun School as Seen in Dunhuang Manuscripts), in Geumgang Daehak bulgyo munhwa yeon'guso, comp., *Jiron shisō no keisei to hen'yō*, pp. 47–48; Ōtake Susumu, "Jironshū no busshinsetsu," pp. 109–110, 126.

27. The Tiantai master Zhiyi 智顗 (538–597) is recorded as identifying a distinction between the Dilun school and the Shelun school, with the former advocating that "dharma nature" (*faxing* 法性; **dharmatā*)—the functional equivalent of suchness—is the basis for all dharmas, and the latter maintaining that everything arises from *ālayavijñāna*. See Zhiyi, *Mohe zhiguan* 摩訶止觀 (The Great Calming and Discernment). T46.1911, 54a23–b8. A problem here is that Zhiyi's works were edited by his disciples, most importantly by Guanding 灌頂 (561–632), and the versions that have come down to us were filtered through Zhanran's 湛然 (711–782) commentaries. There is therefore a question of how much of the information reflects Zhiyi's views and how much came from Guanding or Zhanran.

28. Well before the engagement with the Yogācāra concept of the *ālayavijñāna*, we can discern the genesis of these ideas in the *Tathāgatagarbha-sūtra* (*Dafangguang rulaizang jing* 大方廣如來藏經), written in the second half of the third century. Although the *Tathāgatagarbha-sūtra* was not fully translated into Chinese until the eighth century, its main content—nine analogies illustrating how the *tathāgatagarbha* is covered over by defilements—was already cited in the mid-third century *Ratnagotravibhāga-mahāyānottaratantra-śāstra*, translated into Chinese in 511 by Ratnamati (fl. 508) under the title *Foxing fenbie dasheng jiujing yaoyi lun* 佛性分別大乘究竟要義論 or *Baoxing*

Sui and Tang commentators and doxographers identified the main doctrinal difference between the Northern and Southern branches of the Dilun school to have been whether defiled phenomena arise from the *ālayavijñāna* (the Northern position) or from suchness (the Southern position). If these accounts are taken as accurate, then the *Treatise* appears both consistent with the Northern branch in presenting the *ālayavijñāna*, identified with the gateway of arising and ceasing in the *Treatise*, as the basis for defiled phenomena; and also consistent with the Southern branch in presenting suchness or the *tathāgatagarbha*, which exists in the defiled *ālayavijñāna*, as the basis of everything, no matter defiled or undefiled.[29]

The Influences of the Laṅkāvatāra-sūtra

The Tathāgatagarbha tradition with which the *Treatise* is closely aligned is associated with a cluster of texts that focus on the potential to become a *tathāgata* (buddha), on the innate capacity for buddhahood. One text from this tradition, the *Laṅkāvatāra-sūtra*, has long been identified as having a particularly close connection with the *Treatise*. Already in the sixth century, for example, Huiyuan had commented that the *Treatise* was produced on the basis of the *Laṅkāvatāra-sūtra*.[30]

---

lun 寶性論 (Treatise on the Jewel Nature). Seven of these nine analogies present the *tathāgatagarbha* as fully formed but obscured by defilements.

29. Zhanran, *Fahua xuanyi shiqian* 法華玄義釋籤 (Comments on the *Profound Meaning of the Lotus Sutra*). T33.1717, 942c16–24. See also Keng Ching, "Yogācāra Buddhism Transmitted or Transformed? Paramārtha (499–569) and His Chinese Interpreters" (PhD diss., Harvard University, 2009), pp. 344–345; and Robert M. Gimello, "Chih-yen and the Foundations of Hua-yen Buddhism," pp. 146–147, 211, 294–297.

30. Huiyuan 慧遠 (523–592), *Dasheng qixin lun yishu* 大乘起信論義疏 (Elucidation of the Meaning of the *Treatise on Awakening Mahāyāna Faith*). T44.1843, 176a8.

Composed in India in the fourth or fifth century, there are three surviving Chinese translations of the *Laṅkāvatāra-sūtra*: Guṇabhadra's (394–468) partial translation of 443; Bodhiruci's of 513; and Śikṣānanda's (d.u.) of 700. Bodhiruci's translation has been identified as most likely to have influenced the author of the *Treatise*.[31] For example, the modern Chinese scholar Lü Cheng 呂澂 (1896–1989) argued that Bodhiruci's mistranslation of a number of key ideas in the *Laṅkāvatāra-sūtra* influenced the author of the *Treatise*. So whereas the author of the *Laṅkāvatāra-sūtra* treated the *tathāgatagarbha* as synonymous with the *ālayavijñāna*, Bodhiruci instead understood relevant passages to differentiate the *tathāgatagarbha* from the *ālayavijñāna*. Lü Cheng asserted that this in turn led the author of the *Treatise* to claim, "The arising-and-ceasing mind exists because of dependence on the *tathāgatagarbha*" [576b].[32] Lü maintained that this claim is doctrinally incoherent—because it presents the unconditioned (which is not subject to the laws of cause and effect) as the basis of the conditioned—and became the basis for a slew of problematic ideas proposed in the *Treatise*.[33]

Guṇabhadra's partial translation of the *Laṅkāvatāra-sūtra* adheres most closely to the extant Sanskrit version. An alternative view to that advanced by Lü Cheng is that the section of Guṇabhadra's translation

31. As we indicate in a note to the translation, there is evidence that the author of the *Treatise* possibly also drew on Guṇabhadra's translation of the *Laṅkāvatāra-sūtra*, albeit to a much lesser extent.

32. Numerical references in square brackets are to the text of the *Treatise* in the *Taishō Tripiṭaka* (Taishō Revised Tripiṭaka).

33. See Lü Cheng, "Chanxue shuyuan" 禪學述源 (Tracing the Origins of Chan Learning), in *Lü Cheng Foxue lunzhu xuanji* 呂澂佛學論著選集 (Lü Cheng on Buddhism: Selected Works) 5 vols. (Jinan: Qilu shushe, 1991), vol. 1, 401–403. See also his "Qixin yu Chan—duiyu *Dasheng qixin lun* laili de tantao" 起信與禪—對於大乘起信論來歷的探討 (Awakening Faith and Chan: An Investigation into the Historical Origins of the *Treatise on Awakening Mahāyāna Faith*), reprinted in *Xiandai Fojiao xueshu congkan* 現代佛教學術叢刊 (Modern Buddhist Scholarship Series), vol. 35, Zhang Mantao 張曼濤, ed. (Taipei: Dasheng wenhua chubanshe, 1978), pp. 302–304.

corresponding to the beginning part of chapter 6 of the Sanskrit version may have provided inspiration for some early interpreters of the *Treatise*—if not for the author of the *Treatise*—in understanding the relationship between the *tathāgatagarbha* and the mind that arises and ceases. Insofar as it is concealed, *tathāgatagarbha* (*rulaizang* 如來藏) is associated with the *ālayavijñāna* (*shizang* 識藏), which is the mixture of purity and afflictions produced by ignorance. The term *zang* 藏 therefore referred both to the repository of a *tathāgata* (*tathāgatagarbha; rulaizang*) and to the concealed *tathāgata* (*shizang*).[34] Guṇabhadra maintains that the *tathāgatagarbha* is the conveyor of suchness because it carries potential *tathāgata*-hood, buddhahood.[35] For Guṇabhadra, *tathāgatagarbha* and *ālayavijñāna* are neither exactly the same nor entirely different.

4. IGNORANCE AND PRACTICE

Ignorance

In the *Treatise*, suchness remains concealed due to ignorance (*wuming* 無明):

> How does habituation [by ignorance] give rise to defiled dharmas without interruption?[36] Because it is based on the dharma of suchness, there is ignorance. Because there are the defiled dharmas of ignorance as cause, these then habituate

---

34. *Lengqie abaduoluo baojing* 楞伽阿跋多羅寶經 (Laṅkāvatāra Sutra), trans. Guṇabhadra (394–468). T16.670, 510b26–c10, *passim*.

35. See, for example, Wonhyo 元曉 (617–686), *Gisil lon so* 起信論疏 (Explanation of the *Treatise on Awakening* [*Mahāyāna*] *Faith*). T44.1844, 208b8.

36. *Xunxi* 熏習 (habituation, permeation) is the standard Chinese translation of the Sanskrit term *vāsanā*. The *Treatise* uses the following metaphor: "'Habituation' is like an ordinary piece of clothing that in reality has no scent; but it will acquire a fragrance if someone perfumes it." [578a]

suchness. Because of this habituation, there is the false mind and, since there is the false mind, it then habituates ignorance. Because [the false mind] does not fully discern the dharma of suchness, it is non-awakened and so conceiving arises, presenting false perceptual fields. Because there are the defiled dharmas of false perceptual fields as conditions, these then habituate the false mind, so that conceiving and attachments generate all kinds of karmic action and one experiences all the sufferings of body and mind. [578a]

By claiming that suchness is somehow habituated by ignorance and that the unconditioned is acted upon causally by the conditioned, the *Treatise* stands apart from other texts associated with the Tathāgatagarbha tradition—not to mention from the Indian understanding of the relation between unconditioned dharmas (*wuwei fa* 無為法) and conditioned dharmas (*youwei fa* 有為法). Some early commentaries (see Section 6) maintained that the *Treatise* asks us to accept that although suchness can be habituated (and so, the unconditioned, *per impossibile*, becomes conditioned), this is merely suchness adapting to conditions (*sui yuan* 隨緣); in fact, suchness only appears to be habituated and does not change at all.[37]

The author of the *Treatise* uses a series of analogies to explain the relationship between ignorance and awakening: the dynamic between the wind and the ocean; a disoriented person; the reflections of a mirror. Support for the early commentators' apologist interpretation is readily found in the *Treatise*'s analogy of the wind and the ocean, which attracted particularly close attention from later commentators. Although the wind stirs up the phenomenal appearance of waves

---

37. See, for example, Tanyan 曇延 (516–588), *Qixin lun yishu* 起信論義疏 (Elucidation of the Meaning of the *Treatise on Awakening Mahāyāna Faith*). X45.755, 159b6–22.

and motion, the wet nature of the ocean is not affected and does not change, whether the wind blows or not:

> ... because all the characteristics of the mind and consciousnesses are ignorance and, since the characteristic of ignorance is not separate from the nature of awakening, the mind and consciousnesses are indestructible and destructible.[38] This is like the great ocean, where water moves in waves due to the wind. The characteristics of the water and the wind [as waves] are not separate from one another. Since it is not in the nature of water to move [by itself], its characteristic of movement will cease if the wind ceases, without its wetness ever being destroyed. [576c]

In the *Treatise*'s use of this metaphor, water stands for the mind; the wind stands for ignorance; the wetness of the water stands for the nature of the mind; and the shapes of the waves stand for the characteristics of the mind. When the wind stops, the water is still and there are no waves; when ignorance is dispelled, the mind no longer has characteristics. Here the author tries to resist collapsing ignorance and awakening: he presents them as inseparable but not the same.[39] Wind's characteristic is to move, while the nature of water is wetness. Although the deluded mind is stirred into making erroneous distinctions, in fact its self-nature—suchness—is constant and unchanging. Only ignorance prevents us from realizing this.[40]

---

38. It is destructible because it is ignorance; it is indestructible because it is not separate from the nature of awakening. Huiyuan and *Hane 333V* use the term "the mind" to refer to the seventh consciousness and the term "consciousnesses" to refer to the first six consciousnesses. They claim that both are inherently mired in ignorance.

39. From the time of Wonhyo and Fazang, writing in the seventh century, this distinction was collapsed.

40. As described elsewhere in the *Treatise*, "the nature of the mind neither arises nor ceases. It is solely due to false thoughts that there are distinctions between every dharma; if one is free from false thoughts, then there are none of the characteristics of perceptual fields." [576a]

If the characteristic of movement is exclusively connected to wind, and the wind ceases to blow, then the characteristic of movement was never an actual characteristic of water. Water does not move in waves except when moved by wind. As such, the example is not intended to be an ontological statement about eternities, but about temporary situations—or else movement would be a permanent characteristic of water and not something absent from its nature.

This analogy of the ocean and the wind is also found in Bodhiruci's translation of the *Laṅkāvatāra-sūtra*, but there are significant differences between the use of the analogy in the two works. In the *Laṅkāvatāra-sūtra*, the ocean is represented by the eighth, store consciousness, which is unchanging. The waves are associated with the first seven consciousnesses (the five sense consciousnesses, the sixth consciousness, which coordinates sensory data, and the seventh continuity- and ego-positing consciousness), with a focus on the sixth and seventh. The wind is associated with perceptual fields, which are a function of consciousness and so internal.[41] In the *Treatise*, by contrast, influential commentators from Wonhyo 元曉 (617–686) on identified the wind as an external factor, acting on water to create waves. In so doing, they turned the analogy into a dualist ontology.[42]

The real concern of the *Treatise*, however, is to demonstrate that ignorance can be overcome. Like suchness, ignorance is seen to be without origin; it is simply a given. Ignorance operates at the level of momentary expressions of cognitive functioning. As described in the *Treatise*, "This is explained as beginningless ignorance because

41. *Ru Lengqie jing* 入楞伽經 (Laṅkāvatāra-sūtra), T16.671, 523b19–c19.
42. The earlier commentator, Huiyuan (T44.1843, 185a25–26), had attempted to explain the discrepancies between the *Laṅkāvatāra-sūtra*'s use of the analogy and that found in the *Treatise* by arguing that the association of wind with perceptual fields in the *Laṅkāvatāra-sūtra* is unimportant. According to Huiyuan, the author of the *Treatise* was concerned with the basis of perceptual fields, which is ignorance. Huiyuan does not, however, explain the source of the wind.

thought-moment after thought-moment have always followed one another in a continuous flow and [sentient beings] have never been free from conceiving" [576b–c].[43] As the text explains, ignorance amounts to breaking the constancy of the mind into discrete, successive moments. Beginningless ignorance means that this has always happened—there is no point at which conceiving starts—but that does not preclude one from becoming aware of this and severing one's continuous agitation by ignorance.

In the *Treatise*, the analysis of ignorance concludes by exposing differences between authentic non-empty qualities and inauthentic "characteristics" (*xiang* 相). Suchness is characterized as both empty and non-empty. On the one hand, it is truly empty because it is free of false conceptual and verbal discriminations, and it can disclose what is real when defilements caused by ignorance are removed. Emptiness renders delusion unreal and so discloses the reality of "non-emptiness." On the other hand, suchness is truly non-empty because it is "constantly unchanging and replete with pure dharmas" [576b]. Overturning delusion enables the practitioner to become aware of what is ultimately real. What is important to note is the pragmatic instructiveness of the false. If it were not for delusion, the practitioner would not awaken to what is real, to the fact that the practitioner is already inherently awoken.[44]

shentong (margin note)

(fish and water) (margin note)

---

43. *Nian* 念, translated in this context as conceiving, is an important term with multiple meanings, several of which are used in the *Treatise*. First, it means either "mindfulness" or "memory." Second, it denotes a thought-moment. In Buddhist psychology, thoughts are momentary. Each follows from its predecessor and is conditioned by it. In turn, the successive series tends to perpetuate patterns of thought and conceptual distinctions. Third, *nian* refers to conceiving, a prominent theme in the *Treatise*. In the work, this use of the term has a negative implication because conceiving leads to attachment to perceptual fields as something real through false conceptualization rather than through correct cognition.

44. The non-duality of emptiness and non-emptiness in the *Treatise* follows a distinction similar to that drawn in an earlier Tathāgatagarbha text, the *Śrīmālādevī-siṃhanāda-sūtra* (*Shengman shizi hou yisheng da fangbian fangguang jing* 勝鬘師子吼一乘大方便方廣經; Sutra on the Lion's Roar of Queen Śrīmālā), trans. Guṇabhadra. T12.353, 221c17–19.

Calming and Discernment

The *Treatise* lists five of the perfections (which it refers to as "gateways") that enable one to "perfect faith." It provides only minimal explanations of the first four of these five perfections, probably because these were well known and relatively straightforward.[45] The fifth perfection, however, deals with what broadly speaking might be called meditation, and it is explained in some detail.[46] It consists of calming (*zhi* 止; *śamatha*) and discernment (*guan* 觀; *vipaśyanā*). One calms the mind by focusing and so achieves an alert, calm awareness. This is *śamatha*. *Vipaśyanā* is analytical, observational. With alert focus, one calmly contemplates objects and concepts—compassion, anger, arising, or ceasing, for example—until one understands them as they truly are. Calming and discernment are inseparable and so they form a single perfection.[47] This was probably emphasized in the *Treatise* because, according to Zhiyi (538–597), some meditators practice only calming and others only discernment, which leads to failure.[48] In most Mahāyāna literature, however, calming and discernment are paired.

The *Treatise* describes calming as "stopping the characteristics of all perceptual fields" [582a]. This begins with the removal of

---

45. Elsewhere, the *Treatise* sets out the more standard list of six perfections (*pāramitā*s): giving, discipline, forbearance, vigorous exertion, meditative concentration, and wisdom [582b].

46. See Alan Sponberg's caution over the use of the word "meditation" in his "Meditation in Fa-hsiang Buddhism," in ed. Peter N. Gregory, *Traditions of Meditation in Chinese Buddhism* (Honolulu: University of Hawaii Press, 1986), pp. 18–19.

47. Geshe Sopa, "*Śamathavipaśyanāyudanaddha*: The Two Leading Principles of Buddhist Meditation," in Minoru Kiyota, ed., *Mahāyāna Buddhist Meditation: Theory and Practice* (Honolulu: University of Hawaii Press, 1978), pp. 46–65. The author of the *Treatise* seems to have been influenced in his ideas on the topic by Bodhiruci's translations of the *Laṅkāvatarā-sūtra*, the *Saṃdhinirmocana-sūtra*, and the *Dharmasaṃgīti-sūtra*. See Takemura Makio 竹村牧男, *Kaiteiban* Daijō kishin ron *dokushaku* 改訂版大乗起信論読釈 (Revised Edition of An Interpretative Reading of the *Treatise on Awakening Mahāyāna Faith*) (Tokyo: Sankibō busshorin, 1993), pp. 465, 497, 500.

48. *Mohe zhiguan*. T46.1911, 59a16–21.

all concepts in the thought-moment in which they arise and even rejects the concept of removing concepts. Through this practice one can enter meditative absorption (*samādhi*). This is directed at creating a spontaneous power to habituate or "perfume" sentient beings (as in the analogy of scent and clothing), enabling them to see and hear what they need to see and hear, including various buddhas.

The *Treatise* describes discernment as "discriminating the causes and conditions of arising and ceasing" [582a]. Discernment analyzes how memories and present states are fleeting. This form of examination may be linked to an understanding of the characteristics of thought-moments [576b–c], in which there really are no characteristics of arising, enduring, changing, and ceasing.

Calming and discernment are both necessary for enlightenment, and should be practiced at all times. Not all practitioners are able to be so committed, however, and so an allowance is made for them. They are asked to be mindful of the buddhas and their promises to assist sentient beings, and also to practice single-minded meditation on Amitābha's western paradise.[49] This will aid in improving one's behavior and bring one to rebirth in a buddha-land.

---

49. The Amitābha Buddha is the primary deity of the Pure Land school. He is attributed with infinite merits and is said to expound the Dharma in his pure paradise in the West. Although the *Treatise* neither makes statements about chanting Amitābha's name nor uses the term "pure land," it does talk about a single-minded meditation on Amitābha's western paradise in the context of receiving a transference of merit to be reborn there. These *nian fo* 念佛 (*buddha-anusmṛti*) practices are more likely to be the elaborate rituals and meditations described in the sutras that became foundational for Pure Land, rather than the bare name recitation that came to be synonymous with Pure Land practice.

5. KEY MODELS

One Mind Two Gateways

The *Treatise* presents the mind, or the so-called One Mind, as the ultimate source of reality. The One Mind has two modalities or aspects, which the text calls "gateways":

> There are two gateways based on the dharma of the One Mind. What are they? The first is the gateway of the mind as suchness. The second is the gateway of the mind as arising and ceasing. Each of these two gateways contains all dharmas. Why? Because these two gateways are not separate from one another. [576a]

The gateway of the mind as suchness (*xin zhenru men* 心真如門) is the true mind. It is quiescent, unchanging, unconditioned, and it neither arises nor ceases. It is free of false conceptualizing and distinction making. The gateway of the mind as arising and ceasing (*xin shengmie men* 心生滅門) is cyclic existence (*saṃsāra*), in which the mind's propensity to awaken struggles against the mental and physical behaviors that arise from the mind's defilement by ignorance.

The *Treatise* explains that the combination or integration of the non-arising and non-ceasing aspect with the arising-and-ceasing aspect constitutes the *ālayavijñāna*. The *ālayavijñāna* represents the adaptation of *tathāgatagarbha*, the mind of suchness, to phenomenal conditions and to ignorance. Crucially, *tathāgatagarbha*/suchness—the unconditioned—remains constant, unchanged, undiminished, and undefiled by these phenomenal conditions.

Both the mind as suchness and the mind as arising and ceasing are ultimately the One Mind. Because ignorance obscures realization of the One Mind, however, deluded beings create false perceptions and so become mired in suffering. The mind as arising and ceasing then generates false perceptual distinctions, which in turn provide new conditions for the ongoing defilement of the mind and for the suffering caused by taking the wrong sorts of actions.

The Three Greats

Early in the *Treatise*, the author introduces two aspects of Mahāyāna: dharma and meanings. Dharma refers to the mind of sentient beings, since the mind of sentient beings contains all dharmas, as well as the mind as suchness and as arising and ceasing.

The meanings of Mahāyāna are revealed through the mind of sentient beings. The *Treatise* identifies these as intrinsic reality (*ti* 體), characteristics (*xiang* 相), and function (*yong* 用). They are presented as the three "Greats" denoted by *mahā-* in the word Mahāyāna, "Great Vehicle." This is the first time in the tradition that we find the three used together, and represents a significant modification of the traditional pairing of *ti* and *yong*. This distinction of intrinsic reality, characteristics, and function stands in contrast to the traditional pair of intrinsic reality (*ti*) and function (*yong*).

In the *Treatise*, intrinsic reality refers to the quality of something being so of itself, without relying on anything more fundamental to be what it is. As one of the three Greats it refers to the One Mind and to suchness. It can be experienced only through its characteristics and its functions.

With the mind as suchness, the intrinsic reality of the mind of sentient beings is realized. This intrinsic reality, also known as the One Mind, is the focus of Mahāyāna as a teaching. When suchness adapts to and accords with phenomenal reality, the functioning of the One Mind is revealed. In other words, suchness (*ti*) is realized through phenomenal arising and ceasing (*xiang, yong*).

Three Bodies

The three bodies (*san shen* 三身; *trikāya*), or "threefold embodiment of buddhas," doctrine was a development from an earlier Buddhist doctrine of two bodies, the dharma body (*fashen* 法身; *dharmakāya*), and the form body (*seshen* 色身; *rūpa-kāya*). The dharma body referred to the corpus of teachings the Buddha bequeathed to his monastic community (*saṃgha*); the form body denoted the Buddha's physical body. The development of a doctrine of three bodies occurred in the Yogācāra school associated with the fourth-century CE Indian thinkers Asaṅga and Vasubandhu.[50]

The three bodies are typically presented as the dharma body (*fashen* 法身; *dharmakāya*), the recompense body or bodies (*baoshen* 報身; *saṃbhogakāya*), and the response body or bodies (*yingshen* 應身; *nirmāṇakāya*). In the *Treatise*, however, the three bodies are introduced in an unconventional order: the response body precedes the recompense body.

The *Treatise* describes the dharma body as "eternal, blissful, Self, and pure" [579a]. This set of qualities indicates that the text belongs to the Tathāgatagarbha tradition, since Tathāgatagarbha texts invariably invoke this formula. The dharma body is a buddha's embodiment and understanding of the ultimate. As described in the *Treatise*, it is the realization "there are no perceptual fields; there is only cognition of suchness, which is called the dharma body" [581a]. This realization is beyond what might be achieved even by a bodhisattva, limited only to buddhas. The *Treatise* also describes how the dharma body experiences the dharma realm (*fajie* 法界; *dharmadhātu*), the

---

50. Gadjin M. Nagao, *Mādhyamika and Yogācāra: A Study of Māhāyana Philosophies*, trans. and ed. Leslie S. Kawamura (Albany: State University of New York Press, 1991), p. 107. The earliest text to use the terminology of three bodies is found in the "Bodhi" chapter of the *Mahāyāna-sūtrālaṃkāra*, an early Yogācāra work of the fourth or perhaps the third century. See John J. Makransky, *Buddhahood Embodied: Sources of Controversy in India and Tibet* (Albany: State University of New York Press, 1997), p. 42.

full range of experiential fields. Experiencing, seeing, and perceiving the dharma realm just as it is constitutes an unobstructed way of being in an unobstructed world.

The text goes on to explain that "awakening" means to have an unobstructed mind that pervades everything. The dharma realm and the dharma body are therefore understood to be "pervaded" by the same uniformity of the mind and understanding. When awakening, one eliminates the obstructions hindering one's ability to perceive and to interact with the dharma realm. The unhindered mind, free from delusions and misconceptions, permeates everywhere. This is based on the *Treatise's* earlier claim that "'dharma' refers to the mind of sentient beings" [575c]. It is also a commentary of sorts on the opening to the text's discussion of the mind as suchness:

> ... the nature of the mind neither arises nor ceases. It is solely
> due to false thoughts that there are distinctions between every
> dharma; if one is free from false thoughts, then there are none
> of the characteristics of perceptual fields. Therefore, all dharmas
> have always been free from the characteristics of language,
> naming, and mental perceptions. They are ultimately uniform,
> invariant, and indestructible. [576a]

A recompense body is sometimes also called a reward body.[51] Buddhas begin their careers by taking vows to attain buddhahood, perhaps many eons away, and then work for the benefit of others. One culmination of this process is that they receive a recompense

---

51. The *Treatise* uses the term *baoshen* 報身, meaning "recompense body." The Sanskrit term *saṃbhoga* means "complete enjoyment" or "delight." It is perhaps better reflected in another Chinese translation, *shouyong shen* 受用身, the "enjoyment body." Both Chinese renderings have their justification: *baoshen* emphasizes the "reward body" aspect; *shouyong shen* follows the Sanskrit in emphasizing that this is a thoroughly enjoyable experience for this Buddha and those who interact with it.

body as the fruition of, or reward for, countless eons of cultivation of good karma. These buddhas continue to work for the benefit of others.

The *Treatise*'s main focus is to urge potential bodhisattvas to complete the levels of the bodhisattva path in order one day to see the recompense body in its entirety:

> ... bodhisattvas who have newly aroused the aspiration to awakening are capable of perceiving [the recompense body] to a small extent because they have profound faith in the dharma of suchness. . . . These bodhisattvas still construct their own distinctions, however, because they have yet to enter the stage of the dharma body. If they attain [the level of] pure mind, then what they perceive will be subtle and marvellous and its function will be all the more efficacious, until the bodhisattva levels are completed and they perceive [the recompense body] in its entirety. [579c]

Ordinary people are able to see a recompense body only in its coarse form. Because they each experience it differently, what they actually experience is a response body. Response bodies are the innumerable physical manifestations created by buddhas as a spontaneous response to what will most benefit individuals or specific groups of sentient beings unable to apprehend or relate to the pure forms of recompense bodies. They take on the characteristics of their audiences. For example, humans relate to other humans, and so buddhas will generally create humanoid manifestations for them.

Four Characteristics of Awakening

Mind is, by nature, awareness. Only when the mind is aware of its own aware nature does it coincide with its inherent nature. It is aware

29

It is aware...

not of the abstract notion that something called "a thought-moment" arises, but of actual thought-moments (of anger, passion, or intellectual clarity) as they present themselves. To be aware of these thought-moments, and to recognize that they have no distinct moment in which they initially arise or finally cease, is to be aware of the mind. This is final awakening.

This is not a momentary epiphany, but a continuous, ongoing awareness. For the author of the *Treatise*, the mind has been awakening, within the conditions of conventional reality, from the beginning; awakening is not something subsequently acquired. It coincides with the initial moment of every thought-moment and is simultaneous with the full arising, enduring, changing, and ceasing of each and every thought-moment. Accordingly, the author approaches the process of awakening through the model of the four characteristics of all conditioned things, although he reverses its standard order [576b]:

Four Characteristics	Type of Person	Insight	Resultant Situation	Type of Awakening
1. Ceasing 滅	Ordinary people 凡夫人	Become aware that previous thought-moments gave rise to bad [consequences] 覺知前念起惡	Will be able to stop thought-moments from subsequently arising 能止後念令其不起	Although they may still call this "awakening," it is precisely non-awakening 復名覺即是不覺
2. Changing 異	Those of the Two Vehicles with discerning cognition and bodhisattvas who have newly aroused the aspiration to awakening 二乘觀智初發意菩薩等	Awaken to the fact that as thought-moments [appear to] change, they do not have the characteristic of change 覺於念異念無異相	Have abandoned the characteristics of coarse discriminations and attachments 捨麤分別執著相	This is called "semblance of awakening" 名相似覺

(continued)

Karma

Four Characteristics	Type of Person	Insight	Resultant Situation	Type of Awakening
3. Enduring 住	Dharma-body bodhisattvas 法身菩薩等	Awaken to the fact that as thought-moments [appear to] endure, they do not have the characteristic of enduring 覺於念住念無住相	Are free from the characteristics of discriminations and coarse thought-moments 離分別麤念相	This is called "partial awakening" 名隨分覺
4. Arising 生	Those who have completed the bodhisattva levels, fully accomplished skillful means, and accorded with [suchness] in a single thought-moment 菩薩地盡滿足方便一念相應	Awaken to the fact that as the mind [appears to] arise initially, it has no characteristic of initial [arising] 覺心初起心無初相	Are far removed from subtle thought-moments 遠離微細念	The mind constantly enduring is called "final awakening" 心即常住名究竟覺

Five Names for Mentation and Six Types of Defiled Mind

The *Treatise* distinguishes five names for mentation (*yi* 意; *manas*). They are set in a cyclical sequence. The author revisits this core model several times in the text. The first name given for mentation is karmic consciousness. This refers to the unawakened mind's being set in motion by the force of ignorance. Second, once set in motion, the mind becomes a perceiver. This is the operating consciousness. Third, this leads to the presenting consciousness, in which a perceptual field is created. Fourth, the discerning consciousness discriminates the pure from the impure in that perceptual field. Fifth, the continuing consciousness generates new karma, which returns us to the beginning of the cycle. These five functions of mentation are conventionally associated with the *ālayavijñāna* or store consciousness; their association with *manas* in the *Treatise* highlights an idiosyncratic understanding of standard Yogācāra philosophy.

The author of the *Treatise* also explains six types of defiled mind. Here, he reverses the structure associated with mentation, and adds to it a sixth item, attachment [577c]:

Five names for mentation (*yi* 意)	Six types of defiled mind
1. Karmic consciousness 業識	6. Dissociated defilement of fundamental karmic action 根本業不相應染
2. Operating consciousness 轉識 *(perceiver)*	5. Dissociated defilement of the perceiving mind 能現心不相應染
3. Presenting consciousness 現識	4. Dissociated defilement of presented form 現色不相應染

(*Continued*)

Five names for mentation (*yi* 意)	Six types of defiled mind
4. Discerning consciousness 智識	3. Associated defilement of discriminating cognition 分別智相應染
5. Continuing consciousness 相續識	2. Associated defilement of the uninterrupted [flow of thought moments] 不斷相應染
	1. Associated defilement of attachment 執相應染

The six types of defiled mind are presented as stages of progression along the bodhisattva path, moving from coarse forms of defiled mind to subtle ones. It is only on the basis of first constructing a distinction between cognizer and what is cognized that the first three types of defiled mind can associate cognizer and cognized as being identical. In contrast, the three "dissociated" types of defiled mind are identified as being "without differentiation" because they do not uphold an initial distinction between cognizer and what is cognized. There is no longer any active engagement in false discrimination. The sixth type of defiled mind, the dissociated defilement of fundamental karmic action, is the most subtle. (In light of this, the first of the five types of mentation, karmic consciousness, is the most subtle; those that follow are increasingly coarse.) To rid oneself of this sixth type of defiled mind is to attain buddhahood.

Ten Bhūmis

To become a bodhisattva, in pursuit of awakening (*bodhi*), one must enter the bodhisattva path. Like many other Mahāyāna texts in sixth-century. China, the *Treatise* describes the bodhisattva path in terms of levels (*di* 地; *bhūmi*).[52] As already noted, in 508, Bodhiruci and Ratnamati together translated a commentary by the Yogācāra master Vasubandhu, titled *Daśabhūmi-vyākhyāna* (*Shidi jing lun* 十地經論; Commentary on the Discourse on the Ten Levels [of the Bodhisattva Path]). That translation, popularly called the *Dilun* 地論 (Treatise on Levels), came to dominate much of sixth-century Chinese Buddhist thinking about the levels of the bodhisattva path.

To enter the first level, ordinary people and non-Mahāyāna Buddhists first need to arouse the aspiration both for their own awakening and also for the awakening of all sentient beings, so that all can attain nirvana. The Sanskrit terms for this are *bodhicitta* or *cittotpāda*.[53] The Chinese term often used as an equivalent is *faxin* 發心. For those familiar with Mahāyāna Buddhist usage, this foundational term would have been taken to mean "arousing the aspiration to awakening." But since *xin* 心 is also the standard rendering for *citta*, "mind," its appearance here encouraged some Chinese Buddhists to conflate "mind" and the "aspiration to progress on the path." In a text such as the *Treatise*, grounded in a theory of the mind as the foundation of reality, the affinity between aspiration and mind expressed by *citta* and *xin* would have encouraged such a conflation.

The *Treatise* advances its own particular list of bodhisattva levels. The first is the "level of pure mind." Progress is made by advancing through subsequent levels, each of which comprises a variety of practices and realizations. The eighth level is especially significant, because it is here that one achieves a type of awakening from which

---

52. The *bhūmi*s later came to be subdivided into multiple sub-levels, most prominently the 52- (or 53-) level model adopted by the Huayan school.
53. In Buddhist usage, *citta* usually means "mind," but here it means "aspiration" or "to aspire to." *Bodhi* means "to be awakened." *Bodhicitta* therefore means "to aspire for awakening." In all forms of Mahāyāna Buddhism, having the life-changing experience of *bodhicitta* is the distinguishing feature of entering the Mahāyāna path.

one will not regress. The tenth level is the highest that a bodhi-sattva achieves as a bodhisattva; after the tenth level, one becomes a buddha. The *Treatise* describes the buddha level in terms of the three types of buddha bodies described above: a dharma body, a response body, and a recompense body.

The section dealing with the topic of "six kinds of defiled mind" provides the *Treatise*'s most sustained account of the bodhisattva levels. Elsewhere in the text, there are direct references to these levels and indications of which practices and achievements occur at which levels. The major commentators are even more fastidious than the text's author in connecting items in the *Treatise* with the various levels.

6. EARLY COMMENTARIES

Our understanding of the historical and intellectual contexts of the *Treatise*'s composition (see Section 3) has informed our translation of the text. Our exegesis has paid particular attention to how the text was interpreted in early commentaries, especially sixth-century commentaries. We have also drawn attention to the interpretations of seventh-century commentaries, which were extremely influential on subsequent interpretations of the *Treatise*.

Tanyan's Qixin lun yishu

Tanyan 曇延 (516–588) was a sixth-century monk who achieved high official position under the early Sui state (581–618). He was originally from an area in present-day Shanxi and later lived at the Taihang Baiti Monastery 太行百梯寺. There he composed commentaries on a number of seminal Mahāyāna texts, including his *Niepan jing shu* 涅槃經疏 (Commentary on the *Nirvana*

Sutra). He later did further exegetical work on the *Śrīmālādevī-siṃhanāda-sūtra* (*Shengman shizi hou yisheng da fangbian fangguang jing* 勝鬘師子吼一乘大方便方廣經; Sutra on the Lion's Roar of Queen Śrīmālā) and the *Ren wang jing* 仁王經 (Sutra for Humane Kings).

Only one of two fascicles of Tanyan's *Qixin lun yishu* 起信論義疏 (Elucidation of the Meaning of the *Treatise on Awakening* [*Mahāyāna*] *Faith*; X45.755) survives. Some scholars have doubted that Tanyan composed this work. They have argued that if Tanyan wrote this commentary he could only have done so during the last year of his life, because it refers many times to Paramārtha's translation of the *Mahāyānasaṃgraha-bhāṣya* (*She dasheng lun shi* 攝大乘論釋; Commentary on the *Compendium of the Great Vehicle*), which Tanqian began to teach only in 587.[54] A further argument is that neither Daoxuan's 道宣 (596–667) *Xu Gaoseng zhuan* 續高僧傳 (Supplementary *Biographies of Eminent Monks*) nor any Tang catalogue makes reference to a commentary on the *Treatise* written by Tanyan. Instead, the earliest reference to a commentary on the *Treatise* by "Master Yan" 延法師 is in a Shōsōin 正倉院 document dated 751.[55] Similar descriptions appear in later Japanese Buddhist catalogues edited in 914 and in 1094.[56]

Against this view, the modern scholar Kashiwagi Hiroo suggests that this is the earliest extant commentary on the *Treatise*, and that its author may well be Tanyan.[57] His main reason is that, according

---

54. Kashiwagi Hiroo 柏木弘雄 cites examples of scholars who maintain that the *Qixin lun yishu* was written by Tanqian and not Tanyan. Kashiwagi provides evidence to refute these views. See his *Daijō kishin ron no kenkyū: Daijō kishin ron no seiritsu ni kansuru shiryōronteki kenkyū* 大乘起信論の研究 : 大乘起信論の成立に関する資料論的研究 (Studies on the *Treatise on Awakening Mahāyāna Faith*: Document-Based Studies on the Dating of the *Treatise on Awakening Mahāyāna Faith*) (Tokyo: Shunjūsha, 1981), pp. 185–186.

55. Kashiwagi Hiroo, *Daijō kishin ron no kenkyū*, p. 27.

56. Kashiwagi Hiroo, *Daijō kishin ron no kenkyū*, p. 27.

57. Kashiwagi Hiroo, *Daijō kishin ron no kenkyū*, p. 194.

to the *Xu Gaoseng zhuan*, the earliest transmitters of the *Treatise* also taught Paramārtha's translation of the **Mahāyānasaṃgraha-bhāṣya*. Based on the frequent references to **Mahāyānasaṃgraha-bhāṣya* in this commentary, Kashiwagi claims that its author probably belonged to the earliest group of those who read the *Treatise* in the light of Paramārtha's **Mahāyānasaṃgraha-bhāṣya*. We follow Kashiwagi in accepting that Tanyan is the probable author of *Qixin lun yishu*.[58]

Tanyan emphasizes the identity of the *tathāgatagarbha* with inherent awakening (*benjue* 本覺). The *tathāgatagarbha* is without conceiving (*wu nian* 無念) and its illuminating nature (*zhaoxing* 照性) never changes.[59] He likens inherent awakening to a mirror: when images of defiled objects are reflected in a mirror, they never defile the mirror itself.[60] Commenting on the Two Gateways paradigm, Tanyan claims that when suchness, as the *tathāgatagarbha*, combines with the arising-and-ceasing store consciousness it merely accords with or accommodates habituating conditions (*suixun* 隨薰). It therefore only appears (*xiangsi* 相似) to arise and cease without actually doing so.[61]

Huiyuan's Dasheng qixin lun yishu

Another important early commentary on the *Treatise* is the *Dasheng qixin lun yishu* 大乘起信論義疏 (Elucidation of the Meaning of the *Treatise on Awakening Mahāyāna Faith*; T44.1843). It was traditionally attributed to the Sui monk Huiyuan 慧遠 (523–592), whose later scholarship centered on works seminal to the Dilun and Tathāgatagarbha traditions.

---

58. Kashiwagi Hiroo, *Daijō kishin ron no kenkyū*, pp. 203–204.
59. Tanyan, *Qixin lun shu*. X45.755, 159b12–16.
60. X45.755, 162c20–23.
61. X45.755, 159b15–16.

Modern scholars have come to doubt that Huiyuan wrote *Dasheng qixin lun yishu*.[62] They cite two internal reasons. First, the text refers to "Dharma Master Yuan" 遠法師, which suggests that it was written not by Huiyuan himself, but by a disciple or admirer. Second, Huiyuan's other works adopt a prosody of four-character units. This commentary breaks that stylistic habit. There is also other, circumstantial evidence against Huiyuan's authorship. For example, the *Xu Gaoseng zhuan* reports that Huiyuan was the most senior monk in the audience when Tanqian taught Paramārtha's *Mahāyānasaṃgrahabhāṣya*, but it does not mention that Huiyuan wrote a commentary on the *Treatise*. The earliest catalogue listing a commentary on the *Treatise* by Huiyuan is dated 1091.[63]

Yoshihide Yoshizu 吉津宜英, however, claims that similarities between this commentary on the *Treatise* and Huiyuan's other works suggest a common authorship.[64] Huiyuan is the purported author of a number of exegetical works on major scriptures and at least nine extant works are attributed to him. These include the encyclopedic *Dasheng yizhang* 大乘義章 (A Compendium of the Great Vehicle; T44.1851), in twenty fascicles.[65] The commentary evidences

---

62. See, for example, Kenneth K. Tanaka, *The Dawn of Chinese Pure Land Buddhist Doctrine: Ching-ying Hui-yuan's Commentary on the Visualization Sutra* (Albany: State University of New York Press, 1990), pp. 29–30.

63. *Sinpyeon jejong gyojang chongnok* 新編諸宗教藏總錄 (Newly Compiled *Comprehensive Record of the Canonical* Works of the Various Schools), edited by the Goryeo monk Uicheon 義天 (1055–1101). T55.2184, 1175a2. The commentary is listed as two fascicles. *Tōiki dentō mokuroku* 東域傳燈目錄 (Record of the Transmission of the Lamp to the Eastern Regions), by the Japanese monk Eichō 永超 (1014–1095), also attributes a commentary on the *Treatise* in two fascicles to Huiyuan; T55.2183, 1158c25.

64. Yoshihide Yoshizu, "Eon *Daijō kishin ron gisho* no kenkyū" 慧遠『大乘起信論義疏』の研究 (A Study of Huiyuan's *Elucidation of the Meaning of the Treatise on Awakening Mahāyāna Faith*), *Komazawa daigaku Bukkyō gakubu ronshū kenkyū kiyō* 駒沢大学仏教学部研究紀要 34 (1976): pp. 151–173.

65. For a list and study of Huiyuan's works, see Okamoto Ippei, "Jōyō ji Eon no chosaku no zengo kankei ni kansuru shiron" 淨影寺慧遠の著作の前後関係に関する試論 (On the Chronological Relationship of Writings by Huiyuan of Jingying Monastery),

doctrinal agreement with these other works of Huiyuan and may at least be treated as the work of someone close to him and part of the same Southern branch of the Dilun school. With these considerations in mind, we will continue to refer to the author of *Dasheng qixin lun yishu* as Huiyuan.

Like the commentary attributed to Tanyan, the main doctrinal feature of this commentary is a strict distinction between suchness as unconditioned and phenomena as conditioned. Huiyuan reprises a classic analogy of a rope mistaken to be a snake. In darkness, one mistakenly sees a rope as a snake but in daylight one realizes that it is just a rope; the appearance of a snake arises and ceases, but the rope remains as it is. Huiyuan associates true consciousness (*zhenshi* 真識) with the rope, and false consciousness (*wangshi* 妄識) with the illusion of a snake.[66] Similarly, when discussing the metaphor of ocean and waves in the *Treatise*, Huiyuan insists that true consciousness never changes even if it combines with the winds of ignorance.[67]

Possibly adapting the relationship described in the *Laṅkāvatāra-sūtra* between the eighth, store consciousness and the seven other consciousnesses (*qi shi* 七識),[68] he further maintains that the *tathāgatagarbha* serves as the basis of the eighth consciousness and the eighth consciousness in turn serves as the basis for the seventh consciousness (*di qi shi* 第七識). He describes this relationship between the eighth and the seventh consciousnesses as one resembling a body and its shadow. In turn, he identifies the seventh consciousness as the mind that arises and ceases and the eighth consciousness

---

in Geumgang Daehak bulgyo munhwa yeon'guso, comp., *Jiron shisō no keisei to hen'yō*, pp. 162–183.

66. Huiyuan, *Dasheng qixin lun yishu*. T44.1843, 197a6–9.

67. T44.1843, 185a7–11.

68. T16.670, 484b11–16; T16.671, 523b22–23c1.

as that which accords with the flow of falsehood generated by arising and ceasing.[69]

Huiyuan also employs the idea of a ninth consciousness in this commentary. He associates the gateway of suchness and the gateway of arising and ceasing with the ninth and eighth consciousnesses, respectively. When the ninth consciousness, the gateway of suchness, changes by adjusting to conditions, it comes to be identified as the eighth consciousness.[70] The idea of the ninth consciousness does not appear in Tanyan's commentary, but in the preface to the *Treatise* attributed to Zhikai 智愷 (d. 568)[71] there is reference to a two-fascicle work titled *Jiushi yizhang* 九識義章 (Essays on the Idea of the Ninth Consciousness), claiming Paramārtha as its translator. The *Hane* commentary (see discussion of *Hane 333V*) also attributes a text titled *Jiushi zhang* 九識章 (Essays on the Ninth Consciousness) to Paramārtha.[72]

---

69. Huiyuan, *Dasheng qixin lun yishu*. T44.1843,182b28.
70. T44.1843, 179a20–27.
71. Zhikai was one of Paramārtha's foremost students and amanuenses; see *Xu Gaoseng zhuan*. T50.2060, 430a19, 430c3–11, 431b2–23. The preface to the *Treatise* is unlikely to have been written by Zhikai. It states that Paramārtha was invited to China by the Liang Emperor Wu, who had sent a delegation to Magadha, but there is no record of such a delegation. Rather, there was a delegation sent to Funan (in present-day southern Cambodia and southern Vietnam); see *Xu Gaoseng zhuan*, T50.2060, 429c11–13. There is evidence that Paramārtha was in Funan, and not India, at this time. This suggests that Tanqian had only a partial grasp of the truth or was trying to give Paramārtha and the *Treatise* more Indic credentials. It is possible that the preface was written by Tanqian, who went to south China when the persecution of Buddhism began in 574, studied Paramārtha's theories and translations, and began to teach them in North China in 587. The reference to the *Jiushi yizhang* in the preface, and a similar reference in *Hane 333V*, further supports speculation that Tanqian was the author of both the preface and *Hane 333V*.
72. Ikeda Masanori 池田將則 (이케다 마사노리), "Kyō'u shōku shozō Tonkō bunken *Daijō kishin ron sho* (gidai, *Hane 333V*) ni tsuite" 杏雨書屋所藏敦煌文獻大乘起信論疏 (擬題, 羽333V) について (On the Dunhuang Manuscript *Dasheng qixin lun shu* Held in the Kyō'u Library [provisional title *Hane 333 Verso*]), *Bulgyohak ribyu* 불교학리뷰 (Critical Review for Buddhist Studies) 12 (2012): p. 122.

Hane 333V

A manuscript of this commentary on the *Treatise* was discovered in the collection of Dunhuang manuscripts collected by Haneda Tōru 羽田亨 (1882–1955). It is therefore abbreviated as *Hane 333V*. The extant manuscript is incomplete and carries neither a title nor reference to its author or the date of its composition. It has recently been edited by Ikeda Masanori.[73]

Hane 333V stands in close relation to Tanyan's commentary: some sentences are identical in the two texts. According to Ikeda, this text predates Tanyan's commentary because Tanyan at one point criticizes it. If Ikeda were right, and if Tanyan's commentary were genuine, then *Hane 333V* would have to pre-date Tanyan's death in 588. Yet *Hane 333V* does not seem to be Tanyan's particular focus in the passage on which Ikeda bases his argument (X45.755, 165a1–6), leaving his conclusions tentative at best. Our research on the manuscript and its contents remains preliminary at this point and more work needs to be done to confirm whether or not *Hane 333V* is the oldest commentary on the *Treatise*, as Ikeda suggests.

Wonhyo's Gisil lon so *and* Daeseung gisil lon byeolgi

The Silla commentator Wonhyo 元曉 (617–686) wrote two important commentaries on the *Treatise*: *Gisil lon so* 起信論疏 (Commentary on the *Treatise on Awakening [Mahāyāna] Faith*; T44.1844) and *Daeseung gisil lon byeolgi* 大乘起信論別記 (Further Notes on the *Treatise on Awakening Mahāyāna Faith*; T44.1845). He deemed it uniquely able to reconcile all Buddhist doctrinal debates[74]

---

73. Ikeda Masanori, "Kyō'u shōku shozō Tonkō bunken *Daijō kishin ron sho* (gidai, *Hane 333V*) ni tsuite," pp. 45–167.
74. T44.1845, 226b12.

and to avoid what he presented as an excessive focus on negation or affirmation of the existence of dharmas, which he associated with Madhyamaka and Yogācāra teachings, respectively.[75] Wonhyo also attempted to overcome some of the internal tensions that had developed in Sinitic Buddhism after the pilgrim and monk Xuanzang 玄奘 (596–664) had returned to China from India in 645, bringing new texts of the Yogācāra school as well as retranslating texts originally translated by Bodhiruci, Paramārtha, and others.[76]

Throughout the sixth century, commentators on the *Treatise* had been troubled by the relationship between the *tathāgatagarbha* and the store consciousness, in particular the claim made in the *Treatise* that when the mind as suchness combines with the mind as arising and ceasing, this constitutes the store consciousness [576b]. This claim was seen to bear upon two related doctrinal issues. First, could suchness, an unconditioned dharma—one not subject to the laws of cause and effect—be acted upon causally? In other words, could the mind as suchness, represented by *tathāgatagarbha*, change when combined with the mind as arising and ceasing, represented by the store consciousness? Second, could unconditioned suchness act causally?

Some of the earliest commentators were committed to the fundamental principle of Indian Buddhism that unconditioned dharmas cannot be acted upon casually and so do not change. Huiyuan was particularly prominent in adopting this position, as we have seen. The problem with these accounts, however, is the lingering ambiguity introduced by the term *sui* 隨, variously meaning to follow, to

---

75. T44.1845, 226b5–9.
76. Yoshizu Yoshihide, "Hōzō no *Daijō kishin ron gigi* no seiritsu to tenkai" 法蔵の「大乗起信論義記」の成立と展開 (Date and Development of Fazang's *Notes on the Meaning of the Treatise on Awakening Mahāyāna Faith*) in ed., Hirakawa Akira 平川彰, *Nyoraizō to Daijō kishin ron* 如来蔵と大乗起信論 (*Tathāgatagarbha* and the *Treatise on Awakening Mahāyāna Faith*) (Tokyo: Shunjūsha, 1990), p. 396.

accord with, to accommodate, to respond to, to adapt to. Although early commentators sought to emphasize the non-changing nature of suchness and, by implication, to uphold the doctrinal claim that unconditioned dharmas cannot be causal, their use of the term *sui* carries a connotation of change associated with adaptation.

Wonhyo's intervention marks a watershed in this commentarial tradition. He was perhaps the earliest commentator explicitly to endorse the view that the *Treatise* in fact stated that suchness could be acted upon causally. His understanding of the analogy of the wind acting on the ocean to stir up waves is instructive. He claims that it is not in the self-nature of the ocean to move, yet the ocean moves at the level of waves (representing phenomenal appearance) in response to the wind (ignorance). For Wonhyo, this creates arising and ceasing.[77] He states that the sense in which there is production or generation is an attribute of the gateway of the mind as arising and ceasing, not the gateway of the mind as suchness.[78] He also makes it clear that the *tathāgatagarbha* is associated with both gateways. In the gateway of the mind of suchness, he identifies it as that which neither arises nor ceases.[79] He describes its role in the gateway of the mind of arising and ceasing as follows:

Although this One Mind is inherently awoken, in according with ignorance it generates arising and ceasing. Hence, in this gateway [of arising and ceasing] the *tathāgata*'s nature is hidden and not revealed; it is called the *tathāgatagarbha*. As the [*Laṅkāvatāra-*] *sūtra* says: "The *tathāgatagarbha* is the cause of good and bad. It is able to create rebirth in all types of existence, everywhere. It is like an actor transforming to appear as all manner of sentient

77. T44.1844.208b13; 211b8–9.
78. T44.1844, 208c20–24.
79. T44.1844, 208b12.

existence."[80] These are the meanings to be found in the gateway of arising and ceasing. Hence, what the [*Laṅkāvatāra-*]*sūtra* terms "the One Mind, called the *tathāgatagarbha*" is expressed in the [the *Treatise*] as the gateway of arising and ceasing.[81]

Wonhyo also emphasizes that what arises or ceases shares an intrinsic reality (*ti*) with what does not arise and cease. The former is simply the mode in which the latter is manifest as phenomenal appearance, in response to the winds of ignorance.[82]

Fazang's Dasheng qixin lun yiji

Fazang 法藏 (643–712) was regarded as the third patriarch of the Huayan lineage. He initially based himself at Mount Taibai 太白山, in the southwest of present-day Shaanxi. He later became the disciple of the Huayan master Zhiyan 智儼 (602–668). In 670, two years after Zhiyan's death, Fazang formally entered the monastic community at Taiyuan Monastery 太原寺 in Chang'an. He subsequently became a peripatetic, spreading Huayan doctrines and contributing to various translation projects. He even served as a teacher to Empress Wu Zetian (r. 690–705).

Fazang wrote two commentaries on the *Treatise*: *Dasheng qixin lun yiji* 大乘起信論義記 (Notes on the Meaning of the *Treatise on Awakening Mahāyāna Faith*; T44.1846) and *Dasheng qixin lun bieji* 大乘起信論別記 (Further Notes on the *Treatise on Awakening Mahāyāna Faith*; T44.1847). *Dasheng qixin lun yiji*, in particular, had a substantial influence on later commentators. In it, he cited and adopted much from Wonhyo's *Gisil lon so*; both were students

---

80. Guṇabhadra trans. T16.670, 510b4–6.
81. T44.1844, 206c19–22.
82. T44.1844, 208b13.

of Zhiyan. Fazang was also a close acquaintance of the Silla monk Uisang 義湘 (625–702), founder of Huayan in Korea, who in turn was a friend of Wonhyo.

Inspired by the *Treatise*'s teaching that the mind as suchness retains its own identity when merging with the mind as arising and ceasing, the Huayan master Dushun 杜順 (557–640) had introduced the idea of the non-obstruction suchness and phenomena (*li shi wu ai* 理事無礙).[83] Fazang subsequently identified this doctrine as the characteristic teaching of what he termed "the lineage of the dependent arising out of the *tathāgatagarbha*" (*rulaizang yuanqi zong* 如來藏緣起宗), one of the four Buddhist lineages (*zong* 宗) that he recognized.[84] The doctrine of "the dependent arising out of the *tathāgatagarbha*" effectively turned the theory of dependent arising (*pratītya-samutpāda*)—everything arises from causes and conditions and has no inherent self-nature—into an ontology. It supported the idea that the unconditioned dharma of suchness (*tathāgatagarbha*) is the basis of conditioned and defiled phenomena.

By drawing on analogies that present ignorance as external to suchness, the *Treatise* leaves itself vulnerable to the charge that it introduces a dualist analogy into a monistic ontology. In failing to

---

83. In Sinitic Buddhist contexts, *li* 理 is synonymous with suchness (*tathatā*) when contrasted with *shi* 事 (phenomena). It denotes reality as it truly is, without any conceptual overlay.
84. In his system of doctrinal classification of Buddhist scriptures translated into Chinese, Fazang distinguished four lineages: (1) attachment to dharmas through their characteristics (*suixiang fazhi zong* 隨相法執宗), associated with Hīnayāna scriptures; (2) real emptiness without characteristics (*zhenkong wuxiang zong* 真空無相宗), associated with Prajñā and Madhyamaka scriptures; (3) nothing but consciousness or, alternatively, dharma characteristics (*weishi faxiang zong* 唯識法相宗), associated with Yogācāra scriptures; and (4) the dependent arising out of the *tathāgatagarbha*, associated with the *Laṅkāvatāra* and the *Ghana-vyūha* (*Dasheng miyan jing* 大乘密嚴經; Sutra of the Secret Adornment) sutras, as well as the *Treatise* and the *Ratnagotravibhāga*.

account for the origin of ignorance, the *Treatise* can be construed as also failing to provide a satisfactory account of how badness and suffering arise, thus undermining its own soteriological goal. Fazang advanced an explanation of why it is not possible for ignorance to exist separately from suchness as the intrinsic reality of badness. He did so in response to the *Treatise*'s statement that "all the characteristics of the mind and consciousnesses are ignorance, and the characteristic of ignorance is not separate from the nature of awakening" [576c]. Fazang commented:

> The karmic and other defiled consciousnesses (*xin*)[85] are called cognitive characteristics. Since they are all characteristics of non-awakening [the *Treatise*] states that "all the characteristics of the mind and consciousnesses are ignorance."[86] This remark is not made with respect to the intrinsic reality of the mind (*xin*).
>
> This, however, presents a further objection. Since it is said that the characteristics of all these are ignorance, then the explanation for the cessation of ignorance would be that there is an additional intrinsic nature separate from that of suchness. This is the objection that there is an intrinsic nature that exists apart from suchness.
>
> The response to this objection is as follows. The characteristic of non-awakening [associated with] these consciousnesses is not separate from the nature of inherent awakening as it accords with defilements. It is for this reason that [the *Treatise*]

85. As noted above, in the *Treatise*, karmic consciousness is one of the five names of mentation (*yi* 意), the seventh consciousness: "Mentation has five names. What are they? The first is karmic consciousness, because this means that the unawakened mind is set in motion because of the force of ignorance" [577b].

86. As noted above, early commentators on this passage understood the term "the mind" (*xin* 心) to refer to the seventh consciousness and the term "consciousnesses" (*shi* 識) to refer to the first six consciousnesses.

says: "[The characteristic of ignorance] is not separate from the nature of awakening." The characteristic of ignorance and the nature of inherent awakening are neither the same nor different. Because they are not different, [their nature] is not destructible. Because they are not the same, [the characteristic aspect] is not indestructible.

The idea that [their nature] is not destructible [because] they are not different explains why ignorance is identical to true understanding. So the *Nirvana Sutra* says: "The nature of true understanding and that of ignorance is non-dual. The nature of this non-duality is true nature."[87] The idea that [the characteristic of ignorance] is destructible [because] they[88] are not the same explains why ignorance ceases but the nature of awakening is not destroyed. The meaning of extinguishing delusion can be understood in the light of this.[89]

Although Fazang identifies ignorance as a characteristic associated with the first seven consciousnesses, he interprets the *Treatise* to mean that ignorance is not associated with the intrinsic reality of the mind, with suchness.[90]

This claim introduces a potential difficulty, however: it implies that if ignorance is able to cease, as it must if there is to be initial awakening, it does so due to the cessation of the intrinsic nature (*tixing* 體性) of ignorance. To claim this is to acknowledge the existence of

87. Based on the *Mahāparinirvāṇa-sūtra* (*Da banniepan jing* 大般涅槃經; Nirvana Sutra). T12.374, 410c21–22.
88. True understanding and ignorance.
89. *Dasheng qixin lun yiji* 大乘起信論義記 (Notes on the Meaning of the *Treatise on Awakening Mahāyāna Faith*). T44.1846, 260a19–29.
90. Here he draws on views expressed in the *Treatise*, such as "'Awakening' means that the intrinsic reality of the mind [as suchness] is free from conceiving" [576b].

"a nature that exists apart from suchness," opening up the problem of the origin of ignorance.

Following the lead of the *Treatise*, Fazang presents ignorance as a characteristic (*xiang* 相). He emphasizes that ignorance is therefore an appearance devoid of self-nature. He claims that awakening consists of the realization of this idea, such that "ignorance is identical to true understanding." Ignorance is indestructible only as long as the deluded mind sustains and supports it. This is analogous to the situation where waves (representing the deluded mind) continue to exist only as long as the ocean moves in response to the wind (ignorance). In this analogy, the characteristic of ignorance and the nature of inherent awakening are said not to be different in the same way that the wind is never separated from the ocean, the nature of which is wetness. Once the ocean stops moving, however, the waves cease to exist, and it becomes apparent that the waves and the wetness of the ocean are not the same, since only the ocean has an enduring self-nature. Similarly, ignorance ceases to exist with the realization that one has always been awoken, and so it differs from awakening because it lacks an enduring self-nature.

Fazang further makes the point that ultimately there is only one nature, not two, by citing the *Nirvana sutra*— "The nature of true understanding and of ignorance is non-dual. The nature of this non-duality is true nature." The nature of true understanding and of ignorance is non-dual because there is only one nature. True understanding is the realization that ignorance has no self-nature.

7. A CASE STUDY IN COMMENTARIAL DIFFERENCES: THE MOVEMENT OF SUCHNESS

The issue of whether suchness changes or moves underscores differences between interpretations of the *Treatise* proposed by Wonhyo and Fazang and those articulated in earlier commentaries. Commentaries on three key passages in the *Treatise* evidence these differences.

THE GATEWAY OF ARISING AND CEASING

In the *Treatise*, we find the claim that "the arising-and-ceasing mind exists because it is based on the *tathāgatagarbha*. That is to say, non-arising and non-ceasing combine with arising and ceasing: they are neither the same nor different. This is called the '*ālaya* consciousness'" [576b]. The issue is whether the *tathāgatagarbha*, the un-conditioned, changes when combined with the arising-and-ceasing mind, the conditioned. Commentators expressed different opinions on this claim.

Tanyan, Huiyuan, and *Hane 333V* all emphasized that the *tathāgatagarbha* does not change. Tanyan maintained that the *tathāgatagarbha* is the inherent awakening in which there is no conceiving. Precisely because there is no conceiving, it can adjust to defilements (*sui wang liuzhuan* 隨妄流轉). Yet the *tathāgatagarbha* merely appears to arise and cease when, in fact, its nature (which is to illuminate) never changes.[91] Huiyuan identified the *tathāgatagarbha* as the eighth consciousness—the *ālayavijñāna* or store consciousness—and maintained that the *tathāgatagarbha* "constantly abides" (*chang zhu* 常住; *nitya*) as the intrinsic reality (*ti* 體) of defilement. It remains constant despite its apparent defilement as

---

91. X45.755, 159b12–16.

it adjusts to conditions.⁹² For *Hane 333V*, the *tathāgatagarbha* refers to the state where the nature of the mind remains as it is and does not change.⁹³

In contrast, both Wonhyo and Fazang clearly state that the *tathāgatagarbha*—the non-arising and non-ceasing mind—moves as a whole when combined with arising and ceasing. In other words, they allow that the unconditioned is subject to conditioning.⁹⁴

THE METAPHOR OF THE WIND AND WAVES
The *Treatise* addresses the issue of whether the *tathāgatagarbha* moves or changes with an analogy:

> ... since the characteristic of ignorance is not separate from the nature of awakening, the mind and consciousnesses are inde-structible and destructible. This is like the great ocean, where water moves in waves due to the wind. The characteristics of the water and the wind [as waves] are not separate from one another. Since it is not in the nature of water to move [by itself], its char-acteristic of movement will cease if the wind ceases, without its wetness ever being destroyed. And it is because, in the same way, the intrinsically pristine mind of sentient beings is moved by the wind of ignorance. Both the mind and ignorance lack character-istics of shape, and they are not separate from one another. Since it is not in the nature of the mind to move [by itself], its contin-uous flow will cease if ignorance ceases, without the nature of cognition ever being destroyed. [576c]

---

92. T44.1843, 182b28–c4.
93. Ikeda Masanori, "Kyō'u shōku shozō Tonkō bunken *Daijō kishin ron sho* (gidai, *Hane 333V*) ni tsuite," p. 122.
94. Wonhyo, T44.1844, 208b12–26; Fazang, T44.1846, 254b24–c26.

For Huiyuan, Tanyan, and *Hane 333V*, the text's statement that water retains its wetness, whether calm or agitated, emphasizes the idea that the *tathāgatagarbha* never changes.[95]

By contrast, Wonhyo and Fazang interpret this analogy to mean that the *tathāgatagarbha* changes from a calm to an agitated state. They navigate the difficulty of how the *tathāgatagarbha* can move by explaining that it changes not out of its own self-nature but because it adjusts to, or accords with, ignorance.[96] This reading was made possible by an ambiguity in the formulation of this analogy in the *Treatise*. On the one hand, the text states that the wetness that is the nature of water—and, by analogy, the *tathāgatagarbha*—does not change, whether the water is smooth or agitated. Yet, on the other hand, the *Treatise* also says that "it is not in the nature of water to move [by itself]."

THE HABITUATION OF SUCHNESS

In his *Mahāyānasaṃgraha-śāstra*, the fourth-century Yogācāra master Asaṅga maintains that for something to be habituated, it must be: (1) enduring; (2) indeterminate, giving rise neither to good nor bad; (3) able to be habituated; and (4) exist at the same time and locus as that which habituates.[97] In the seventh century, both Xuanzang and Wonhyo drew attention to the third item on this list, insisting that Asaṅga's implication is that because suchness is an unconditioned dharma therefore it cannot be habituated.[98] In contrast, the *Treatise*

95. Huiyuan, T44.1843, 185a9–11; Tanyan, X45.755, 161c24–162a4; Ikeda, "Kyō'u shōku shozō Tonkō bunken *Daijō kishin ron sho* (gidai, *Hane 333V*) ni tsuite," p. 135.
96. The key phrase here is 非自性動, 但隨他動. See Wonhyo, T44.1844, 211b8–10; Fazang, T44.1846, 260b5–8.
97. *She dasheng lun* 攝大乘論 (Compendium of the Great Vehicle), trans. Paramārtha. T31.1593, 115c5–6.
98. Xuanzang, *Cheng weishi lun* 成唯識論 (Demonstration of Nothing but Consciousness). T31.1585, 9c13–15; Wonhyo, *Daeseung gisil lon byeolgi*. T44.1845, 239a21–26.

recurrently uses the phrase "habituate suchness" (*xunxi zhenru* 熏習真如) [578a, 578b, 579a]. This seems to run counter to the basic Yogācāra idea that suchness is unconditioned.[99]

Commenting on this phrase, Tanyan states: "When ignorance has arisen, it does not have the power to sustain itself, and so it must depend on suchness to habituate [something else]."[100] The phrase "habituate suchness," however, also leaves room for Wonhyo and Fazang to suggest that suchness itself can be habituated; once agitated, it becomes karmic consciousness (*yeshi* 業識). As Fazang says: "[T]he mind as karmic consciousness arises because ignorance habituates and moves suchness."[101]

These three examples highlight contrasts between two lines of interpretation of the *Treatise*, but they leave several problems unresolved. For example, in the interpretations of earlier commentators such as Tanyan and Huiyuan, what exactly does it mean to claim that the *tathāgatagarbha*, which constantly abides and does not change, adjusts to conditions? One explanation is that the *tathāgatagarbha* remains unchanged despite serving as the basis of false conceptualization. This is where the classic analogy of the rope and the snake has a role to play. So when Tanyan comments on the phrase in the *Treatise* that "the mind constantly endures" (心即常住) [576b], he states: "[The mind] has always relied upon habituation by false conceptualizing and [appears to be] impermanent and nonenduring, just as water relies upon wind [and appears to have waves].

99. In *abhidharma* ("higher doctrine") literature, which Yogācāra follows, there are two unconditioned dharmas: nirvana and space (*ākāśa*). Nirvana is freedom from all affliction and suffering. Space neither displaces nor is displaced by any object; it permeates rather than obstructs. Something conditioned is subject to causes and conditions and is impermanent. Unconditioned dharmas are not, and that is what makes them unconditioned.
100. X45.755, 168b11–12.
101. T44.1846, 270c5–6.

When the energy of false conceptualizing is depleted, then 'the mind constantly endures,' just as when the wind ceases, then the water is calm."[102] This line of interpretation is consistent with the doctrine of Indian Yogācāra.

If interpreted in this way, however, the *Treatise* still presents a fundamental conundrum. The text seeks to establish a close relation between defiled phenomena and the undefiled (suchness, *tathāgatagarbha*). It therefore posits the store consciousness as merely an intermediate state in which suchness is combined with ignorance. In this model, the store consciousness cannot be considered a consciousness in the usual sense because suchness is unconditioned. Being unconditioned it cannot be causal and therefore cannot serve the function of producing defiled phenomena. Yet the *Treatise* is clear that the store consciousness is "the collector and producer of all dharmas" [576b]. As a result, it appears as unconditioned yet also conditioned, introducing a sharp aporia.[103] For this model to work, the store consciousness has to be taken to be a real consciousness, since a real consciousness serves as the basis for producing phenomena. In the analogy of the ocean waves that the text introduces to discuss this model, the store consciousness should therefore be likened not to the water of the ocean but to the wetness that is the nature of water. The metaphor in the *Treatise* would then lack anything that might correspond to water, and so the only way to make the model work is to concede that the store consciousness plays the roles of both the water and the wetness that is its nature. By

---

102. X45.755, 160c21–22.
103. Huiyuan's proposal to take the store consciousness as "true consciousness" (*zhenshi* 真識) on the one hand, and as ocean water on the other, is problematic. In the analogy, ocean water is transformed into waves. By contrast, the store consciousness as true consciousness cannot be transformed into the seven consciousnesses; see T44.1843, 185a7–11.

extension, it must be understood as both unconditioned (identical with suchness) and conditioned (serving the function of producing phenomena).

Wonhyo and Fazang correctly discerned this conundrum. They addressed it by abandoning the distinction between unconditioned and conditioned dharmas and, as a result, their interpretation is less problematic than that of earlier commentators. After Fazang, Chengguan 澄觀 (557–640), and Zongmi 宗密 (780–841), this line of interpretation emerged as the dominant reading of the *Treatise*. As a result, the interpretations of Tanyan and Huiyuan fell into disuse and the distinction between unconditioned and conditioned was effaced.

Treatise on Awakening Mahāyāna Faith

Preface to the Treatise on Awakening Mahāyāna Faith

COMPOSED BY THE MONK ZHIKAI
OF YANGZHOU[1]

[575a] The *Treatise on Awakening Mahāyāna Faith* is an extremely profound and recondite scripture of the ultimate Great Vehicle. It discloses the meaning of dependent arising as it really is. [Dependent arising] is deep and expansive in import; tranquil, it is without characteristics. It is extensive and vast in application; broad, it is without bounds.[2] It is the basis for ordinary people and sages, and

---

1. As discussed in the introduction, the *Treatise* is a Chinese apocryphon but it has been widely accepted as an authentic Indian text in East Asia. The purported author of its preface, Zhikai 智愷 (518–568), claims to provide an account of its composition in India and its subsequent transmission to and translation in China. In so doing, he imitates prefaces appended to texts actually written in India and later translated into Chinese. He refers to real historical events but misconstrues others.
2. An understanding of dependent arising constituted the core of the Buddha's awakening. It was classically summarized as "if this arises, that comes to be; in the absence of this, that ceases," and was presented as a chain of twelve causal links beginning with ignorance and ending with death. It explains the arising of suffering and supplies its antidote, the elimination of ignorance. The *Treatise* largely ignores the twelve-link presentation of dependent

the foundation of the multitude of dharmas.[3] Yet very few had faith since the texts of the Great Vehicle are profound and their import is remote. Therefore, for over six hundred years after the Tathāgata's decease,[4] various paths emerged in chaotic profusion and *māra* demons vied to stir things up, incessantly maligning the True Dharma of the Buddha.[5]

At that time, a certain monk of eminent virtue, named Aśvaghoṣa, was in profound accord with the Great Vehicle and had a thorough comprehension of the dharma nature.[6] He was suffused with great compassion and revealed [the True Dharma] in accordance with the varying capacities of [his audience]. Because he took pity on beings who had long since strayed, he composed this treatise. He caused the Three Jewels to flourish and the Buddha's Sun to rise once more,[7] giving rise to faith so that before long people turned away from what was wrong and entered true understanding. He caused the true scriptures of the Great Vehicle to be revealed again to his contemporaries and the profound principle of dependent arising to be made evident again to later ages. The masses

arising. Instead, the text introduces its own dynamic version of the idea as a conflict between ignorance and habituation on the one hand, and the purifying power of the *tathāgatagarbha* and the capacity of sentient beings to become buddhas on the other.

3. Dharma (*fa* 法) is an important and recurring term in the *Treatise*. It has a wide range of connotations in Buddhist literature. These include: Buddhist doctrine, the basic factors of experience, mental and physical constituents, good qualities, principles, rules or laws, practices, ways of understanding reality, and truth. In its most expansive sense, it can encompass all reality. These and other possible meanings may be simultaneously at work in the *Treatise* in any given instance.

4. This interval of six hundred years after the Buddha is linked to Aśvaghoṣa (first century CE) on the testimony of Kumārajīva. See Stuart H. Young, *Conceiving the Indian Buddhist Patriarchs in China*, pp. 45–46.

5. *Māras*, literally "causing death," are demons who tempt Buddhist practitioners to deviate from the path that leads to enlightenment.

6. The dharma nature (*faxing* 法性) refers to the true nature of reality. It is equivalent to suchness (*zhenru* 真如). The following Prayer of Homage makes this connection.

7. The Three Jewels are the Buddha, Dharma, and Monastic Community. One becomes a Buddhist by formally "taking refuge" in these three.

who had strayed and those with heterodox views abandoned them and took refuge in [the Three Jewels]; the benighted and the biased abandoned the attachments that they had and rallied to [the Three Jewels].

From early times, [the *Treatise*] has long been hidden in the Western Regions, without being transmitted to Xia of the East.[8] The time was just right for it to be propagated in translation, so the late Emperor Wu of Liang (r. 502–549) dispatched an emissary on an official visit to the state of Magadha in central India[9] to collect scriptures and Dharma masters. The emissary met the Tripiṭaka master Kulānanda, known by the Chinese name Zhendi (Paramārtha).[10] In his youth, this man had widely collected and thoroughly read the scriptures, but his understanding of the Great Vehicle had been particularly incisive, profound, and far-reaching. So now the king of that state [Magadha] responded by immediately sending him [to Liang]. The Dharma master vehemently declined, but to no avail, so he boarded a sailing ship. With Gautama and many attendants and

8. "Xia of the East" here refers to what we would now recognize as China.
9. Magadha was a major region of India in Buddha's time, roughly corresponding to the southern part of present-day Bihār. It was considered to have been Buddha's home for much of his life. In the time of Emperor Wu, in the first half of the sixth century, Magadha was an important region of the Gupta Empire. *Zhong Tianzhu* 中天竺, translated here as "central India," refers specifically to Madhyadeśa, the area of north central India bounded by the Himālayas to the north and the Vindhya mountains to the south.
10. Mochizuki Shinkō 望月信亨 argues that Paramārtha was not in India, but in Funan, in the area of present-day southern Cambodia and southern Vietnam. Mochizuki therefore suggests that the preface conflates two events here. See *Kōjutsu Daijō kishin ron* 講述大乘起信論 (An Account of the *Treatise on Awakening Mahāyāna Faith*) (Tokyo: Fuzanbō, 1938), sec. 2, p. 12. On Paramārtha's residence in Funan and the circumstances of his invitation to Liang, see also Diana Y. Paul, *Philosophy of Mind in Sixth-Century China*, p. 23. See also the discussion in the introduction to this volume on the issue of Paramārtha relationship to the *Treatise*. Tripiṭaka refers to the traditional division of the Indian Buddhist canon into three "baskets": 1) monastic discipline (*vinaya*); 2) discourses (*sūtra*); and 3) *abhidharma*, a general term referring to scholastic presentations of Buddhist doctrine based on discourses attributed to the Buddha.

followers,[11] they all delivered a storax Buddha image to the [Liang] court.[12]

Within ten days of their arrival, they encountered Hou Jing's invasion and uprising.[13] The flow of the Dharma master's splendid accomplishments was obstructed before he had yet spoken of the treasures that he held within himself. With the Sun of Wisdom temporarily eclipsed, he wished to return [to Magadha].

In due course, he was called on to meet the brilliant and worthy men of the capital: Huixian; Zhishao; Zhikai; Tanzhen; Huimin; and the Commander Commissioned with the Golden Axe and Grand Protector, Xiao Bo. In the third year of the *chengsheng* period of Great Liang, a *guiyou* year, on the tenth day of the ninth month,[14] the Dharma master was respectfully invited to expound the Great Vehicle in the Jianxing Temple of Shixing Commandery in Hengzhou,[15] in order to promulgate its recondite scriptures and to instruct and guide disciples who had strayed into confusion. In due course, he translated this treatise in one scroll and, to clarify the meaning of the treatise, [he also composed] a "profound text" commentary in twenty scrolls,[16] a "profound text" commentary on the

---

11. Gautama appears to be the name of a Buddhist monk, but his exact identity is unclear.

12. Storax is a fragrant resin made from the small tree *styrax officinalis*. It was used to make medicines, perfumes, and incense.

13. Hou Jing 侯景 (d. 552) was a general from the state of Eastern Wei. Having fled south to Liang, he led a rebellion and captured its capital in 549. Two months after Hou Jing's victory, the Liang ruler, Emperor Wu, died in captivity. On January 1, 552, Hou Jing proclaimed himself emperor, but on February 28, Liang troops forced him to flee the capital. He was murdered on May 26.

14. No such date exists in the Chinese calendar. If one were to take this as the second, not the third, year of the *chengsheng* period, then the equivalent date would be October 2, 553.

15. Shixing Commandery was near modern Shaoguan, in northern Guangdong Province. First established as a commandery in 265, it was abolished in 581 when the northern state of Sui conquered its southern rival, Chen.

16. Possibly a reference to *Dasheng qixin lun xuanwen* 大乘起信論玄文 (A "Profound Text" Commentary on the *Treatise on Awakening Mahāyāna Faith*). A work in twenty scrolls under this title appears both in the *Kegonshū shōsho narabini inmyō roku* 華嚴宗章疏并因明録 (A Record of Commentaries and Logic Texts of the Huayan School) by Enchō 圓超

Great Perfection of Wisdom Discourse in four scrolls,[17] the *Twelve Links of Dependent Arising Scripture* in two scrolls, and *Essays on the Idea of the Ninth Consciousness* in two scrolls.[18] **[575b]** The oral translators included Upaśūnya,[19] from the Indic regions, and others. The scribes included Zhikai and others. From beginning to end, it was completed only after two full years.

When Aśvaghoṣa's capacious purpose shone forth again at that time, those with wrong views submitted to the true persuasion. Although I lament not having met the sage [Aśvaghoṣa], I rejoice in having come across his profound purpose. I extol his subtle tenets. My affection and adoration are without end. I have casually written this record without heed to my own ignorance. Should a wise man come across it, may he deign to correct what I have written.

(fl. early tenth century); and in the eleventh-century *Tōiki dentō mokuroku*, by the Japanese monk Eichō. It is attributed to Paramārtha in both. See T55.2177, 1133a9; T55.2183, 1158c14.

17. Possibly a contracted form of the title *Mahāprajñāpāramitā-sūtra* (*Dapin bore jing* 大品般若經).

18. None of the texts in this list has been firmly identified, or associated with Paramārtha, except by the author of this preface and by those who subsequently cited it. With the final item, there is a reference to a *Jiu shi zhang* 九識章 (Essay on the Ninth Consciousness) in *Hane 333V*; see Ikeda Masanori, "Kyō'u shōku shozō Tonkō bunken *Daijō kishin ron sho* (gidai, *Hane 333V*) ni tsuite," p. 122, col. 43; see also pp. 81–82, 88–90. But there is on-going scholarly debate about the exact identity of the *Treatise's* reference to *Jiu shi yi zhang*.

19. This identification follows Mochizuki Shinkō, who suggests that *yuezhi shouna* 月支首那 should read *yuepo shouna* 月婆首那; see Mochizuki Shinkō, *Kōjutsu Daijō kishin ron*, sec. 2, p. 12. Upaśūnya was a prince of Ujjain in Central India. In the mid-sixth century, he worked as a translator first in the Eastern Wei capital of Ye, then in the Liang capital of Jiankang, and finally in Jiangzhou. See *Da Tang neidian lu* 大唐內典錄 (Record of Buddhist Scriptures in the Great Tang), T55.2149, 274a11–26.

Treatise on Awakening Mahāyāna Faith, in One Fascicle

COMPOSED BY THE BODHISATTVA AŚVAGHOṢA.
TRANSLATED BY THE WESTERN INDIAN TRIPIṬAKA
DHARMA MASTER PARAMĀRTHA, OF LIANG.

PRAYER OF HOMAGE

I take refuge in [the Buddha] who pervades all ten directions,[20]
Whose actions are supreme, who is omniscient,[21]
Whose form is unhindered and unimpeded—
The One of Great Compassion who saves the world.

20. Before this time, the phrase "I take refuge in [the Buddha] who pervades all ten directions" (*guiming jin shifang* 歸命盡十方) is attested only in the translation of Vasubandhu's *Sukhāvatīvyūhopadeśa* that Bodhiruci made under the title *Wuliangshou jing youbotishe* 無量壽經優波提舍 (Commentary on the Sutra of Limitless Life). T26.1524, 230c17–18.
21. In his *Dasheng qixin lun yishu* (T44.1843, 176b27–176c2) the sixth-century commentator Huiyuan understands this line as a reference to three of the ten epithets of the response body, one of the three bodies of buddhas. See introduction for a discussion of the three bodies.

And I take refuge in the intrinsic reality and characteristics
of his body,[22] of Dharma

The ocean of suchness—the dharma nature—[23]

And the store of countless merits.[24]

And I take refuge in those who practice in accordance with
what is real.

This is because I wish to have sentient beings

Eliminate doubts and abandon wrongly held views,

And give rise to correct Mahāyāna faith,

Leaving the buddha-lineage uninterrupted.

22. The author plays on the connotations of several terms with overlapping associations. This part of the prayer refers to the Dharma, which comprises the corpus—the body— of teachings and practices of the Buddha. The term *ti* 體 also has connotations of a body and, as translated here, can further refer to the intrinsic reality of something. The term *xiang* 相 can refer to the characteristics of something. When applied to the bodies of buddhas, it refers specifically to the 32 major and 80 minor distinctive marks that indicate their supreme attainments. For Huiyuan, this line indicates veneration of the three kinds of buddha body: "And his [body]" (*ji bi* 及彼) refers to the response body; the "intrinsic reality of the body" (*shen ti* 身體) refers to the dharma body; and the "characteristics of the body" (*xiang* 相) refers to the recompense body. See T44.1843, 176c15–20. By contrast, Wonhyo comments in his seventh-century *Gisil lon so* that "this refers to the bodies of the Tathāgata. These bodies are precisely the recompense [bodies] of the Buddha, and are exactly the dharma realm, which serves as its own intrinsic reality." See T44.1844, 203c27–28. In other words, the dharma realm is the intrinsic reality (*ti*) of the Buddha, and the recompense bodies are its phenomenal characteristics (*xiang*).

23. This is a key term in the *Treatise* and in Mahāyāna generally. The text later describes the dharma nature: "The dharma nature is extensive and vast and it pervades all sentient beings. This is because it is uniform and non-dual, cannot be conceived in terms of distinctions between this or that, and is ultimately quiescent" [581a].

24. "Store" here translates *zang* 藏, one of the several meanings of the term. It is part of *rulaizang* 如來藏, *tathāgatagarbha*, a central term in the *Treatise* (see introduction). "Merit" translates *gongde* 功德, which is typically used as an equivalent of either *puṇya* (merit) or *guṇa* (qualities). *Gongde* is often understood in medieval Chinese literature as something acquired. That is how Huiyuan glosses its use in this passage of the *Treatise*. T44.1843, 177a7. However, later commentators on the *Treatise* generally take it to refer to innate qualities in the mind of all sentient beings. These are the qualities of buddhas.

OUTLINE OF THE TREATISE

The *Treatise* states: There is a Dharma able to give rise to the roots of Mahāyāna faith.[25] It therefore ought to be explained. The explanation has five parts. What are they?

Part 1. Reasons [for composing the treatise]

Part 2. Establishing the meaning

Part 3. Elucidation

Part 4. Cultivation of the commitment to faith

Part 5. Exhortation to practice and to reap the benefits

PART 1: REASONS FOR COMPOSING THE TREATISE

First, I will explain the "reasons [for composing the treatise]."

Question: What are the reasons for composing this treatise?

Answer: There are eight reasons. What are they?

The first is the main reason—that is to say, to free sentient beings from all suffering in order to attain ultimate happiness, and not to seek fame, profit, respect, or honor in the mundane world.

The second is that I wish to elucidate the Tathāgata's fundamental meaning in order to enable sentient beings to have a true understanding of it and not to make mistakes.

---

25. Huiyuan comments: "Faith is the root of practices, so it says that one should 'give rise to correct Mahāyāna faith.'... Faith is a necessary cause for becoming a reward buddha." T44.1843, 177b29–177c4. Wonhyo understands the use of "Dharma" here in the *Treatise* to refer to the One Mind teaching. T44.1844, 204c9.

The third is to cause sentient beings whose virtuous roots have reached maturity to remain firm in the Mahāyāna Dharma, without relapsing in their faith.[26]

The fourth is to cause sentient beings of few virtuous roots to cultivate a commitment to faith.

[575c] The fifth is to show skillful means to eliminate the hindrances of evil karmic actions, to protect the mind well, to set misconception and arrogance at a far remove, and to escape from the net of wrong doctrines.[27]

The sixth is to show how to practice calming and discernment, which are antidotes to the mental faults of ordinary people and adherents of the Two Vehicles.[28]

The seventh is to show the skillful means of concentrated mindfulness so that one will be born in the presence of a buddha and inevitably establish a non-relapsing commitment to faith.[29]

The eighth is to show the benefits of practice and to encourage it.

It is for such reasons that I have composed this treatise.

Question: The sutras are replete with these dharmas. Why must you expound them again?

---

26. In the agricultural metaphor of virtuous roots, one sows or stores seeds for future actions by engaging in wholesome activities. Like seeds, these activities mature over time to produce fruitful consequences and virtues such as compassion, generosity, and patience.

27. "Skillful means" (*fangbian* 方便) refers to the ability of buddhas and advanced bodhisattvas to assist sentient beings by adapting Buddhist teachings to their specific capacities, needs, and proclivities.

28. Calming and discernment are two central practices in Buddhist meditation. Calming involves cultivating a state of fixed attention on a meditative object, without restless agitation or sleepiness. Discernment refers to meditative analysis of an object or concept to understand what it truly is and what its implications might be. The reference to the "Two Vehicles" here alludes to the division of Buddhist teachings into various "vehicles." As noted in the introduction, Mahāyāna Buddhists speak of three vehicles. In this scheme, the "Two Vehicles" are the "Lesser Vehicles" (*Hīnayāna*) of hearers (*śrāvaka*) and solitary realizers (*pratyekabuddha*).

29. For a discussion of *nian* 念, see the introduction. Here, it refers to mindfulness of Amitābha, the buddha of the Western Paradise.

Answer: Although the sutras contain these dharmas, [I expound them again here] since sentient beings are not equal in their capacities and cultivation, and vary in their predispositions for receiving and understanding. That is to say, when the Tathāgata was in the world, sentient beings had keen faculties and the Teacher excelled in actions of body and mind. There was no need for a treatise since his perfect voice had only to sound once for the different kinds of beings to have an equal understanding.[30]

Ever since the Tathāgata's decease, there have been some sentient beings who, entirely through their own powers, have been able to gain an understanding by listening extensively [to sutras]. There have been some sentient beings who, also through their own powers, have heard a little yet understood much. And there have been some sentient beings who, without any intrinsic mental powers, have attained an understanding from expanded treatises.[31] Of course, there have also been sentient beings who, finding the wordiness of expanded treatises frustrating, have been able to gain understanding because their minds have taken pleasure in drawing out much meaning from *aide-memoires* and succinct texts.[32] Because a treatise such as this aims to summarize the idea that the Tathāgata's extensive, great, and profound dharma is boundless, I ought to expound it.

30. The Buddha's "perfect voice" refers to an idea, found in many Buddhist works, that he was like a skilled physician who correctly diagnosed the spiritual maladies of each person he encountered and prescribed the ideal antidote in his teachings. When he spoke to a crowd, each person heard exactly what would be most beneficial.
31. "Expanded treatises" refers both to large canonical texts, which elaborate details abbreviated in shorter works, and to commentaries on sutras.
32. *Zong chi* 總持, rendered here as "*aide-memoires*," is often used to translate the Sanskrit term *dhāranī*. These are condensed formulas that summarize complex doctrinal ideas. They were probably designed to facilitate memory, and so the Chinese preserves the idea of "retention" that is part of the Sanskrit etymology.

PART 2: ESTABLISHING THE MEANING

Having explained the "reasons [for composing the treatise]," I will next explain "establishing the meaning."

In general terms, there are two aspects of Mahāyāna. What are they?

The first is Dharma.

The second is the meanings.

"Dharma" refers to the mind of sentient beings. This mind includes all mundane and supramundane dharmas. The meaning of Mahāyāna is disclosed on the basis of this mind. Why? Because the aspect of this mind as suchness directly reveals Mahāyāna's intrinsic reality; and because the aspect of this mind as the cause and condition of arising and ceasing is the revealer of Mahāyāna's own intrinsic reality (*ziti*), characteristics (*xiang*), and function (*yong*).[33]

There are three "meanings" [of *mahā-*, "great," in the word Mahāyāna, "Great Vehicle"]. What are they?

33. This anticipates the two aspects, or "gateways," of the One Mind that appear later in the text: the aspect of the mind as suchness; and the aspect of the mind as arising and ceasing. The aspect of the mind as suchness reveals the intrinsic reality of Mahāyāna directly. The aspect of the mind as arising and ceasing reveals it indirectly. To reinforce the idea that the intrinsic reality of Mahāyāna is constant in both aspects, the text introduces the term "its own intrinsic reality" (*zi ti*). This indicates that the meaning of Mahāyāna remains unchanged in its arising-and-ceasing aspect although it is revealed only indirectly. This would have been important to the author of the *Treatise*. Since this teaching can occur only in the aspect of the mind as arising and ceasing, if it is to be genuine, he needed to emphasize that it still gives access to the intrinsic reality of Mahāyāna.

In his *Dasheng qixin lun yishu*, the sixth-century commentator Tanyan explains that Mahāyāna "has its own intrinsic reality (*zi ti* 自體), characteristics (*xiang* 相), and functions (*yong* 用)." He identifies Mahāyāna with the eighth, store consciousness. The eighth consciousness enables the other consciousnesses to have characteristics and functions; the other consciousnesses do not have their own intrinsic reality to produce characteristics and functions. Mahāyāna cannot be revealed until the intrinsic reality associated with the eighth consciousness causes characteristics and functions to be expressed through the other consciousnesses. X45.755, 156b22–156c3. Huiyuan frames this distinction instead in terms of the eighth and ninth consciousnesses. T44.1843, 179a20–179b1. See the discussion of this point in the introduction.

The first is that Mahāyāna's intrinsic reality is great because the suchness of all dharmas is uniform, neither increasing nor decreasing.

The second is that its characteristics are great because the *tathāgatagarbha* is replete with countless merits.

The third is that its functions are great because it is the producer of all good causes and effects, both mundane and supramundane.

That is why Mahāyāna [the "Great Vehicle"] is that on which all buddhas have always ridden and why all bodhisattvas ride on this Dharma until they arrive at the level of *tathāgatas*.[34]

PART 3: ELUCIDATION

[576a] Having explained "establishing the meaning," I will next explain the "elucidation."

The elucidation is threefold. What are its three sections?

The first discloses the correct meaning.

The second is on the antidotes to wrongly held views.

The third discriminates characteristics for embarking on the Way.

For Wonhyo, the mind that "reveals Mahāyāna's own intrinsic reality (*zi ti*)" refers to what he calls the "inherently awoken mind" (*benjue xin* 本覺心). This is in the gateway of arising and ceasing. Wonhyo further identifies this inherently awoken mind as the One Mind. "It is both the intrinsic reality and the cause of arising and ceasing and, for this reason, it is in the gateway of arising and ceasing," he says. "In the gateway of suchness, Mahāyāna as intrinsic reality (*ti*) is spoken of directly; but in the gateway of arising and ceasing, it is spoken of as 'its own intrinsic reality' (*zi ti*)." In other words, the referent of *ti* in the gateway of suchness and of *zi ti* in the gateway of arising and ceasing is the same—the One Mind. T44.1844, 206b13–15. In his *Dasheng qixin lun yiji*, Fazang follows this distinction between "intrinsic reality" (*ti*) and "its own intrinsic reality" (*zi ti*). T44.1846, 250c25–251a6.

34. Having explained *mahā-* of Mahāyāna, this passage explores the connotations of *yāna*, meaning "a vehicle" or "to ride." Mahāyāna is a teaching, a method, or a set of illuminating instructions. It is the "vehicle" to transport all bodhisattvas to buddhahood.

SECTION 1: THE CORRECT MEANING OF MAHĀYĀNA DOCTRINE: ONE MIND TWO GATEWAYS

With disclosing the correct meaning, there are two gateways based on the dharma of the One Mind.[35] What are they?

The first is the gateway of the mind as suchness.

The second is the gateway of the mind as arising and ceasing.

Each of these two gateways contains all dharmas. Why? Because these two gateways are not separate from one another.[36]

1.1 The Mind as Suchness

The mind as suchness is precisely the dharma-gate reality,[37] which is the overarching characteristic of the unified dharma

---

35. The doctrine of the One Mind was highly influential in East Asia, but it has no clear Sanskrit antecedent. The closest Sanskrit terms, *ekacitta* or *cittaikāgratā*, generally refer to concentrated mental focus, not to the expansive notion of a unified consciousness that pervades the universe, which we find in the *Treatise*. Huiyuan comments that reference to the two "gateways" here denotes the aspects (*xiang* 相) of the One Mind. T44.1843, 180a10–12.

36. There would be an apparent doctrinal inconsistency if this passage were read literally: it would imply that conditioned dharmas are contained in the unconditioned realm of suchness. For the attempts by various commentators to explain this problem in terms of the relationship between intrinsic reality, characteristics, and functions, see note 33.

37. In the *Jin'gangxian lun*, a translation traditionally attributed to Bodhiruci (although a number of modern scholars contest this claim), dharma (*fa* 法) is defined as a rule that prevents people from falling into evil and so allows them to reach buddhahood. The gateway (*men* 門) allows beings to pass through and reach buddhahood. Its reality (*ti* 體) is principle and teaching, and is the Dharma jewel. T25.1512, 799a28–30, 799b6–12. Bodhiruci's translation of the *Laṅkāvatāra-sūtra*, titled *Ru Lengqie jing*, combines these ideas into the term "dharma-gate reality," which denotes all the teachings of Buddhism. T16.671, 524b7–8. As the *Treatise* here refers to the dharma realm and to all dharmas, it is playing on the word "dharma" to mean both teaching or principle and the constituents of existence. For a brief discussion of the term "dharma gate" and its Sanskrit equivalent, *dharma-paryāya*, see Gadjin M. Nagao, *Mādhyamika and Yogācāra: A Study of Mahāyāna Philosophies*, p. 132.

realm.[38] That is to say, the nature of the mind neither arises nor ceases. It is solely due to false thoughts that there are distinctions between every dharma; if one is free from false thoughts, then there are none of the characteristics of perceptual fields.[39] Therefore, all dharmas have always been free from the characteristics of language, naming, and mental perceptions.[40] They are ultimately uniform, invariant, and indestructible. They are nothing but this One Mind and are therefore called "suchness." [By contrast,] all [dharmas] designated by language lack real referents because they follow only from false thoughts and cannot be apprehended.

"Suchness" (zhenru) is also devoid of characteristics. That is to say, it is at the point where language runs out. We use words to refute words, but there is nothing in suchness itself that might be refuted because all dharmas are entirely "real" (zhen). There is also nothing in suchness itself that might be posited because all dharmas are

---

38. The dharma realm (dharma-dhātu) denotes the field of sensory and mental experience. Initially, Buddhists listed eighteen components, dhātu: six sense faculties (the five senses and the mind); six kinds of cognitive fields (visible, auditory, gustatory, olfactory, tactile, and ideational); and six kinds of corresponding "consciousnesses" (vision, hearing, taste, smell, touch, and thinking). In later Mahāyāna discourse, these were subsumed under the dharma realm. The present passage similarly reduces the multiplicity of realms in Buddhist cosmology to a single, absolute reality. Huiyuan (T44.1843, 180a24–25) and Wonhyo (T44.1844, 4.207a25) identify the absolute dharma realm with the One Mind. Huiyuan (T44.1843, 186b07–08) draws an analogy between suchness and the fine particles of clay that constitute all earthen vessels. These particles pervade all such vessels; without them, there would be no pottery. In this sense, they are a general characteristic, just as suchness is the general characteristic of the mind and pervades cyclic existence.

39. Huiyuan draws a common analogy to a defect of the eyes: "It is like spots before the eyes, which exist because of damage to the eyes. If the eyes are cured then the spots will not exist." For Huiyuan, the spots are superimposed on what is actually there. Huiyuan further states that it is only through practice that one "will know that the false does not exist and will clearly comprehend the truth." T44.1843, 180b10–14.

40. Bodhiruci's translation of the Laṅkāvatāra-sūtra carries an identical reference to being "free from the characteristics of language and naming." It continues this list not with cognitive objects, but with the characteristics of perceptual fields and of phenomena. T15.671, 527c13–14.

equally "as such" (*ru*). One should know that all dharmas are called "suchness" because it is impossible to speak of or conceive of them.⁴¹

Question: This is the meaning of "suchness." To what should sentient beings conform in order to be able to obtain entry [through this gateway]?

Answer: If one knows that, although all dharmas are spoken of and conceived, there are in fact no speakers and nothing that might be spoken of, and no conceivers and nothing that might be conceived, it is called "conforming." And if one is free from conceiving, it is called "obtaining entry."

Moreover, two senses of suchness are distinguished through language. What are they?

The first is empty in accordance with what is real. This is because it is ultimately able to reveal what is real.

The second is non-empty in accordance with what is real. This is because it has its own intrinsic reality, which is replete with untainted qualities.⁴²

Suchness is "empty" because it has always been dissociated from all defiled dharmas. That is, it is free from the characteristics that differentiate all dharmas because it has none of the thoughts that the false mind has. One should know that the self-nature of suchness is not existent, non-existent, both existent and non-existent, [**576b**] or neither existent nor non-existent; and it is not the same, different,

---

41. This passage attempts to supply an etymology of the Chinese term *zhenru* 真如, by dividing it into two constituent parts. To "refute" (*qian* 遣) something suggests that one or more of its qualities is deemed to be not real or true. Because the *Treatise* tells us that all dharmas are suchness, it is impossible to reject any dharma as being unreal or untrue. To "posit" (*li* 立) has the sense of affirming one or more dharmas over other dharmas. But because all dharmas are undifferentiated—all dharmas are suchness—there is no dharma that might be posited as distinct from, or in preference to, another dharma.

42. A distinction between the empty and the non-empty aspects of the *tathāgatagarbha* appears in the translation of the *Śrīmālādevī-siṃhanāda-sūtra* made by Guṇabhadra (394–468) in 436. T12.353, 221c16–18.

both the same and different, or neither the same nor different.[43] So, in general terms, it is said to be empty because it is dissociated from any of the discriminations that sentient beings, with their false minds, create with each thought-moment. This is because there is really nothing to be emptied when one is free from a false mind.

Suchness is "non-empty" because dharmas are intrinsically empty and without falsity, as has already been shown. It is precisely the true mind—constantly unchanging and replete with pure dharmas—and so it is called non-empty. It also has no characteristics to be grasped because it is only by being free from conceiving and [the characteristics of] perceptual fields that realization accords with [suchness].

1.2 The Mind as Arising and Ceasing

The arising-and-ceasing mind exists because it is based on the *tathāgatagarbha*.[44] That is to say, non-arising and non-ceasing combine with arising and ceasing: they are neither the same nor different.[45]

---

43. This invokes the Indian logical formula known as the "four-cornered" negation, or tetralemma (*catuṣkoṭi*).

44. Tanyan writes that the *tathāgatagarbha* adapts to, or accords with, the arising and ceasing of phenomena. It neither arises nor ceases itself but only appears to do so. See X45.755, 159b13–16. Huiyuan comments that the mind as arising and ceasing and the *tathāgatagarbha* are simultaneous. He likens their relationship to that of a shadow and the shape that it casts. T44.1843, 182b29–c1. Wonhyo here glosses the tathāgatagarbha as the "intrinsically untainted mind," a term that the main text of the *Treatise* introduces below. T44.1844, 208b8.

45. Tanyan claims that "combine" refers to the combination of suchness with the store consciousness; the former is non-arising and non-ceasing, the latter arises and ceases. He links this to the analogy of the wind and the waves, which appears later in the main text. X45.755, 159b15–16, 19–22. In his *Gisil lon so*, Wonhyo comments: "The mind that is non-arising and non-ceasing moves as a whole, and so this mind is not separate from the characteristics of arising and ceasing. All the characteristics of arising and ceasing are intuited, and so arising and ceasing are not separate from the characteristics of the mind. Not being apart, they are said to be 'combined.' This is the combination of the mind that is non-arising and non-ceasing with [the characteristics of] arising and ceasing; it does not mean that arising and ceasing and non-arising and non-ceasing combine. 'Neither the same nor different': the mind that is non-arising and non-ceasing moves as a whole, and

This is called the "ālaya consciousness."[46] As the collector and producer of all dharmas, this consciousness has two senses. What
are they?

The first is awakening.

The second is non-awakening.

1.2.1 AWAKENING

"Awakening" means that the intrinsic reality of the mind [as
suchness] is free from conceiving. To be free from the characteristics of conceiving is to be identical to the realm of space: it is to
be all-pervasive.[47] The unitary characteristic of the dharma realm is
precisely the uniform dharma body of tathāgatas.[48] It is on the basis
of this dharma body that one speaks of inherent awakening. Why?
The meaning of "inherent awakening" is spoken of in relation to the
meaning of initial awakening since initial awakening is precisely the
same as inherent awakening.[49] The meaning of "initial awakening"

---

so it never loses its nature of non-arising and non-ceasing, although it is not different from
arising and ceasing. So arising and ceasing and the mind are not the same." T44.1844,
208b17–22.

46. See the introduction for a discussion of this key term.

47. The "realm of space" is a frequent image in Buddhist texts. The equivalent Sanskrit term,
ākāśa, does not refer to simple physical "space," in which objects cannot share the same
space at the same time. Rather ākāśa neither displaces nor is displaced by any object; it
permeates rather than obstructs. Here, the Treatise suggests that when the mind is freed
from obstructive notions, it permeates everything.

48. On the relationship between the dharma realm and the dharma body, see the introduction. There are echoes of Bodhiruci's phrasing in this sentence. There is reference to "the
uniform dharma body of tathāgatas" in his translation of the Saddharmapuṇḍarīkopadeśa,
titled Miaofa lianhua jing youbotishe 妙法蓮華經憂波提舍 (Commentary on the Lotus
Sutra). For example, T26.1519, 7c7.

49. Huiyuan states that the intrinsic reality of initial awakening and inherent awakening
is the same. The only difference is whether awakening is hidden or revealed. He cites
the *Śrīmālādevī-siṃhanāda-sūtra to suggest that when awakening is hidden it is the
tathāgatagarbha, and when it is revealed it is the dharma body. He indicates that the transition from hidden to revealed awakening requires antidotes to ignorance, and so the process is not a purely spontaneous occurrence. T44.1843, 183b12–22.

is this: because of inherent awakening, there is non-awakening; and because of non-awakening, one speaks of there being initial awakening.[50] In addition, it is called final awakening because one has awoken to the fountainhead of the mind; but it is not final awakening if one has still not awoken to the fountainhead of the mind. Why? It is because ordinary people will be able to stop thought-moments from subsequently arising because they become aware that previous thought-moments gave rise to bad [consequences]. Although they may still call this "awakening," it is precisely non-awakening.[51]

As for those of the Two Vehicles with discerning cognition and bodhisattvas who have newly aroused the aspiration to awakening, because they have abandoned the characteristics of coarse discriminations and attachments, they awaken to the fact that as thought-moments [appear to] change, they do not have the characteristic of change. This is called "semblance of awakening."[52]

---

50. The first move in this logical sequence from inherent awakening to non-awakening appears paradoxical. Yinshun 印順 (1906–2005) explains it through the analogy of defective eyesight—a commonplace in Buddhist literature, and also evident in its recurring use in commentaries on the *Treatise*. See his *Dasheng qixin lun jiangji* 大乘起信論講記 (Lecture Notes on the *Treatise on Awakening Mahāyāna Faith*) (Beijing: Zhonghua shuju, 2010), pp. 73–74. In the present application of the analogy, eyesight is the capacity to see, analogous to being inherently awoken. If one's eyesight were harmed, one would no longer be able to see. This is analogous to being non-awoken. For a capacity such as eyesight to be damaged, however, that capacity (such as the capacity to see) must have existed in the first place. To extend Yinshun's analogy, just as a damaged eye begins to return to a state of normal function after treatment, so too there is a sense in which awakening "initially" occurs on the basis of non-awakening.

51. As Huiyuan suggests in his commentary, however, to have hindsight is not to be awakened. T44.1843, 183c3. For example, after being angry, one may think that it would have been better not to have become angry and decide that in the future one will avoid doing so. This may sound like an enlightened attitude. In reality, however, resolving to avoid anger does not make one immune from the triggers of one's anger.

52. Although thought-moments are perceived to change, in fact each thought-moment is instantaneous and so has no capacity for change. Thought-moments therefore lack any characteristic of change. In terms of ethical awareness, and the example given in the preceding note, it is like the point at which one's anger diminishes and one decides to calm down. By recognizing that a thought-moment, like being angry, is non-enduring and could instantaneously be otherwise, one can quickly eliminate it. Like the previous

As for dharma-body bodhisattvas, because they are free from the characteristics of discriminations and coarse thought-moments, they awaken to the fact that as thought-moments [appear to] endure, they do not have the characteristic of enduring. This is called "partial awakening."[53]

As for those who have completed the bodhisattva levels, fully accomplished skillful means, and accorded with [suchness] in a single thought-moment, because they are far removed from subtle thought-moments, they awaken to the fact that as the mind [appears to] arise initially, it has no characteristic of initial [arising]. They manage to see the nature of the mind, which is that the mind constantly endures. This is called "final awakening."[54]

A sutra therefore states: "When there are sentient beings capable of discerning without conceiving, it is because they are headed towards buddha wisdom."[55]

In addition, the arising of the mind has no characteristic of initial [arising] to be known, so to speak of knowing the characteristic of initial [arising, which is that there are no characteristics of initial arising,] means precisely being "without conceiving." [As the sutra

example, however, this is not true awakening; it is only a semblance of awakening because it occurs only after the anger has already begun to subside, not as it starts or during its peak.

53. A dharma-body bodhisattva is one who has achieved the level (bhūmi) of seeing the dharma body. The dharma body is suchness directly perceived at the first level, and so a dharma-body bodhisattva refers to a bodhisattva above the first level. "Partial awakening" varies for bodhisattvas in this group according to the degrees of their individual accomplishment.

54. The preceding passage describes a sequence of practice. Each stage in the sequence corresponds to the four characteristics (lakṣaṇa), which appear in the reverse of the standard order: cessation; change; endurance; and arising.

55. Huiyuan (T44.1843, 184b16) identifies this as a passage from the Laṅkāvatāra-sūtra. No such phrasing can be found in extant versions of either Guṇabhadra's or Bodhiruci's translations of the Laṅkāvatāra-sūtra, however. Wonhyo interprets this to mean that sentient beings "are incapable of discerning the principle of non-conceiving." T44.1844, 210b27.

infers,] therefore, not all sentient beings are called "awakened." This is explained as beginningless ignorance because thought-moment after thought-moment [576c] have always followed one another in a continuous flow and [sentient beings] have never been free from conceiving. If they manage to be without conceiving, then they will recognize the mind's characteristics as arising, enduring, changing, and ceasing. Because they are without conceiving and so on, there is really no difference from initial awakening. This is because the four characteristics exist simultaneously and are not established by [sentient beings] themselves; they have always been uniform and are one and the same awakening.[56]

Moreover, when inherent awakening accords with defilements, it produces two kinds of characteristic through discrimination. They are not separate from inherent awakening. What are they?

The first is the characteristic of purity of cognition.

The second is the characteristic of inconceivable karmic action.[57]

56. This traces a trajectory from initial awakening to more advanced levels of realization. A bodhisattva who attains initial awakening recognizes that the mind is unitary and that all reality has a single nature, despite appearances of multiplicity. Although there appear to be the four characteristics of arising, enduring, changing, and ceasing, in reality there is only the One Mind, which is coextensive with final awakening. In his *Daeseung gisil lon byeolgi*, Wonhyo draws on a variation of the analogy of the ocean and waves to make the point: "It is just like the movement of the ocean water, which is said to be waves. Because waves have no self-nature, however, there is no movement of waves. Because water has self-nature, there is movement of water. The mind and the four characteristics are also like this." T44.1845, 232c19–21.

Huiyuan states that all awakening, both inherent and initial, is the same; like suchness, it is uniform. The four characteristics appear to have sequence and continuity, but this is merely their functioning as characteristics. If there were a sequence, it would mean that awakening (and, by extension, suchness) is differentiated. However, these characteristics must be simultaneous and, "not being established by themselves," they lack intrinsic reality, like a dream. This can only be known through the absence of conceiving. T44.1843, 184b18–184c8. In his version of the *Treatise*, Śikṣānanda (fl. 700) makes a similar point. T32.1667, 585a26–29.

57. Huiyuan identifies these two characteristics with the dharma body and recompense bodies, respectively. T44.1843, 184c15–18.

"The characteristic of purity of cognition" means that one practices in accordance with what is real, based on habituation by the power of the Dharma, because one has fully accomplished skillful means. And one destroys the characteristics of the combined consciousness[58] and extinguishes the characteristics of the continuously flowing mind because one has revealed the dharma body and one's cognition has become unadulterated and pure.[59]

Why? It is because all the characteristics of the mind and consciousnesses are ignorance and, since the characteristic of ignorance is not separate from the nature of awakening, the mind and consciousnesses are both indestructible and destructible.[60] This is like the great ocean, where water moves in waves due to the wind. The characteristics of the water and the wind [as waves] are not separate

58. In his *Daeseung gisil lon byeolgi*, Wonhyo glosses the "combined consciousness" as "the combination of [the mind of] arising and ceasing and [the mind of] non-arising and non-ceasing." T44.1845, 208c18–19. *Hane 333V* corresponds with Wonhyo; see Ikeda Masanori, "Kyō'u shōku shozō Tonkō bunken *Daijō kishin ron sho* (gidai, *Hane 333V*) ni tsuite," p. 122, cols. 39–41.

59. This passage offers a response to the key question in the *Treatise*: How might sentient beings be intrinsically awakened yet also enmeshed in ignorance? Its central elements are likely to have derived from Bodhiruci's translation of the *Laṅkāvatāra-sūtra*. In particular, that text discusses "the extinction of characteristics" (*xiang mie* 相滅) and "the extinction of continuous flow" (*xiangxu mie* 相續滅). With "the extinction of characteristics," the operations of the sense faculties cease when habituation of the *ālaya* (store) consciousness by the false discriminations ceases. Reference to "the extinction of continuous flow" in Bodhiruci's translation parallels the idea discussed here of "extinguishing the characteristics of the continuously flowing mind." T16.671, 521c23–522a27.

60. Following Tanyan in taking this to mean that the nature aspect of the mind and the consciousnesses—inherent awakening—are indestructible, but the characteristic aspect of mind and the consciousnesses—ignorance—are destructible. X45.755.161c16–17. Huiyuan (T44.1843, 184c27–185a6) and *Hane 333V* (Ikeda Masanori, "Kyō'u shōku shozō Tonkō bunken *Daijō kishin ron sho* (gidai, *Hane 333V*) ni tsuite," p. 134, col. 143) use the term "the mind" to refer to the seventh consciousness and the term "consciousnesses" to refer to the first six consciousnesses. They claim that both are inherently mired in ignorance. Tanyan makes a similar identification. By associating "the mind" with the seventh consciousness, he identifies two aspects—nature and characteristics—that enable him to describe nature as pure mind and characteristics as false discrimination. X45.755, 161c11–13. Wonhyo draws a similar distinction between nature and characteristics. T44.1844, 211a29–b3.

from one another. Since it is not in the nature of water to move [by itself], its characteristic of movement will cease if the wind ceases, without its wetness ever being destroyed. And it is because, in the same way, the intrinsically pristine mind of sentient beings is moved by the wind of ignorance. Both the mind and ignorance lack characteristics of shape, and they are not separate from one another. Since it is not in the nature of the mind to move [by itself], its continuous flow will cease if ignorance ceases, without the nature of cognition ever being destroyed.[61]

"The characteristic of inconceivable karmic action" is the creator of all sublime perceptual fields [as it accords with the defilements of sentient beings], based on the purity of cognition. That is to say, the characteristics of countless qualities are constantly uninterrupted. This is because the characteristic of inconceivable karmic action accords with the capacities of sentient beings as a matter of course. It manifests itself in all kinds of ways, from which sentient beings obtain benefit.

Moreover, there are four significant senses of the characteristic of awakening as intrinsic reality, in which it is identical to space and like a clear mirror.[62] What are the four senses?

61. The metaphor of the ocean and the wind appears in Bodhiruci's translation of the *Laṅkāvatāra-sūtra*, although with significant differences in its application. T16.671, 538c8–9. See also the introduction for a further discussion of this point. Wonhyo comments on the *Treatise*: "In the analogy it is stated that 'it is not in the nature of water to move.' This shows that, although the water may be moving now, it is not the self-nature of water to move. Rather, it is merely according with external conditions. If it were in the nature of water to move, then when the characteristic of movement ceased, its wetness would accordingly cease. Yet it merely accords with external conditions and so its wetness is not destroyed, even when the characteristic of movement ceases." T44.1844, 211b8–10.

62. There is reference to "the characteristic of awakening as intrinsic reality" (*jue ti xiang* 覺體相) in the *Tipo pusa po Lengqie jingzhong waidao xiaosheng sizong lun* 提婆菩薩破楞伽經中外道小乘四宗論 (The Critique of Deva Bodhisattva of the Four Tenets of the Non-Buddhists and Hīnayānists in the *Laṅkāvatāra-sūtra*), a translation that Bodhiruci made between 508 and 535. T32.1639, 155b3–4. The term *jing* 淨,

First, it is a truly empty mirror. Because it is not awakening that illuminates [dharmas], awakening is far removed from all images of the mind's perceptual fields and no dharma may appear in it.

Second, it is a mirror as cause for habituation. This means that it is truly non-empty. All mundane perceptual fields appear in it without leaving or entering, disappearing or being destroyed. They constantly endure in the One Mind because all dharmas are precisely the nature of reality. In addition, [awakening] is something that no defiled dharma is able to defile because the intrinsic reality of cognition does not move and, replete with untainted dharmas, it habituates sentient beings.[63]

Third, it is a mirror in which dharmas transcend and leave behind [obstructions]. This means that, because it is unsullied, clear, and bright, non-empty dharmas [of suchness] transcend the afflictive and cognitive obstructions, leaving behind images of the combined.[64]

Fourth, it is a mirror as condition for habituation. This means that, because [non-empty] dharmas have transcended and left

rendered here as "clear," is used elsewhere in the *Treatise* to refer to dharmas, cognition, and the mind. In these cases, it has been translated as "pure." Its use here draws a connection between the analogy of the mirror and the "purified mind."

63. Following the metaphor of the wind and the waves, the idea that "the intrinsic reality of cognition does not move" means that the intrinsic reality of the mind—suchness—remains undisturbed by ignorance or afflictions. Tanyan argues that defiled objects can never tarnish a clear mirror. Although images in the mirror may change, the nature of the mirror itself never changes. X45.755, 162c20–163a1. For a related interpretation by a later commentator, see Hanshan Deqing 憨山德清 (1546–1623), *Qixin lun zhijie* 起信論直解 (Direct Interpretation of the *Treatise on Awakening Mahāyāna Faith*), X45.766, 493b15–493c3.

64. Reference to "the combined" is shorthand for the combined consciousness. As noted above, Wonhyo glosses this as "the combination of [the mind of] arising and ceasing and [the mind of] non-arising and non-ceasing," T44.1845, 208c18–19. "The afflictive and cognitive obstructions" are technical terms in Buddhist soteriology. They have to be overcome to attain full awakening. The afflictive obstructions are primarily emotions and attitudes that obscure how one understands and reacts to situations. The cognitive obstructions prevent one from seeing things as they truly are. They are often summarized as the false attachment to the view of selfhood. They are considered to be more problematic than the afflictive obstructions. Some Mahāyāna polemical literature allows that Hīnayāna practitioners can overcome the afflictive obstructions, but only Mahāyāna bodhisattvas can fully extirpate cognitive obstructions. The *Treatise* offers a positive vision

behind [obstructions], it universally illuminates the minds of sentient beings, revealing in every thought-moment the roots of the cultivation of virtue.[65]

1.2.2 NON-AWAKENING

[577a] "Non-awakening" means that a non-awakened mind arises and has its thought-moments because one does not know the unitary nature of the dharma of suchness in accordance with what is real. Its thought-moments lack intrinsic characteristics and are not apart from inherent awakening.[66] This is just like a disoriented person, who becomes disoriented because there are directions. Once apart from directions, there is no becoming disoriented.[67] Sentient beings are also like this: they become disoriented because there is awakening. Once apart from awakening, there is no non-awakening. [Sentient beings] are only able to presume that names and definitions serve to

here: There is something true and positive to be known, and there are countless undefiled dharmas that can be cultivated and habituated, removing the veils that prevent one from seeing everything as it is.

65. This passage traces a sequence by which the awakening dimension of the *ālaya* (store) consciousness develops. Through the analogy of the mirror, it describes how this awakening process works in the case of a bodhisattva. It starts with a mind in which cognition does not operate and so reflects nothing—a blank mirror. It then moves to a mind aligned with the perception of all things as they truly are. Next is a mind that transcends the obstructions that seem to prevent the accurate and complete reflection of reality as it truly is. It concludes with an awakened mind, which has developed to the point of providing conditions conducive to the enlightenment of other sentient beings.

66. "Intrinsic characteristics" is a technical term for the specific features that distinguish something as belonging to a defined class. A recurring example in Indian Buddhist literature is the dewlap of a cow, which only a cow would have.

67. Commentators have differed in their interpretations of this phrase. *Hane 333V*, for example, takes it to mean that a person is disoriented with respect to the correct direction; see Ikeda Masanori, "Kyō'u shōku shozō Tonkō bunken *Daijō kishin ron sho* (gidai, *Hane 333V*) ni tsuite," p. 142, cols. 210–212. Others have suggested that a person is disoriented with respect to direction in general—that is, the very idea of direction is the precondition for being disoriented. Wonhyo (T44.1844, 212a5–8) and Hanshan Deqing (X45.766, 494a7–8) adopt this interpretation.

explain true awakening because there is the non-awakened and falsely conceptualizing mind. Once apart from the non-awakened mind, there is no intrinsic characteristic of true awakening to be spoken of.

Moreover, three kinds of characteristics are produced because of non-awakening. They are associated with, and not apart from, non-awakening.[68] What are they?

The first is the characteristic of the karmic action of ignorance. The mind moves because of non-awakening, and this is termed "karmic action." When awakened, it does not move. When it does move, there is suffering because effect is not separate from cause.[69]

The second is the characteristic of the perceiver. There is a perceiver because of movement [in the mind].[70] When it does not move, there is no perceiving.

The third is the characteristic of perceptual fields.[71] Perceptual fields falsely appear because of the perceiver. When apart from perceiving, there are no perceptual fields.

Because there are perceptual fields that serve as conditions, six further characteristics are produced.[72] What are they?

---

68. Wonhyo identifies what follows as a list of subtle and coarse characteristics. The first three are subtle, the following six coarse. T44.1844, 212a19.

69. In his translation of the *Dazhidu lun* 大智度論 (Treatise on the Great Perfection of Wisdom), Kumārajīva uses identical phrasing to suggest that the perfection of wisdom occurs when "effect is not separate from cause" (果不離因) and cause not separate from effect, when conditioned and unconditioned are not separate, and when the perfection of wisdom (*prajñāpāramitā*) and all dharmas are not separate. T25.1509, 520a19–23. Commenting on the present passage in the *Treatise*, Wonhyo explains that ignorance causes suffering and so, as soon as ignorance ceases, suffering gives way to pleasure, and this is when awakening begins. T44.1844, 212a27–b1.

70. This interpretation is supported by a textual variant, which reads 以依心動故能見. Elsewhere, 以 is replaced by 心. See T32.1666, 577a10–11; Frédéric Girard, trans., *Traité sur l'acte de foi dans le Grand Véhicule* (Tokyo: Keio University Press, 2004), p. 42.

71. In his translation of the *Laṅkāvatāra-sūtra*, Bodhiruci frequently uses the term "the characteristic of perceptual fields" in relation to misperception. See, for example, T16.671, 544b4–5.

72. Much of the following argument seems to derive from a discussion in Bodhiruci's translation of the *Laṅkāvatāra-sūtra* of three kinds of consciousness—the consciousnesses of

The first is the characteristic of cognition because, based on perceptual fields, the mind gives rise to discriminating likes and dislikes.[73]

The second is the characteristic of continuous flow because, based on the production of pain and pleasure due to cognition, sensations give rise to thought-moments, which are associated with [those sensations] without interruption.[74]

The third is the characteristic of attachment and grasping because, based on continuous flow, one takes perceptual fields as cognitive objects, endures pain and pleasure, and the mind gives rise to attachments.

The fourth is the characteristic of devising names because, based on falsely held views, one discriminates between the characteristics of names and words that have only been provisionally designated.[75]

The fifth is the characteristic of giving rise to karmic action because, based on names and labels, one pursues those names and words and becomes attached to them, creating all kinds of karmic action.

The sixth is the characteristic of suffering through the bondage of karmic action because, based on karmic action, one experiences the effects [of one's actions] without any control over them.

[In sum,] one should know that ignorance is the producer of all defiled dharmas because all defiled dharmas are characteristics of non-awakening.[76]

---

continuity, of the characteristics of karmic action, and of the characteristics of cognition—and of the cessation of consciousness. T16.671, 521c25–522a1.

73. Wonhyo gives an alternative reading of this line: "Arising on the basis of perceptual fields, the mind discriminates likes and dislikes." T44.1844, 212c5–10, esp. 212c7.

74. Part of this argument seems to stand in relation to Bodhiruci's translation of the *Laṅkāvatāra-sūtra*. See, especially, T16.671, 545a24–545b1. Wonhyo suggests that "the characteristic of continuous flow" refers to how attachments continue from past to future due to illusory discrimination. T44.1844, 213a7–9. We have followed Yinshun in understanding *juexin* 覺心 here to mean "sensations." *Dasheng qixin lun jiangji*, p. 104.

75. The contrast here is between what exists only nominally (*prajñapti*) and what exists in reality (*dravya*).

76. The preceding six characteristics appear here in a cyclical sequence. First, there is cognition of perceptual objects. Then, one becomes attached to those objects and names them

1.2.3 THE RELATIONSHIP OF AWAKENING AND NON-AWAKENING

Moreover, the relationship of awakening and non-awakening has two characteristics. What are they?

The first is the characteristic of sameness.

The second is the characteristic of difference.

The characteristic of sameness can be compared to various kinds of pottery vessels, which all share the intrinsic characteristic of being [composed of] atoms.[77] In the same way, various kinds of illusion of karmic action,[78] whether untainted or ignorant, all share the intrinsic characteristic of being [composed of] suchness.

On the basis of this idea of suchness, a sutra therefore says that all sentient beings have always constantly abided in and entered nirvana.[79] The dharma of *bodhi* (awakening) is neither a characteristic that can be cultivated nor one that can be constructed. It is ultimately

---

because of the perception of continuous flow. This gives rise to karmic action, which in turn produces suffering. This cycle resembles the model of the links of dependent arising, which also operates in a cyclical way.

77. In this analogy, pieces of pottery are seen to have various shapes and sizes and so appear to be different entities. Since they are all composed of clay, however, they share the same nature.

78. The term "illusion of karmic action" (*yehuan* 業幻) is rare in texts that pre-date the *Treatise*. It appears only in Bodhiruci's translation of the *Laṅkāvatāra-sūtra* (T16.671, 528a13–17); in Bodhiruci's translation of Vasubandhu's *Daśabhūmi-vyākhyāna*, or *Dilun* (T26.1522, 139c14–15); and in the translation of the *Saddharmasmṛtyupasthāna-sūtra* made by Gautama Prajñāruci (fl. 538–543), titled *Zhengfa nianchu jing* 正法念處經 (Sutra on the Bases of Mindfulness of the True Dharma; T17.721, 148b17–18, 202a24–26, 231a4–5).

79. Fazang associates this scriptural reference with the *Vimalakīrti-nirdeśa-sūtra*, a translation of which was made by Kumārajīva in 406, under the title *Weimojie suoshuo jing* 維摩詰所說經 (The Sutra Preached by Vimalakīrti). Fazang comments that buddha wisdom is not newly acquired; sentient beings have been buddhas since beginningless time. T44.1846, 263c29–264a15. For the source of Fazang's quotation from the *Vimalakīrti-nirdeśa-sūtra*, see T14.475, 542b17–19. By contrast, Wonhyo traces the scriptural quotation to the translation of the *Mahāprajñāpāramitā-sūtra* by Kumārajīva, titled *Mohe bore boluomi jing* 摩訶般若波羅蜜經. T44.1844, 213b9. For its appearance in the *Mohe bore boluomi jing*, see T8.223, 379a18–22, 401b7–10.

inapprehensible and, indeed, has no perceptible characteristics of form.[80] Where there are characteristics of perceptible form, they are constructed only by illusions of karmic action in accordance with defilements; they are not cognition of the non-empty nature of form [that is suchness]. This is because none of the characteristics of the cognition [of suchness] is perceptible.

[577b] The characteristic of difference is like various kinds of pottery vessels, each of which is not the same. In the same way the untainted and ignorance are differentiated by according with defilement and illusion. This is because their natures are differentiated [on the basis of] defilement and illusion.[81]

1.2.4 THE CAUSE AND CONDITION OF ARISING AND CEASING

Moreover, "the cause and condition of arising and ceasing"[82] refers to sentient beings, because mentation (*manas*) and mental consciousness (*manovijñāna*) operate on the basis of the mind.[83]

---

80. This phrasing echoes two passages in the *Jin'gangxian lun*, attributed to Bodhiruci. T25.1512, 856c25–26 and 858c13–14.
81. The idea that suchness adapts to phenomenal conditions is discussed in the introduction.
82. This follows the majority of early commentators, who identify "the cause and condition" as singular. Tanyan claims, for example, that "the seeds internal to the store consciousness are the cause, and the unreal appearances of the three realms [i.e., the Form Realm, the Formless Realm, and the Desire Realm] are the condition." X45.755, 164c23. By contrast, Fazang identifies two causes and two conditions. According to Fazang, the first cause of arising and ceasing is that the suchness aspect of the *ālaya*, or store, consciousness does not preserve its self-nature. The second cause is entrenched ignorance (*wuming zhudi* 無明住地; *avidyāvāsa-bhūmi*). The two conditions that Fazang identifies are habituation of the suchness aspect of the *ālaya* consciousness by fundamental ignorance (*genben wuming* 根本無明); and the stirring of cognitive activity by false perceptual fields. As with other early commentators, Fazang emphasizes that the "causes and conditions" are based solely on the intrinsic reality of the mind. T44.1846, 264b15–23.
83. Following the interpretation of Tanyan on the relationship between the mind, mentation, and mental consciousness. X45.755, 164c24–165a6. This reading was taken up by such later commentators as Huiyuan, *Hane 333V*, Wonhyo, and Fazang.

What does this mean? It is talked about as mentation because it is said that on the basis of the *ālaya* consciousness there is ignorance and non-awakening, which give rise to the perceiver, the presenter, and the apprehender of perceptual fields. These in turn give rise to thought-moments in a continuous flow.

In addition, mentation has five names. What are they?

The first is karmic consciousness because this means that the non-awakened mind is set in motion by the force of ignorance.[84]

The second is called the operating consciousness because there is the characteristic of a perceiver based on the moving mind.

The third is called the presenting consciousness because this means that it is the presenter of all perceptual fields.[85] And just as a bright mirror presents the images of visible forms, so too the presenting consciousness directly presents the five kinds of sensory objects as they come before it, without any sequence of before and after; it spontaneously arises whenever [an object] is before it.

The fourth is called the discerning consciousness because it discriminates defiled and pure dharmas.

The fifth is called the continuously flowing consciousness because thought-moments are associated with [karmic action] without interruption; because it sustains the good and bad karmic action of countless past times, preserving that karmic action without loss; and, moreover, because it is able to bring to maturity the recompense of pain and pleasure in the present and future without disparity or contradiction. It is able to cause one suddenly to conceive of past and present events and to have non-awakened and false concerns about future events.

84. This reading follows such commentators as Tanyan (X45.755, 165a24–165b2) and Huiyuan (T44.1843, 187a2–3).

85. The term "presenting consciousness" (*xianshi* 現識), an equivalent of the Sanskrit term *khyāti-vijñāna*, appears in the translation of the *Laṅkāvatāra-sūtra* that Guṇabhadra made in 443. T16.670, 483a15–20. By contrast, it does not occur in Bodhiruci's translation of the same text. This is consistent with the possibility that the author of the *Treatise* drew on both translations of the *Laṅkāvatāra-sūtra*, not only Bodhiruci's.

Therefore, the three worlds are illusory constructs, created by the mind alone.[86] The perceptual fields of the six sensory and conceptual fields do not exist apart from the mind.[87] Why? There are no characteristics to be apprehended for the mind does not see the mind, since all dharmas are produced from the mind's giving rise to false thoughts and since all discriminations are precisely the mind's discriminating itself.[88]

One should know that all mundane perceptual fields can be sustained based only on the ignorance and false minds of sentient beings. Therefore, all dharmas, like images in a mirror, have no intrinsic reality that can be apprehended. They are nothing but falsehoods of the mind. This is because when the mind arises, all kinds of dharmas arise; and when the mind ceases, all kinds of dharmas cease.

Moreover, what is termed the "mental consciousness" is really none other than the continuously flowing consciousness since, as ordinary people become ever more profoundly attached [to the mind's own discriminations], they posit "self" and "what pertains to self" and, through all manner of falsely held view, they follow after things and take them as cognitive objects. In discriminating the six

---

86. The three realms (*traidhātuka*) are the Desire Realm (*kāma-dhātu*), the Form Realm (*rūpa-dhātu*), and the Formless Realm (*ārūpya-dhātu*). They appear in several, slightly different formulations, which have produced much controversy. On the one hand is a position of metaphysical idealism, which holds that the mind creates the three realms. On the other hand is a position that lends itself to an epistemic interpretation by claiming that the mind "is" the three realms. The *Treatise* here adopts the first position. An early statement of this position appears in the earliest translation of the *Daśabhūmika-sūtra*, the *Jianbei yiqie zhide jing* 漸備一切智德經 (Sutra on Gradually Obtaining the Virtue of Omniscience), made by Dharmarakṣa (c. 230–316) in 297. T10.285, 476b9–10. A close parallel of both the doctrinal perspective and the phrasing of the *Treatise* appears in the translation of the *Avataṃsaka-sūtra* by Buddhabhadra (358–429), titled *Dafangguangfo huayan jing* 大方廣佛華嚴經 (Flower Garland Sutra). T9.278, 558c10. Bodhiruci's translation of the *Di lun* quotes this sutra with only minor variation, and gives an explanation of it. T26.1522, 169a15–20.

87. The six sensory and conceptual fields, *ṣaḍ-viṣaya* in Sanskrit, refer to the five sensory fields and the mental field.

88. This echoes Bodhiruci's translation of the *Laṅkāvatāra-sūtra*. T16.671, 522b12–13.

sensory and conceptual fields, [the continuously flowing consciousness] is called "mental consciousness;" it is also called the "separating consciousness."[89] In addition, it is further termed the "phenomena-discriminating consciousness" because of the idea that it intensifies due to afflictions of views and cravings.[90] This consciousness, which arises on the basis of habituation by ignorance, is something that neither ordinary people are capable of knowing, nor the insights of the Two Vehicles are aware of.

It is said that [577c] if bodhisattvas directly experience the dharma body, they manage to do so to a small extent, based on the fact that they arouse the aspiration to awakening and investigate [how ignorance produces these consciousnesses] from the first stage of correct faith. Even when they reach the final bodhisattva level, they are unable to know it completely, since only buddhas discern it thoroughly. Why? The mind has always been intrinsically pristine, yet there is ignorance. When defiled by ignorance, there is the defiled mind. Yet, although there is the defiled mind, [the nature of the mind] is constantly unchanging. Therefore, only buddhas are capable of knowing what this means.[91] That is to say, the

---

89. On the basis of a sense of "self," the "mental consciousness" imputes false interpretations to the six sensory and conceptual fields (*liu chen* 六塵)—visual, auditory, olfactory, gustatory, tactile, and mental objects. In standard Yogācāra doctrine it is the sixth consciousness (*manovijñāna*) that brings together, and differentiates, sensory impressions from the five sensory consciousnesses. It can think about what the other five consciousnesses perceive; the five consciousnesses themselves do not have this reflexive capacity. The seventh consciousness (*manas*) is the source of self-attachment.

90. The earliest extant use of the term "the phenomena-discriminating consciousness" (*fenbie shi shi* 分別事識) is in Bodhiruci's translation of the *Laṅkāvatāra-sūtra*, where it appears in relation to cause and habituation. T16.671, 522a1–7. "Afflictions of views and cravings" probably denotes the afflictive and cognitive obstructions to which the *Treatise* refers above.

91. The phrasing of this passage contains several verbal echoes from the explanation of the *tathāgatagarbha* given in the translation of the *Aṅgulimālīya-sūtra* by Guṇabhadra, titled *Yangjuemoluo jing* 央掘魔羅經 (Sutra of Aṅgulimāla). T2.120, 538b20–27. In his commentary on the *Treatise*, Huiyuan suggests that true consciousness, or suchness, becomes false if it follows conditions. He therefore argues that ignorance is a kind of consciousness.

nature of the mind is called "unchanging" because it is constantly without conceiving. The minds [of beings other than buddhas] do not accord with it, and suddenly give rise to conceiving, because they do not comprehend the unified dharma realm. This is termed "ignorance."[92]

There are six kinds of defiled mind.[93] What are they?

The first is the associated defilement of attachment. This is because [the defiled mind of novice practitioners] is far removed even from the liberation of the Two Vehicles or the level associated with faith.[94]

The second is the associated defilement of the uninterrupted [flow of thought-moments]. This is because [bodhisattvas] are eventually able to abandon this defilement through the cultivation of skillful means at the level associated with faith and they become finally free from it on attaining the level of pure mind.[95]

Huiyuan goes on to state: "Even when there is a defiled mind, [the nature of the mind] is constantly unchanging. Even when the characteristics [of the nature of the mind] become defiled, its true nature does not alter. In the *Śrīmālādevī-siṃhanāda-sūtra*, it therefore says: 'It is difficult to comprehend fully that the intrinsically pristine mind is defiled by afflictions.' [The mind] is true [i.e., suchness] but becomes false; but actually it only appears to be false and is always true [i.e., suchness]. This principle is thoroughly comprehended by buddhas; it is not something that cognition can discern." T44.1843, 187b28–c9. For the original phrase in the *Śrīmālādevī-siṃhanāda-sūtra*, see T12.353, 222b28–29.

92. This passage elaborates on the claim made earlier in the *Treatise* that "the unitary characteristic of the dharma realm is precisely the uniform dharma body of *tathāgatas*" [576b].

93. The following explanation traces advancement along the bodhisattva path, moving from coarse minds to subtle ones. See the introduction, under "Five Names for Mentation and Six Kinds of Defiled Mind," for a more detailed account of this sequence.

94. For Tanyan (X45.755, 166c18–21) and Huiyuan (T44.1843, 187c20–22), this kind of defiled mind is associated with practitioners who have not yet reached the first of the ten bodhisattva levels. The *Treatise* engages in polemic by implying that the highest achievement of those who follow the path of the Two Vehicles—their liberation—is equal only to the achievement of those at the initial stage of the Mahāyāna path.

95. Tanyan (X45.755, 166c24) and Huiyuan (T44.1843, 187c22–24) identify "the level of pure mind" with the first of the ten bodhisattva levels. Later commentators, such as Wonhyo (T44.1844, 215a19–21) and Fazang (T44.1846, 267b28–267c1), follow this identification.

The third is the associated defilement of discriminating cognition. This is because [bodhisattvas] gradually free themselves from this defilement at the level of being in full possession of monastic precepts and they become finally free from it by the time they reach the level of skillful means devoid of characteristics.[96]

The fourth is the dissociated defilement of presented form. This is because [bodhisattvas] are able to become free from this defilement only at the level of unimpeded form.[97]

The fifth is the dissociated defilement of the perceiving mind. This is because [bodhisattvas] are able to become free from this defilement only at the level of the sovereign mind.[98]

The sixth is the dissociated defilement of fundamental karmic action. This is because [bodhisattvas] are able to become free from this defilement only when they obtain entry into the level of *tathāgatas* from the ultimate bodhisattva level.

"[Beings other than buddhas] do not fully comprehend the meaning of a unified dharma realm" means that they investigate [defilements] and cut them off through study at the level associated with faith.[99] On entering the level of pure mind, they manage to free themselves partially [from defilements], according to their

---

96. Tanyan (X45.755, 167a2–3) and Huiyuan (T44.1843, 187c24–25) identify "the level of being in full possession of monastic precepts" with the second bodhisattva level, and "the level of skillful means devoid of characteristics" with the seventh level. Wonhyo (T44.1844, 215a22–27) and Fazang (T44.1846, 267c2–12) offer a similar account.

97. Tanyan (X45.755, 167a3–7) and Huiyuan (T44.1843, 187c26–27) identify "the level of unimpeded form" with the eighth bodhisattva level. Wonhyo (T44.1844, 215a27–215b2) and Fazang (T44.1846, 267c13–19) follow the early commentators. They further comment that bodhisattvas at this level are free from delusions relating to external objects and their minds are like clear mirrors that manifest forms.

98. Tanyan (X45.755, 167a7–10) and Huiyuan (T44.1843, 187c28) identify "the level of the sovereign mind" with the ninth bodhisattva level. Wonhyo (T44.1844, 215b2–4) and Fazang (T44.1846, 267c20–26) make the same identification.

99. This revisits the phrase "they do not comprehend the unified dharma realm" 不達一法界 [577c].

accomplishments, until they reach the level of *tathāgatas* because they have been able to become finally free from them.

"Associated" is so-called because [in the first three kinds of defiled mind] the cognizing aspect and the aspect taken as cognitive object are identical,[100] even though these [kinds of] mind differ from the dharmas that they conceive based on differentiations in their degrees of defilement and purity.

"Dissociated" is so-called because [the fourth, fifth, and sixth kinds of] defiled mind, being non-awakened, are constantly without differentiation and do not posit identity between the cognizing aspect and the aspect taken as cognitive object.[101]

In addition, "the defiled mind" is called an "afflictive obstruction" because it impedes fundamental cognition of suchness. "Ignorance" is called a "cognitive obstruction" because it impedes cognition of how karmic action operates as a matter of course in the mundane world.[102] Why? Because one cannot conform with any kind of [conventional] knowledge of any of the mundane perceptual fields.[103]

---

100. It is only on the basis of first making a distinction between cognizer and what is cognized that the first three kinds of defiled mind can associate them as identical. So Huiyuan states that "identical" here means that "the [defiled] mind itself is the cognizer and its defiled function is also the cognizer." They stand in a *ti–yong* relationship. See T44.1843, 188a14.

101. The three "dissociated" kinds of defiled mind are not actively engaged in false conceptual construction, unlike the three "associated" kinds of defiled mind. The "dissociated" kinds of defiled mind are identified as being "without differentiation" because they do not uphold an initial distinction between cognizer and what is cognized. This interpretation of the discussion of "associated" and "dissociated" follows Tanyan (X45.755, 163c6–11, 167b16–22) and Huiyuan (T44.1843, 188a8–18).

102. According to Wonhyo, the *Treatise*'s presentation of the two obstructions diverges from that generally found in Buddhist scriptures and treatises. In the standard account, afflictive obstructions inhibit the training of both Hīnayānists and Mahāyānists. Cognitive obstructions are particularly problematic for Mahāyānists because they prevent the attainment of omniscience, a core quality of buddhahood. In the *Treatise*, by contrast, the associations of these two kinds of affliction are reversed. Wonhyo questions this move. T44.1845, 237c18–28.

103. This interpretation has been informed by Huiyuan. T44.1843, 191b27–28.

This is because, being based on the defiled mind, the perceiver, the presenter, and the apprehender of perceptual fields run counter to the uniformity [of suchness].[104] And it is because all dharmas are always quiescent and have no characteristic of arising, and the falsehoods of ignorance and non-awakening run counter to those dharmas.[105]

1.2.5 THE CHARACTERISTICS OF ARISING AND CEASING

Moreover, there are two distinguishable characteristics of arising and ceasing. What are they?

The first is coarse because it is associated with the mind.

The second is subtle because it is dissociated from the mind.

In addition, the coarsest of the coarse is the perceptual field of ordinary people. The subtlest of the coarse and coarsest of the subtle are the perceptual fields of bodhisattvas [as they progress]. The subtlest of the subtle is the perceptual field of buddhas.

These two kinds of arising and ceasing [**578a**] exist on the basis of habituation by ignorance—that is, on the basis of causes and on the basis of conditions.[106] [Arising and ceasing] exists on the basis of causes because of non-awakening. It exists on the basis of conditions because of falsely constructed perceptual fields.[107] If causes cease,

---

104. Reading 能取 for 妄取, based on the earlier use of the phrase "the perceiver, the presenter, and the apprehender of perceptual fields" 能見能現能取境界 [577b]. The defiled mind runs counter to uniformity because it produces a false dichotomy between the perceiver and what is perceived.

105. Ignorance and non-awakening run counter to the quiescent state of dharmas because they are active and moving.

106. This passage has a possible source in Bodhiruci's translation of the Laṅkāvatāra-sūtra, where coarse defilements, ignorance, and stages of practice receive mention. T16.671, 526c14–17.

107. Huiyuan interprets "conditions" as a reference to the six sensory and conceptual fields and their objects. He adds: "There being these causes and conditions, arising and ceasing

then conditions cease.[108] Because causes cease, the mind dissoci-ated from [the subtle characteristics of arising and ceasing] ceases. Because conditions cease, the mind associated with [the coarse char-acteristics of arising and ceasing] ceases.

Question: If the mind ceases, then how can it continuously flow? Or, if it continuously flows, then how can it be said ultimately to cease?[109]

Answer: What we have talked about as "ceasing" is only cessa-tion of the mind's characteristics; it is not cessation of the intrinsic reality of the mind. It is like the wind, which has the characteristic of movement based on [there being water]. If water were to cease [to be], then the wind's characteristic would be eliminated, having no basis. But since water does not cease [to be], the wind's characteristic continues. It is only because the wind ceases that the characteristic of movement accordingly ceases. It is not that water ceases [to be]. It is the same with ignorance, which is based on the intrinsic reality of the mind to move. If the intrinsic reality of the mind were to cease [to

come to be established." T44.1843, 191c14–15. Huiyuan seems to have drawn this idea from a later passage in the *Treatise*, which refers to "the defiled dharmas of false perceptual fields as conditions" [578a].

108. When the causes of something are eliminated, cooperating conditions become irrelevant and are no longer effective in contributing to its production. With a seed that sprouts, for example, the seed is the cause of the sprout and such conditions as rain and sun con-tribute to its burgeoning. Without a seed, however, there is no possibility for rain or sun to assist in the growth of a sprout.

109. This question introduces an explication of a claim made earlier in the *Treatise*: "If one manages to be without conceiving, then one will recognize the mind's characteristics as arising, enduring, changing, and ceasing. Because one is without conceiving and so on, there is really no difference from initial awakening. This is because the four characteristics exist simultaneously and are not established by themselves; they have always been uni-form and are one and the same awakening" [576c]. From this point on, the text makes it increasingly explicit that the problem under consideration is the overlay of conceiving (*nian*) on the mind. Conceiving prevents one from perceiving the underlying uniformity and unity of the two gateways of mind. It obscures this uniformity by applying con-ceptual characteristics (*xiang*). It starts with the four characteristics of all conditioned things: arising, enduring, changing, and ceasing. Conceiving and conceptual characteris-tics therefore need to be eliminated.

be], then sentient beings would be eliminated, having no basis [for sentience]. But since the intrinsic reality of the mind does not cease [to be], the [arising-and-ceasing] mind can continue. It is only because delusion ceases [to be] that the characteristics of the [arising-and-ceasing] mind accordingly cease [to be]. It is not that the mind's [nature of] cognition ceases [to be].[110]

1.2.6 HABITUATION

Moreover, defiled and pure dharmas arise without interruption because there is habituation by four kinds of dharma.[111] What are they?

The first is the pure dharma, called suchness.

The second is the cause of all defilements, called ignorance.

The third is the false mind, called karmic consciousness.[112]

The fourth is falsely [constructed] perceptual fields—that is, the six sensory and conceptual fields.

"Habituation" is like an ordinary piece of clothing that in reality has no scent; but it will acquire a fragrance if someone perfumes it. This is just the same. The pure dharma of suchness in reality has no defilements; it only has defiled characteristics because of habituation by ignorance.[113] The defiled dharma of ignorance in reality has no

110. Cf. the earlier statement that "since it is not in the nature of the mind to move [by itself], its continuous flow will cease if ignorance ceases, without the nature of cognition ever being destroyed" [576c]. Huiyuan comments: "The complete loss of false consciousness does not stop true [consciousness] from existing. Because true consciousness always exists, it is not that sentient existence is cut off. And because false consciousness ultimately ceases, sentient beings attain true consciousness. 'Wind' is a metaphor for ignorance. 'Water' is a metaphor for true consciousness. 'Movement' is a metaphor for false consciousness." T44.1843, 191c28–192a1.

111. For a comparable idea, see the discussion of seeds and habituation in the translation of Asaṅga's fourth-century Mahāyānasaṃgraha-śāstra (She dasheng lun 攝大乘論; Compendium of the Great Vehicle) made in 531 by Buddhaśanta (fl. 525–539). T31.1592, 98b21–24.

112. This refers to the first of the five names for mentation [577b].

113. As Wonhyo notes in his Daeseung gisil lon byeolgi, Paramārtha's translation of the Mahāyānasaṃgraha-śāstra, the so-called Shelun, states that unconditioned dharmas

pure karmic action; it has a purifying function only because of habituation by suchness.[114]

How does habituation [by ignorance] give rise to defiled dharmas without interruption? Because it is based on the dharma of suchness, there is ignorance. Because there are the defiled dharmas of ignorance as causes, they then habituate suchness. Because of this habituation, there is the false mind and, since there is the false mind, it then habituates ignorance. Because [the false mind] does not fully discern the dharma of suchness, it is non-awakened and so conceiving arises, presenting false perceptual fields.[115] Because there are the defiled dharmas of false perceptual fields as conditions, these then habituate the false mind, so that conceiving and attachments generate all kinds

cannot be habituated. T44.1845, 239a21–26. See the introduction for an account of Wonhyo's view that the *Treatise* is in fact stating that suchness can be acted upon causally. Fazang elaborates Wonhyo's apologist account in his *Huayan yisheng jiaoyi fenqi zhang* 華嚴一乘教義分齊章 (Essay on the Five Teachings of Huayan). Commenting on the *Treatise*, Fazang refers to suchness as "constant," but he qualifies this by suggesting that "it is not what is meant by 'constant' in ordinary speech." He emphasizes that suchness remains unchanged even as it adapts to conditioned realities. Fazang refers to suchness as "the inconceivable constant" since the unconditioned and the conditioned merge to be neither the same nor different. T45.1866, 485a9–15.

114. Here, suchness is given a role in the arising-and-ceasing aspect of the One Mind, but it is not the static, immobile role expounded in much of the literature on which the author of the *Treatise* drew. Instead, it actively infiltrates the arising-and-ceasing aspect of the One Mind and rights everything that is wrong there. Suchness makes its appearance at this point in the *Treatise* not in terms of its intrinsic reality (*ti*), but in terms of its function (*yong*)—the countless positive qualities of non-empty suchness. In what follows, both suchness as intrinsic reality and its functions are retained as a solution to the problem of ignorance, but its characteristics (*xiang*) are eliminated. The tension between habituation by suchness and habituation by ignorance shapes the "dynamic" version of dependent arising that the author of the *Treatise* introduces.

115. Wonhyo explains this as follows: "Due to habituation by ignorance there is the mind of karmic consciousness. Because this deluded mind then habituates ignorance, increasing it without end, [the deluded mind] becomes the operating consciousness and the manifesting consciousness, and so on. So it is said: 'it is non-awakened and so conceiving arises, presenting false perceptual fields.'" T44.1844, 217b15–17.

of karmic action and one experiences all the sufferings of body and mind.[116]

There are two senses of habituation by false perceptual fields. What are they?

The first is habituation that increases conceiving.

The second is habituation that increases grasping.

There are two senses of habituation by the false mind. [578b] What are they?

The first is fundamental habituation by the karmic consciousness, because one experiences the sufferings of the births and deaths of arhats, *pratyekabuddhas*, and bodhisattvas.[117]

The second is habituation that increases the phenomena-discriminating consciousness, because one experiences ordinary people's sufferings of the bondage of karmic action.

There are two senses of habituation by ignorance.[118] What are they?

116. Before the *Treatise*, the phrase "all the sufferings of body and mind" is attested only in the translation of Śuddhamati's *Pratītyasamutpāda-śāstra* (*Shier yinyuan lun* 十二因緣論; Treatise on the Twelve Links of Dependent Arising) made by Bodhiruci between 508 and 535. T32.1651, 481c20–21.

117. These are the three main kinds of Buddhist adepts according to Mahāyāna. Arhats are practitioners destined to attain nirvana in their present lives. The arhats described in the Pāli canon are mainly disciples of the Buddha who heard his words. They eliminated afflictions and cultivated wisdom through meditation. Their path ends with a personal nirvana. *Pratyekabuddhas*, literally "solitary buddhas," are born in a time when there is no buddha. They attain nirvana through their own efforts. Their path is longer and more difficult than that of the arhats, and so they are superior in wisdom and supernatural powers. Bodhisattvas are Mahāyānists. Because of their "great compassion" they reject the paths of arhats and *pratyekabuddhas*. Their path aims to attain buddhahood for the benefit of other sentient beings. This passage indicates that they still have residual karma, which leads them to experience suffering as a result of past actions.

118. The only two attested uses of the phrase "habituation by ignorance" (*wuming xunxi* 無明熏習) before the *Treatise* both appear in Bodhiruci's translation of the

The first is fundamental habituation, because it is able to bring the karmic consciousness to realization.[119]

The second is habituation by [false] views and cravings that are aroused, because it is able to bring the phenomena-discriminating consciousness to realization.[120]

How does habituation give rise to pure dharmas without interruption? Because there is the dharma of suchness, it is able to habituate ignorance. Because of the power of [suchness] to habituate causes and conditions, [sentient beings'] false minds are made to weary of the sufferings of [the cycle of] birth and death and to take pleasure in seeking nirvana.[121] Because there are causes and conditions for these false minds to weary of [the cycle of birth and death] and to seek nirvana, they then habituate suchness.[122]

By trusting in one's own nature, one knows that the mind moves falsely [even] when there are no perceptual fields before it and so one cultivates the dharma of being far removed from [habituation by ignorance]. All sorts of skillful means give rise to practices that conform to [this dharma] because, in accordance with what is real,

---

Laṅkāvatāra-sūtra. The most apposite refers to the inability of the śravakas to divorce themselves from "habituation by ignorance." T16.671, 526c15–16; see also T16.671, 568b3.

119. This is because the non-awakened mind is set in motion on the basis of the force of ignorance.

120. "[False] views and cravings" are two fundamental categories of affliction, considered root causes of suffering. Similar reference to "habituation by [false] views and passions" appears in connection with a discussion of the ālaya, or store, consciousness in the translation of Vasubandhu's fourth-century Mahāyānasaṃgraha-bhāṣya made by Paramārtha in the fifth century, under the title She dasheng lun shi. T31.1595, 178b17–19.

121. This phrase appears in Guṇabhadra's translation of the *Śrīmālādevī-siṃhanāda-sūtra: "If there were no tathāgatagarbha, one could not weary of sufferings or take pleasure in seeking nirvana" 不得厭苦樂求涅槃. T32.353, 222b14–15. The same basic idea also appears elsewhere in the *Śrīmālādevī-siṃhanāda-sūtra.

122. This echoes the phrasing of the translation of the Ratnagotravibhāga-mahāyānottaratantra-śāstra made by Ratnamati (fl. 508) in 511, under the abbreviated title Baoxing lun. That text makes the same connection to the tathāgatagarbha as the Treatise. T31.1611, 831a9–10.

one knows that there are no perceptual fields before [the mind]. One neither grasps nor conceives until at last ignorance ceases because of the power of long habituation [by suchness]. Because ignorance has ceased, the mind has no arising. Because it has no arising, perceptual fields subsequently cease. Because the causes and conditions [of ignorance and perceptual fields] have both ceased, the mind's characteristics all end. This is called attaining nirvana and achieving [cognition of how] karmic action operates as a matter of course.

There are two senses of habituation by the false mind. What are they?

The first is habituation by the phenomena-discriminating consciousness. Because ordinary people and followers of the Two Vehicles weary of the sufferings of [the cycle of] birth and death they gradually advance toward the peerless Way in accordance with the capacities of their respective abilities.

The second is habituation by mentation. Because bodhisattvas' aspiration to awakening is courageous they rapidly advance toward nirvana.[123]

There are two senses of habituation by suchness. What are they?

The first is habituation by [suchness'] own intrinsic reality and characteristic.

The second is habituation by its function.[124]

Habituation by its own intrinsic reality and characteristics [means that] from beginningless time [suchness] has been endowed with a

123. Fazang states that bodhisattvas realize that all dharmas are aspects of cognition, and so they overcome the belief that they are external. They comprehend suchness through this, which leads them to attain nirvana quickly. Because bodhisattvas are aware of the store consciousness, they understand the origin of the phenomena of experience, and so they are farther along the path than other beings. T44.1846, 271b12–271c2.

124. Huiyuan identifies this with the power to motivate sentient beings to cultivate good qualities through understanding that buddhas and boddhisattvas have personally experienced suchness. T44.1843, 193b27–29.

full complement of untainted dharmas, has possessed inconceivable karmic action, and has created the nature of [purified] perceptual fields.¹²⁵ Based on these two senses, there is perpetual habituation. Because [suchness] has this power, it is capable of inducing sentient beings to weary of the sufferings of [the cycle of] birth and death and take pleasure in seeking nirvana, to believe that they themselves have the dharma of suchness, and to arouse the aspiration to awakening and cultivate practice.

Question: If these are the senses [of habituation by suchness], then all sentient beings have suchness and all are equally habituated.¹²⁶ Why, then, are there countless distinctions of precedence among those with faith and those without faith?¹²⁷ They all ought to know at the same time that they themselves have the dharma of suchness [and so] strive to cultivate skillful means and equally enter nirvana.

Answer: Although suchness is intrinsically uniform, there are nevertheless countless and boundless [forms of] ignorance because there have always been differences in the degrees and grades of [sentient beings'] self-nature. [578c] On the basis of ignorance, severe afflictions more numerous than the sands of the Ganges give rise to distinctions. And, also on the basis of ignorance, afflictions of the view of self and the defilement of craving give rise to distinctions. All such afflictions arise on the basis of ignorance because there are countless distinctions of prior and subsequent [karmic action], which only buddhas are capable of knowing.

In addition, the dharmas of buddhas have causes and conditions; only when replete with causes and conditions can those dharmas be

---

125. For Huiyuan, these untainted dharmas are associated with the dharma body and inconceivable activity is associated with the recompense body/bodies. He notes that delusion becomes severed because of the habituating power of these two buddha bodies. T44.1843, 193a12–14.

126. In the *Jin'gangxian lun* we find a similar claim that all sentient beings have buddha-nature, which is suchness. T25.1512, 841c16–17.

127. "Precedence" refers to the fact that some practitioners are more advanced than others.

brought to maturity. It is like the combustible nature of wood being the direct cause of fire.[128] If there is no one who knows this, then people will have no recourse to the means necessary [to ignite the wood]—and it is impossible that the wood will be able burn by itself. It is just the same with sentient beings. Even though they may possess the power of habituation by the direct cause [of suchness], it will be impossible for them to be able to eliminate afflictions or enter nirvana by themselves unless they encounter buddhas, bodhisattvas, or good teachers and use them as conditions.[129] And even though they may have the power of external conditions, those whose internal pure dharmas still lack the power to habituate will ultimately be incapable of wearying of the sufferings of [the cycle of] birth and death or of taking pleasure in seeking nirvana.

"Replete with causes and conditions" means that [sentient beings] are capable of arousing a mind weary of suffering, have faith that nirvana exists, and cultivate virtuous roots because they themselves possess both the power of habituation [by the intrinsic reality and characteristics of suchness] and the compassionate vows of protection by buddhas and bodhisattvas. They encounter the benefits and joys of the instructions of buddhas and bodhisattvas because

---

128. Wood has the capacity to burn, but this will only happen if that capacity is realized. The capacity to burn is described here as the direct cause of fire. Similarly, all sentient beings equally have buddha-nature. This inherent buddha-nature is the direct cause of buddhahood and of the good qualities of buddhas and bodhisattvas. Yet it is not a sufficient cause for realizing buddhahood. In order to be sparked, sentient beings need to encounter buddhas or bodhisattvas, who will employ skillful means to enable sentient beings to realize their potential. For Fazang, this means that there must be a sufficiency of conditions for the constant operation of suchness to have a positive effect. The obstacle to this is the mental afflictions of sentient beings. T44.1846, 272a18–24.

129. The idea that good teachers serve as external conditions appears also in the translation of Vasubandhu's *Viśeṣacintābrahmaparipṛcchā-śāstra* that Bodhiruci made in 531, titled *Sheng siwei fantian suowen jinglun* 勝思惟梵天所問經論 (Treatise on the Sutra of the Questions of Viśeṣacintābrahma). T26.1532, 341b9–10.

their virtuous roots are cultivated to maturity. Only then are they able to advance along the path to nirvana.[130]

Habituation by the function [of suchness][131] is precisely the power of external conditions [exerted on] sentient beings. Such external conditions have countless meanings, but in general terms there are two kinds. What are they?

The first is the conditions of differentiation.[132]

The second is the conditions of uniformity.

The conditions of differentiation refer to the period of time from when a person, relying on buddhas and bodhisattvas, expresses an intention to begin to seek the Way right through to when they attain buddhahood. During this period, if that person should perceive or be mindful of [buddhas and bodhisattvas], some [of these buddhas and bodhisattvas] will take the form of that person's kinsmen, parents, or relatives, some of their attendants, some of their good friends, and some of their enemies. Others will employ the four methods for winning people over, right through to all of the conditions produced for countless practices.[133] This is because these conditions give rise to the

130. The emphasis of this passage is on sentient beings' continuous effort, which, as it yields fruit, encourages and helps them to advance further. Buddhas and bodhisattvas compassionately protect sentient beings and promise them that there is such a thing as nirvana. Yet it is only by continuous practice and effort that sentient beings strengthen the good roots with which they are endowed. As sentient beings' good roots mature, the buddhas' promises are shown to be genuine. This encourages sentient beings to strive further for nirvana.

131. Huiyuan identifies this with response bodies (nirmāṇa-kāya). T44.1843, 193b29.

132. All sentient beings have an equal capacity for buddhahood, but they differ in terms of whether they encounter buddhas, bodhisattvas, and good teachers. They also differ in terms of their relative level of ignorance, which affects how they respond to such encounters. Fazang comments that all people encounter various kinds of beings who have the potential to have a positive effect on them. He states that this is part of the pervasive conditioning of suchness. T44.1846, 272c1–7.

133. The four means of winning people over (saṃgraha-vastu) are methods used by Buddhist teachers to attract and motivate students. They are: 1) generosity (dāna), which can

power of habituation by compassion and are able to cause sentient beings to increase their virtuous roots and to obtain benefits if they should see or hear [buddhas and bodhisattvas].

These conditions [of differentiation] are divided into two kinds. What are they?

The first is proximate conditions, which enable one to attain salvation rapidly.

The second is remote conditions, which enable one to attain salvation over a long period.[134]

These two conditions, the proximate and the remote, are further divided into [579a] two kinds. What are they?

The first is conditions that promote practice.

The second is conditions for receiving the Way.

The conditions of uniformity are that all buddhas and bodhisattvas vow to liberate all sentient beings and never to abandon spontaneous habituation.[135] They manifest deeds and actions in accordance with what sentient beings see and hear because of the power of

involve giving material things as well as Dharma (teachings), or anything that might be of benefit; 2) speaking kindly (*priya-vacana*), in a reassuring and beneficial manner; 3) beneficial conduct (*artha-kṛtya*), which involves benefitting others through actions of body, speech, and mind, and acting in accordance with one's own words; and 4) acting together (*samānārthatā*), in which one puts oneself on the same level as others and works alongside them.

134. The terms "proximate conditions" (*jinyuan* 近緣) and "remote conditions" (*yuanyuan* 遠緣) refer to how close one is to achieving full awakening. They also appear, in the context of a discussion of discernment (*guan* 觀), in Gautama Parajñāruci's translation of the *Saddharmasmṛtyupasthāna-sūtra*, titled *Zhengfa nianchu jing*. T17.721, 192c15–16. Unlike in the *Treatise*, however, there is no clear association in that text between the two conditions and the time taken to attain salvation.

135. "Spontaneous" here does not have the sense of being sporadic or arbitrary. Instead, it means that buddhas and bodhisattvas constantly work for the benefit of sentient beings in countless ways. During their training, bodhisattvas become so conditioned to this sort

their cognition that they share an intrinsic reality [with all sentient beings]. This means that sentient beings manage uniformly to perceive buddhas on the basis of *samādhi* (meditative absorption).[136]

Habituation by the function of the intrinsic reality [of suchness] is further divided into two kinds. What are they?

The first does not yet accord [with the intrinsic reality of suchness]. This means that even though ordinary people, followers of the Two Vehicles, and bodhisattvas who have newly aroused the intention to awaken are habituated by mentation and the mental consciousness, nevertheless they are capable of cultivating practice because of the power of faith.[137] This is because they have not yet attained a mind free from discrimination or yet accorded with the intrinsic reality of [suchness]. And it is because they have not yet attained mastery over the cultivation of karmic action or yet accorded with this function [of the intrinsic reality of suchness].[138]

of activity that it becomes wholly spontaneous and does not require any deliberation on their part.

136. The virtuous roots of sentient beings mature through constant habituation by buddhas and bodhisattvas. Buddhas and bodhisattvas respond to sentient beings in ways that enable them to receive benefits. As a result, sentient beings gain greater insight into their innate nature, which is suchness. This is an important sense of the One Mind. When sentient beings are sufficiently advanced, they can successfully engage in meditation and attain progressively greater wisdom and insight.

137. The author of the *Treatise* seems to draw on Bodhiruci's translation of the *Laṅkāvatāra-sūtra* here: "Ordinary people discriminate good and bad dharmas because they rely on habituation of the mind, mentation, and mental consciousness [by suchness]." T16.671, 559b19–20.

138. This refers to meditative absorption as a function of suchness. It is effective precisely because all sentient beings are innately endowed with buddha-nature. They can then engage in effective meditative practice on the basis of habituation. According to Fazang, the *Treatise* is referring here to beginners who are incapable of comprehending the essence of the dharma body and do not have "post-enlightenment cognition" 後得智 (*pṛṣṭha-labdha-jñāna*)—or "cognition of how karmic action operates as a matter of course" 自然業智 in the phrasing of the *Treatise*. Fazang goes on to state that these beginning practitioners are unable to benefit fully from the activities of buddhas' recompense bodies due to their own inadequacies. T44.1846, 273a13–16.

The second already accords [with the intrinsic reality of suchness]. This means that dharma-body bodhisattvas attain a non-discriminatory mind and accord with the function of buddha wisdom, based on nothing but the power of the Dharma to cultivate practice as a matter of course.[139] This is because they have been habituated by suchness and have extinguished ignorance.

Moreover, from beginningless time habituation by defiled dharmas has never been interrupted; there is only interruption after one has become a buddha. Habituation by pure dharmas has never been interrupted [either], and it will not be exhausted in the future. Why? The false mind ceases and the dharma body appears because the dharma of suchness constantly habituates. And there is no interruption because suchness gives rise to habituation by its function.

1.2.7 THE FUNCTIONING OF SUCHNESS IN THE MIND AS ARISING AND CEASING

Moreover, suchness' own intrinsic reality and characteristics neither increase nor decrease for any ordinary people, hearers (*śrāvaka*), solitary realizers (*pratyekabuddha*), bodhisattvas, or buddhas. It is neither that suchness arose in a former time, nor that it will cease at some future time. It is absolutely constant. It has always been inherently replete with all qualities. It means this because of the idea that [suchness'] own intrinsic reality is imbued with the light of great wisdom; that it pervasively illuminates the dharma realm; that it is the recognition of reality; that it is the intrinsically pristine mind; that it is eternal, blissful, Self, and pure;[140] and that it is cool, unchanging,

---

139. Fazang comments that these bodhisattvas are in harmony with the essence of suchness, and so they no longer need to rely solely on faith. T44.1846, 273a16–24.

140. This refers to the four results of meritorious activity (*guo de* 果德) mentioned in texts associated with the Tathāgatagarbha tradition. In this tradition, the motto characterizes the true nature of dharmas and reality. The *locus classicus* is the *Mahāparinirvāṇa-sūtra*; see, for example, T12.374, 377c3.

and sovereign [that is, nirvana]. And it is because [suchness' own intrinsic reality] is replete with inconceivable buddha dharmas more numerous than the sands of the Ganges, which are not separate, not cut off from, and not different from it, to the extent that it is perfect and lacks nothing. It is called the *tathāgatagarbha*; it is also called the dharma body of *tathāgatas*.[141]

Question: Earlier, you stated that the intrinsic reality of suchness is uniform and free from all characteristics.[142] How, then, can you also state that this intrinsic reality has such various kinds of qualities?

Answer: Although suchness truly has these qualities, it has no characteristics of differentiation. It is homogeneous and of one taste: there is only one suchness.[143] Why? Since it is without any discriminating [function], and so free from the characteristics of discrimination, it is therefore non-dual.

[Question:] So how can you also talk of differentiation?

[Answer:] Since the characteristics of arising and ceasing are revealed on the basis of the karmic consciousness. How are they revealed? Since there is the false mind, which, being unawakened, gives rise to conceiving and perceives perceptual fields. This is despite the fact that all dharmas have always been nothing but the mind, which in reality is devoid of conceiving. One therefore talks of ignorance.

141. This echoes a discussion in Guṇabhadra's translation of the *Śrīmālādevī-siṃhanāda-sūtra*: "World-Honored One! When inconceivable buddha dharmas more numerous than the sands of the Ganges, which are not separate, not apart, and not different [from the dharma body], are perfected, they are called the dharma body of *tathāgatas*. World-Honored One! As such when the dharma body of *tathāgatas* is not separate from the store of afflictions, it is called the *tathāgatagarbha*." T12.353, 221c9–11. This is consistent with the One Mind Two Gateways model of the *Treatise*, in which suchness in its unconditioned mode corresponds to the dharma body of *tathāgatas*.

142. This refers to an earlier passage in the *Treatise*, which reads: ". . . all dharmas have always been free from the characteristics of language, naming, and mental perceptions. They are ultimately uniform, invariant, and indestructible. They are nothing but this One Mind and are therefore called 'suchness.'" [576a]

143. See also the reference to "only one suchness" (*weiyi zhenru* 唯一真如) in the *Jin'gangxian lun*. T25.1512, 873b23–24.

The nature of the mind is not subject to arising, precisely because it is the light of great wisdom. If the mind were to give rise to perceiving, then there would be characteristics [of cognitive objects] that it does not perceive. But the nature of the mind [**579b**] is free from perceiving, precisely because it pervasively illuminates the dharma realm.[144] If the mind were to move, then it would not be the recognition of reality; it would not have self-nature; it would not be eternal, blissful, Self, or pure; it would be tormented, it would decay, and so it would no longer be sovereign, to the extent that it would be endowed with falsehoods and defilements more numerous than the sands of the Ganges. Because, conversely, the nature of the mind has no movement, the many characteristics of its pure qualities, more numerous than the sands of the Ganges, are revealed.

If the mind were subject to arising and if it were also to perceive the dharmas in front of it as things that could be conceived, then it would be deficient. [By contrast,] such countless qualities of pure dharmas are precisely this One Mind, and there is nothing further to conceive. Therefore, the mind is complete and it is called the dharma body or the store of *tathāgatas* (*tathāgatagarbha*).[145]

Moreover, the function of suchness refers to the buddhas—the *tathāgatas*—who, when they were originally at the causal levels,[146] gave rise to great compassion [for practitioners], cultivated the *pāramitās* (perfections),[147] converted sentient beings, and took the

144. Here the *Treatise* contrasts limited perception, which applies to all sentient beings, with omniscience, which applies only to fully awakened beings. The nature of the mind is potentially omniscient, but its usual mental functions, including perception, are not.

145. The present passage is similar in both theme and phrasing with the *Jin'gangxian lun*. T25.1512, 859a23–859b1.

146. This refers to the training period following their resolve to attain buddhahood in order to benefit sentient beings. They take vows to pursue the path before cultivating the perfections and engaging in various meritorious acts and meditative practices to fulfill their aspiration to awakening.

147. The *pāramitās*, or perfections, are the six—sometimes ten—qualities in which bodhisattvas train on the path to buddhahood. They are: giving, moral discipline, forbearance, vigorous exertion, concentration, and wisdom. See also the introduction.

great vow—all with the intention of liberating the realms of sentient beings equally. They neither impose a limit on the number of future *kalpa*s (eons) required to complete this, because they regard all sentient beings as just like themselves, nor become attached to the characteristics of sentient beings.[148] Why? It means that this is because, in accordance with what is real, they know that all sentient beings and they themselves are true suchness, uniform and without difference. Since they have such wisdom of great skillful means, they eliminate ignorance and reveal the inherent dharma body. As a matter of course, they perform various kinds of inconceivable karmic function. That is, being the same as suchness, they are all-pervading. In addition, they also lack any characteristics of function that can be apprehended.[149] Why? Because the buddhas—the *tathāgatas*—are nothing but the dharma body, the body of the characteristic of wisdom. To be at [the level of] ultimate truth is to be devoid of the perceptual fields of conventional truth and free from actively bestowing benefit; it is only by their according with what sentient beings see and hear that sentient beings acquire benefit.[150] One therefore talks of function.

There are two kinds of function. What are they?

The first is based on the phenomena-discriminating consciousness. What the minds of ordinary people and the followers of the Two Vehicles perceive is called the response body.[151] This is because

---

148. In the *Jin'gangxian lun*, a line in the *Diamond Sutra* is taken to "show that *tathāgatas* have no attachment to the characteristics of sentient beings, yet wish to liberate them." T25.1512, 862b22–23. Huiyuan comments that if buddhas are attached to the characteristics of sentient beings they will be unable to save them. T44.1843, 195b7–8.

149. Similarly in the *Jin'gangxian lun* we find the statement that "the dharma body does not show the excellent characteristics of function that constitute it." T25.1512, 856b6–7.

150. Buddhas accommodate the needs of each sentient being as a matter of course, without plan or calculation, yet always appropriately and effectively.

151. For a discussion of the "response body" (*yingshen* 應身), see the introduction. A similar distinction between the three bodies identified in what follows—the dharma body, the response body, and the recompense body—appears in the *Jin'gangxian lun*. See, especially, T25.1512, 855a18–855b9.

they perceive this body as coming from outside because they do not know that it is a manifestation of the operating consciousness.[152] And it is because, being attached to boundaries of form, they are incapable of knowing all [of the buddha bodies].

The second is based on the karmic consciousness. That is, what is perceived by the minds of bodhisattvas from the initial intention [for awakening] right up to the final bodhisattva level is called the recompense body. This body has countless forms, the forms have countless [major] characteristics, and the characteristics have count-less [minor] features.[153] Based on the effects [of karmic action], its abode also has countless kinds of ornamentation, according to what-ever form it displays. The [body] itself is boundless, is inexhaustible, is free from the characteristic of boundaries, and accords with what-ever it encounters. It is able to be sustained constantly; it neither is destroyed nor disappears.[154] All such qualities are established due to habituation by the untainted activity and the inconceivable [karmic action] of the *pāramitās* (perfections). [**579c**] Because [the body] is replete with the countless characteristics of unlimited pleasure, it is said to be the recompense body.[155] In addition, what ordinary beings perceive are the coarse forms [of the buddha body]. What they each perceive will differ, depending on which of the six paths they are on.[156] Because these various different kinds of being do not

152. The operating consciousness is one of the five names for mentation [577b].
153. For Fazang, these are the characteristics (*lakṣaṇa*) that adorn buddhas' bodies as a result of their past cultivation of virtue. They attract beings, who then draw close to buddhas and become their disciples. T44.1846, 275b8–11.
154. For a similar description of the recompense body, see the *Jin'gangxian lun.* T25.1512, 829a28–829b6.
155. Cultivation of the perfections is an integrated process. Practice of each affects the others and enhances them. This appears to be the function of habituation: as one improves cultivation of ethics, for example, one improves one's ability to cultivate the other perfections.
156. These are the six paths (*gati*) onto which sentient beings are reborn: gods, demigods, humans, animals, hungry ghosts, and hell beings. None is a final destination; one is re-peatedly reborn on one of these until attaining final liberation.

experience [the recompense body's] characteristics of [unlimited] pleasure, what they do experience is said to be the response body.

Moreover, bodhisattvas who have newly aroused the aspiration to awakening are capable of perceiving [the recompense body] to a small extent because they have profound faith in the dharma of suchness. They know that its characteristics of form and its ornamentations are without coming or going, and free from boundaries. And they know that these characteristics appear only on the basis of the mind and are inseparable from suchness.[157] These bodhisattvas still construct their own distinctions, however, because they have yet to enter the stage of the dharma body. If they attain [the level of] pure mind,[158] then what they perceive will be subtle and marvellous and its function will be all the more efficacious, until the bodhisattva levels are completed and they perceive [the recompense body] in its entirety. Once they free themselves from the karmic consciousness, there are no characteristics to be perceived because the dharma body of buddhas does not have characteristics of any particular form that might enable them to perceive one another.

Question: How is the dharma body of buddhas able to appear through a characteristic of form if it is free from any characteristic of form?

Answer: It is able to appear through form because precisely this dharma body is the intrinsic reality of form. That is to say, form and mind have always been non-dual. The intrinsic reality of form is shapeless because the nature of form is cognitive; it is termed the cognitive body.[159] And it is termed the dharma body because the nature

157. In the *Jin'gangxian lun* there is the similar claim that bodhisattvas will "know that they are not separate from the dharma realm of suchness" once they have "made up their minds to practice and liberate sentient beings to enter nirvana" and have "cultivated the Pure Land Practice." T25.1512, 850b29–850c1.
158. This is the first of the ten bodhisattva levels.
159. The "nature of form" is understood to be cognitive because form is reducible to cognition—it is visible, touchable, and so on. Like cognition, it is shapeless and

of cognition is form.[160] The dharma body pervades everywhere and the forms in which it appears have no boundaries. It is capable of revealing at will the countless bodhisattvas, the countless recompense bodies, and the countless ornamentations of the worlds of the ten directions.[161] Each is differentiated yet none impedes the others for they have no boundaries. This is not something that the distinctions of mind and consciousnesses are capable of knowing because it is the sovereign functioning of suchness.[162]

Moreover, I will disclose how to enter directly into the gateway of suchness from the gateway of arising and ceasing. That is to say, when one inquires after the five aggregates, there are aggregates of form and mental aggregates. In the final analysis, there is nothing to be conceived in the perceptual fields of the six sensory and conceptual fields. The mind can never be apprehended, even if one seeks it in the ten directions, because it lacks the characteristic of shape. It is like a person who has become disoriented and therefore deems east to be west, when in reality the directions have not been reversed.[163] Sentient beings are the same. Being ignorant and disoriented, they will therefore deem the mind to

permeates everywhere. Form and mind are conceived as non-dual. In his version of the *Treatise*, Śikṣānanda writes that "the inherent nature of form is termed the cognitive body, since it is precisely the self-nature of the mind." T32.1667, 588a13–14.

160. "Form," *se* 色 (*rūpa*), is used in Buddhist literature in a more general sense than simply material form, although that is also included in its meaning. It refers to all the physical things that one senses—the visible, the audible, the gustatory, the olfactory, and the tactile. According to the *Treatise*, although we experience these as sensory, and so in some sense physically, they are in fact cognitive. Since cognition requires a medium for it to exist, there is no cognition without "form."

161. In Bodhiruci's translation of the *Dilun*, those receptive to teaching are seen to "reveal the buddha body at will." T26.1522, 140c18–19.

162. As discussed previously, early commentators take "the mind" to refer to the seventh consciousness and "consciousnesses" to refer to the first six consciousnesses. The phrasing that the author of the *Treatise* uses here is redolent of the *Jin'gangxian lun*. That text refers twice to "the sovereignty of suchness" (*zhenru zizai* 眞如自在) in discussions of how the mind of the Buddha is in all sentient beings. T25.1512, 804c12, 806a11.

163. This simile also appears in Buddhabhadra's fifth-century translation of the *Avataṃsaka-sūtra*. T9.278, 721a2–3.

be [the activity of] conceiving but, [unlike conceiving,] the mind really does not move. If they are able to investigate, they will know that the mind is without conceiving. Then they will readily enter the gateway of suchness.

SECTION 2: ANTIDOTES TO WRONGLY HELD VIEWS

With "antidotes to wrongly held views," all wrongly held views are based on views of self. One will have no wrongly held views if one frees oneself from [views of] self. There are two kinds of view of self. What are they?

The first is the view of an inherently existing self.

The second is the view of inherently existing dharmas.[164]

There are five kinds of view of an inherently existing self as expressed by ordinary people.[165] What are they?

The first is they think that empty space is the nature of *tathāgata*s. This is because, when they hear the sutra explain that [**580a**] the dharma body of *tathāgata*s is ultimately quiescent and like empty space, they do not know that this is said to destroy attachments.[166]

---

164. A hallmark of Mahāyāna is the claim that not only persons lack selfhood (*ren wu wo* 人無我; *pudgala-nairātmya*), but dharmas are also devoid of self (*fa wu wo* 法無我; *dharma-nairātmya*). Non-Mahāyāna Buddhists sometimes argued for non-self (*anātman*) by reducing a person to the dharmas that constitute that person, such as the aggregates. Mahāyāna, by contrast, went on to insist dharmas also lack selfhood.

165. Buddhism has a long and detailed discourse on the problems of the view of an inherently existing self (*wo jian* 我見; *ātma-dṛṣṭi*). The five views listed here are unusual in that discourse, however. They have mostly been drawn from texts related to the Tathāgatagarbha tradition.

166. Here, ordinary people think that the nature of buddhas is permanent, like empty space: they take it to be an affirming quality. Ōtake Susumu 大竹晋 suspects that the sutra referred to here is *Ru zhufo jingjie zhiguangming zhuangyan jing* 入諸佛境界智

What is the antidote? It is to make it clear that the characteristics of space are false dharmas; they embody nothing and are not real, but exist only because they are contrasted with [the characteristics of] form. These characteristics [of form], which might be perceived, cause the mind to arise and cease. In reality, however, there are no external forms, since all material dharmas have always been mental. If there are no forms, then there will be no characteristics of space. That is to say, all perceptual fields exist only because the mind falsely arises; all perceptual fields will cease if the mind is free from false movement. Only the One True Mind is all-pervasive. This refers to the ultimate extent of a *tathāgata*'s extensive and great wisdom, which is not like the characteristics of space.[167]

The second is they think that the nature of suchness and nirvana is nothing but emptiness. This is because, when they hear the sutra explain that the ultimate reality of mundane dharmas is empty, that even the dharmas of nirvana and suchness are ultimately empty, and that they have always been intrinsically empty and free from all characteristics, they do not know that this [is said] to destroy attachments.[168]

光明莊嚴經 (*Sarvabuddhaviṣayāvatārajñānālokālaṃkāra-sūtra*; The Ornament of the Light of Awareness that Enters the Domain of All the Buddhas), as cited by Ratnamati in his *Baoxing lun* (T31.1611, 842a28–842b1). See Ōtake Susumu, "*Daijō kishin ron* no inyō bunken" 大乗起信論の引用文献 (Sources Cited in the *Treatise on Awakening Mahāyāna Faith*), *Tetsugaku shisō ronsō* 哲学・思想論叢 22 (2004): p. 55.

167. Here space is presented as a mental concept constructed in contrast to material forms. For example, east and west are mutually entailing constructs and do not exist independently of one another. Perceived physicality and space are ultimately mental constructions and so they are reduced to the mind, which is a synonym for buddhas' omniscient cognition. There are frequent comparisons between the dharma body and space in the *Jin'gangxian lun*; but the antidote suggested there differs from that proposed in the *Treatise*. See, for example, T25.1512, 855a12, 855a24–25, 858c11–17, *inter alia*.

168. Ordinary people think that emptiness is an affirming quality of the nature of suchness. A possible source for this scriptural reference is the *Mahāprajñāpāramitā-sūtra*. T8.223, 224b28–c1, 276b7. A similar reference to the intrinsic emptiness of dharmas (citing the *Mahāprajñāpāramitā-sūtra*) appears in a discussion of the self in the *Jin'gangxian lun*.

What is the antidote? It is to make it clear that the dharma body of suchness' own intrinsic reality is not empty, but replete with countless qualities.

The third is they think that the store of a *tathāgata* has distinctions in its intrinsic characteristics [associated with] material and mental dharmas. This is because, when they hear the sutra explain that the store of a *tathāgata* neither increases nor decreases and intrinsically has a full complement of all dharmas of [good] qualities, they do not understand it.[169]

What is the antidote? It is to demonstrate and explain distinctions through the doctrine of the defilements of arising and ceasing because [the sutra] explains things only on the basis of the doctrine of suchness.

The fourth is they think that the *tathāgatagarbha*'s own intrinsic reality possesses all the dharmas of birth and death in the mundane world. This is because, when they hear the sutra explain that all defiled dharmas of birth and death in the mundane world exist on the basis of the *tathāgatagarbha* and that none of the dharmas is separate from suchness, they do not understand it.[170]

T25.1512, 813c20–814a4, 869a13–14. See Ōtake Susumu, "*Daijō kishin ron no inyō bunken,*" pp. 56–57.

169. Takemura Makio traces this scriptural reference to *Foshuo buzeng bujian jing* 佛說不增不減經. T16.668, 467a19–21, 467c7–10. See Takemura Makio, *Kaiteiban Daijō kishin ron dokushaku*, pp. 356–357, 400. There is also reference to "intrinsically having a full complement of" good qualities in the *Jin'gangxian lun*. T25.1512, 819c19–20.

170. Takemura Makio traces the first part of this scriptural reference to Guṇabhadra's translation of the **Śrīmālādevī-siṃhanāda-sūtra* (T12.353, 222b5–12) and Bodhiruci's translation of the *Laṅkāvatāra-sūtra* (T16.670, 556b22–25). Ōtake Susumu notes that Ratnamati's *Baoxing lun* cites the relevant passage from the **Śrīmālādevī-siṃhanāda-sūtra* (T31.1611, 839b1–3). The *Baoxing lun* seems most pertinent to the *Treatise*. Its citation of the **Śrīmālādevī-siṃhanāda-sūtra* claims that birth and death depend on the *tathāgatagarbha*. If the *tathāgatagarbha* did not exist, there would be no motivation to hate suffering and pursue nirvana. In suggesting that the *tathāgatagarbha* is free of differentiation, like the dharma body, it further addresses themes already covered in this section of the *Treatise*. See Takemura Makio, *Kaiteiban Daijō kishin ron dokushaku*, p. 400; Ōtake Susumu, "*Daijō kishin ron no inyō bunken,*" pp. 59–60.

What is the antidote? It is to explain that it would be an impossibility for the *tathāgatagarbha* to be intrinsically replete with false dharmas and yet be capable of causing realization and forever putting an end to falsity. This is because the *tathāgatagarbha* has always been nothing but pure qualities more numerous than the sands of the Ganges, which are not separate from, cut off from, or different from suchness. And it is because afflictions and defiled dharmas more numerous than the sands of the Ganges only have a false existence, their natures are intrinsically non-existent, and they have never had an association with the *tathāgatagarbha* from beginningless time.

The fifth is they think that sentient beings have a beginning. This is because, when they hear the sutra explain that both [rebirth in the cycle of] birth and death and the attainment of nirvana are also based on the *tathāgatagarbha*, they do not understand it.[171] And they further think that the nirvana attained by buddhas has an end, after which [buddhas] return to become sentient beings, because they perceive [that sentient beings have] a beginning.

What is the antidote? It is to explain that the characteristics of ignorance have no beginning because the *tathāgatagarbha* has no starting [580b] point. If one were to claim that there are other sentient beings who first arise outside the three realms, this would be precisely what non-Buddhist scriptures claim. In addition, the *tathāgatagarbha* has no endpoint. Given this, the nirvana attained by buddhas, which is associated with it, also has no endpoint.

With the view of inherently existing dharmas, the Tathāgata merely taught that people do not have an inherent self [and not that all dharmas lack inherent existence] because of the dull faculties of followers of the Two Vehicles. Since this doctrine is not

---

171. Takemura Makio traces this scriptural reference to the quotation of the *Śrīmālādevī-siṃhanāda-sūtra* that appears in Ratnamati's *Baoxing lun* (T31.1611, 839b3–4). See Takemura Makio, *Kaiteiban Daijō kishin ron dokushaku*, pp. 400–401.

definitive, followers of the Two Vehicles perceive the arising-and-ceasing dharmas of the five aggregates, fearing birth and death and falsely grasping nirvana.

What is the antidote? It is to explain that is there is no cessation of the self-nature of dharmas, which is the five aggregates, since that self-nature does not arise; it has always been nirvanic.

Moreover, those who have completely freed themselves from falsely held views should know that all defiled and pure dharmas are mutually dependent and do not have intrinsic characteristics that might be spoken of. Therefore, no dharma has ever been material or mental, [the subject of] cognition or consciousness, existent or non-existent—ultimately, dharmas cannot be spoken of. And [those who have completely freed themselves from falsely held views] should know that when language is used [it is because] the Tathāgata, who was accomplished in skillful means, was guiding sentient beings by provisional means of this language. His intentions all served to free them from conceiving and return them to suchness, because conceiving of any dharma causes the mind to arise and cease, preventing it from cognizing things as they really are.

SECTION 3: THREE KINDS OF ASPIRATION TO AWAKENING

"Discriminating the characteristics for embarking on the Way" is so-called because it refers to the idea of the Way realized by all buddhas, which all bodhisattvas aspire to awaken, to cultivate, and to progress towards. In general terms, there are three kinds of aspiration to awakening. What are they?

The first is the aspiration to awakening through the consummation of faith.

The second is the aspiration to awakening through understanding and practicing [the Way].

The third is the aspiration to awakening through realizing [the Way].

3.1 Aspiration to Awakening through the Consummation of Faith

With the aspiration to awakening through the consummation of faith, what sort of person, doing what sort of practices, manages to consummate faith and is capable of arousing the aspiration to awaken? They are sentient beings of the group not certain to achieve awakening.[172] Because they have the power of the virtuous roots to which they have been habituated, they believe in the retributive effects of karmic action; they are capable of giving rise to the ten kinds of wholesome behavior;[173] they are weary of the sufferings of [the cycle of] birth and death; they arouse the aspiration to supreme *bodhi* (awakening); they manage to encounter buddhas, become their attendants and make offerings to them; and they cultivate a commitment to faith.[174] Because [these sentient beings] have been consummating their commitment to faith for ten thousand

---

172. These beings are not fixed in their commitment to Mahāyāna and may revert to Hīnayāna tendencies unless they encounter the sorts of conditions that will keep them on the bodhisattva path.

173. The ten kinds of wholesome behavior are: not killing living beings, not stealing, not engaging in sexual misconduct, not speaking falsely, not slandering, not speaking divisively, not gossiping, not being greedy, not feeling anger, and not subscribing to wrong views.

174. Mahāyāna texts propose various ways of "encountering buddhas" when none is alive during one's own lifetime. One fervently practices in order to be reborn in the presence of a buddha, either when a buddha is on earth once more, or through rebirth in a buddha land, such as Amitābha's Pure Land. Additionally, the *tathāgatagarbha* signifies a capacity to project response-body buddhas who can respond in various ways to the needs of a practitioner, including appearing in physical form. Another way to "encounter buddhas" is by being "mindful of buddhas" (*nian fo* 念佛; *buddhānusmṛti*), through such practices as visualizing buddhas, reciting their names, and so on.

*kalpa*s (eons), buddhas and bodhisattvas instruct them in arousing their aspiration to awakening. Some will be capable of arousing this aspiration on their own because of great compassion. Others will be capable of arousing this aspiration on their own to preserve the causes and conditions of the true Dharma as it is on the verge of ceasing.[175] Those who consummate a commitment to faith and manage to arouse the aspiration to awakening like this will join the group of beings certain to achieve awakening and will ultimately not regress.[176] They are referred to as being associated with the correct cause through abiding in the lineage of *tathāgatha*s.

[By contrast,] if there are sentient beings with scant virtuous roots, who have had profound afflictions for a long time, they will only produce either seeds [for rebirth as] a human or god,[177] or seeds [for becoming an adherent of] the Two Vehicles, even if they encounter a buddha and also manage to make offerings. Should there be some who seek the Great Vehicle, they may either progress or regress because their roots are indeterminate.[178] [580c] Some who make offerings to buddhas for less than ten thousand *kalpa*s (eons) may also arouse the aspiration to awakening if they encounter the right conditions during this time. That is to say, they will arouse

---

175. There are various predictions in Buddhist literature of the decline and eclipse of the true Dharma. See Jan Nattier, *Once Upon a Future Time: Studies in a Buddhist Prophecy of Decline* (Berkeley, CA: Asian Humanities Press, 1991).
176. A similar division, between the group of beings certain to achieve awakening and those who are still not certain of achieving awakening, appears in Ratnamati's *Baoxing lun*. T31.1611, 829a12–15.
177. The consequence of meeting buddhas and making offerings is positive: rebirth as a human or god is desirable because it provides additional opportunities to increase the roots of good virtues and so advance on the Way. Such opportunities are limited for these sentient beings, however; they are not sufficient for rebirth as a bodhisattva, for example.
178. Fazang cites the *She dasheng lun shi*, which indicates that many novice practitioners on the bodhisattva path still lack sufficient compassion for sentient beings and so they willingly abandon the basic Mahāyāna vows in favor of the Hīnayāna path. T44.1846, 278c17–19. For the section of the *She dasheng lun shi* to which Fazang refers, see T31.1595, 265a4–7.

this aspiration by seeing the physical image of a buddha.[179] Some will arouse their aspiration to awakening by making offerings to the monastic community. Some will arouse this aspiration through the instruction of followers of the Two Vehicles. Some will arouse this aspiration by learning from others. Since all these kinds [of sentient being who] arouse the aspiration to awakening are of the indeterminate group, some may regress and fall to the level of the Two Vehicles on meeting with bad causes and conditions.[180]

Moreover, when one arouses the aspiration to awakening (*faxin*) through the consummation of faith, what sorts of mind (*xin*) does one arouse (*fa*)? Briefly explained, there are three kinds of mind. What are they?

The first is a directly focused mind, because one is true in one's mindfulness of the dharma of suchness.[181]

The second is a profound mind, because one takes pleasure in amassing all good deeds.

The third is a mind of great compassion, because one wishes to eliminate the sufferings of all sentient beings.[182]

Question: Earlier you explained the unitary characteristic of the dharma realm and the non-duality of buddhahood. So why is it not enough simply to be mindful of suchness? Why is there the further need to seek to learn from good deeds?

---

179. This refers either to seeing an image of a buddha, such as a painting or statue, or to visualization practices.

180. The use of "level" (*di* 地) here does not refer to one of the ten levels, or *bhūmis*, on the bodhisattva path; it precedes entry into Mahāyāna faith. One who has aroused the aspiration to awakening may regress, but only to the level of the Two Vehicles.

181. In his translation of the *Laṅkāvatāra-sūtra*, Bodhiruci identifies being mindful of suchness as one of the four forms of meditative absorption. T16.671, 533a3; see also the discussion at T16.671, 533a14–17.

182. In his translation of the *Dilun*, Bodhiruci refers to different kinds of mind—the upright mind (*zhixin* 直心), the profound mind (*shenxin* 深心), the mind of great compassion (*dabei* 大悲)—in identical phrasing to the *Treatise*, although not as a list. T26.1522, 135b2–4.

[need for UPAYA]

Answer: It is like a great *maṇi*, a jewel, which has been encrusted with impurities of ore although it is bright and pure by its own nature.[183] Even if someone were mindful of its precious nature, he would ultimately fail to recover its purity without using the skillful means of various kinds of polishing. In the same way, the dharma of suchness in sentient beings has countless afflictions and impurities although it is empty and pure by its own nature. Even if someone were mindful of suchness, he too would nevertheless fail to recover its purity without using the skillful means of various kinds of habituation and practice. Because impurities are countless and pervade all dharmas, one should use all good deeds as an antidote. This is because, as a matter of course, one will return to the dharma of suchness if one practices all good dharmas.[184]

Briefly explained, there are four kinds of skillful means. What are they?

(1) The first is skillful means that are the fundamentals of practice. That is to say, by discerning that the self-nature of all dharmas is *insight* non-arising, one frees oneself from false views and does not abide *wisdom* in [the cycle of] birth and death. And, by discerning that the causes and conditions of all dharmas are combinations and that the effects of karmic action are unfailing, one gives rise to great compassion, cultivates beneficial qualities, converts sentient beings, and does not abide in nirvana.[185] This is because one conforms to the dharma nature without abiding in it.

183. The *maṇi* jewel is commonly associated with the *tathāgatagarbha* in Buddhist literature. This image is similar in language and theme to its use in Ratnamati's *Baoxing lun*. T31.1611, 834b5–7.

184. This final phrase echoes Bodhiruci's translation of the *Laṅkāvatāra-sūtra*. T16.671, 573c18.

185. By "not abiding in nirvana" (*apratiṣṭhita-nirvāṇa*), one is free from the cycle of birth and death (*saṃsāra*) while still able to act within it. In Mahāyāna, this is one way in which the highest-level bodhisattvas could voluntarily continue to assist sentient beings without advancing to final nirvana.

2. The second is the skillful means that are able to stop [all bad dharmas]. That is to say, feeling ashamed of and repenting one's transgressions, one is able to stop all bad dharmas and prevent them from increasing. This is because one conforms to the dharma nature and frees oneself from transgressions.

3. The third is the skillful means by which the virtuous roots that have been initiated increase. That is to say, one diligently makes offerings to and worships the Three Jewels, and one praises, rejoices in, and implores buddhas. One's faith manages to increase and one is then able to fix one's resolve to seek the unsurpassed Way because one reveres the Three Jewels with a sincere mind. In addition, one is able to extinguish the hindrances of karmic actions and one's virtuous roots do not regress because one is protected by the power of the Buddha, the Dharma, and the Monastic Community. This is because one conforms to the dharma nature and frees oneself from the obstacles of nescience.[186]

4. The fourth is the skillful means of the great vow to [save all beings] uniformly. [581a] That is to say, one vows forever to liberate all sentient beings, without exceptions, causing all to attain nirvana without remainder.[187] This is because one conforms to the dharma nature, which is never cut off.[188]

The dharma nature is extensive and vast and it pervades all sentient beings. This is because it is uniform and non-dual, cannot be conceived in terms of distinctions between this and that, and is ultimately quiescent. Because bodhisattvas arouse this aspiration to

186. Nescience (*chi* 癡; *moha*) is the third of the three poisons, considered more deep-seated and harder to extirpate than the other two. A consistent theme of the *Treatise* is how ignorance is the root cause of suffering and so needs to be remedied.

187. This skillful means enables the transition to nirvana without remainder (*nirupadhiśeṣa-nirvāṇa*), in which all residue of one's karmic actions is extinguished.

188. The *Treatise* reminds its readers that dharma nature is never extinguished, and that nirvana never ends, to avoid the misconception that nirvana without remainder entails annihilation or absolute nonexistence.

awakening, they manage to perceive the dharma body to a small extent. And because they perceive the dharma body according to the power of their vows, they are capable of displaying the eight stages of a buddha's life for the benefit of sentient beings. That is to say, [a bodhisattva] descends from the Tuṣita Heaven, enters the womb, stays in the womb, leaves the womb, leaves the home life, attains awakening, turns the wheel of Dharma, and enters nirvana.[189] However, these bodhisattvas are not yet called the dharma body because they have not yet been able definitively to eliminate [the residue of] their contaminated karmic actions from countless past ages; they still have an association with mild suffering according to the circumstances of their birth.[190] This is not the bondage of karmic action, however, because they have the power of mastery of the great vow. As it is explained by some of the sutras, there are [bodhisattvas] who regress and fall into the bad destinies.[191] It is not that they actually regress. Instead, it is meant only for those novice bodhisattvas who have become lazy, not yet having entered the correct stage, because they are spurred on to heroic efforts through fear.[192] In addition, these bodhisattvas

189. This list of the main episodes in the life of the Buddha is close to that found in Bodhiruci's translation of the *Dilun*. T26.1522, 197c24–25. These eight episodes later became standard in visual depictions of the Buddha's life.

190. This may refer to traditions relating to the Buddha's past lives as a bodhisattva, according to which negative events in his final life were attributed to the residual effects of bad karma from his past. See Mary E. Lilley, ed., *The Apadāna of the Khuddaka Nikāya* (London: Pali Text Society, 1925), pp. 299–301.

191. These "bad destinies" are animals, hungry ghosts, and hell beings.

192. Huiyuan says that this refers to the "indeterminate group." T44.1843, 199c16. When discussing this passage in his *Daeseung gisil lon byeolgi*, Wonhyo draws a connection with the *Pusa yingluo benye jing* 菩薩瓔珞本業經 (Sutra on the Primary Activities that are the Necklaces of the Bodhisattvas), traditionally attributed to Zhu Fonian 竺佛念 (fourth century). T44.1845, 240b20–24. For the relevant passage in *Pusa yingluo benye jing*, see T24.1485, 1014c4–5, 1014c7–11. Takemura Makio and Ōtake Susumu claim that this scriptural allusion comes from the translation of the *Bodhisattvabhūmi-sūtra* by the Central Indian translator-monk Dharmakṣema (385–433), titled *Pusa dichi jing* 菩薩地持經 (Bodhisattva Levels Sutra). T30.1581, 889b8. This, in turn, seems to derive from *Jin'gangxian lun*. T25.1512, 803b27–29. See Takemura Makio, *Kaiteiban Daijō kishin ron dokushaku*, pp. 426–428; Ōtake Susumu, "*Daijō kishin ron no inyō bunken*," pp. 60–63.

become far removed from timidity as soon as they have aroused the aspiration to awakening until, in the end, they are no longer afraid that they may fall to the level of the Two Vehicles. Indeed, even if they hear that it will take countless, boundless *asaṃkhyeya-kalpa* (incalculable eons) of painful, difficult practice before attaining nirvana, they will not be timid because they [now] believe and know that all dharmas have always been intrinsically nirvanic.

3.2 Aspiration to Awakening through Understanding and Practicing the Way

With the aspiration to awakening through understanding and practicing [the Way], one should know that it is a change for the better.[193] This is because, from the first stage of correct faith, these bodhisattvas intend to complete this level in the first *asaṃkhyeya-kalpa* (incalculable eon). Through the dharma of suchness, they profoundly understand what appears before them, since what they cultivate is free from characteristics. They conform to and practice *dāna-pāramitā* (the perfection of giving) because they know that the dharma nature is intrinsically devoid of greed. They conform to and practice *śīla-pāramitā* (the perfection of discipline) because they know that the dharma nature is devoid of defilement and free from the errors of the five desires [for the objects of the senses]. They conform to and practice *kṣānti-pāramitā* (the perfection of forbearance) because they know that the dharma nature is devoid of suffering and

193. Bodhiruci identifies four stages of aspiration to awakening in his translation of the *Gayāśīrṣa-sūtra*, titled *Jiaye shanding jing* 伽耶山頂經 (Summit of Mt. Gaja Sutra). The second is the stage of understanding and practice (*jie xing* 解行). T14.467, 490c1–4. "A change for the better" (*zhuansheng* 轉勝) indicates progressive improvement, which is the core import of the heroic effort expected of bodhisattvas, as mentioned above. In his translation of the *Dilun*, Bodhiruci states that the sixth bodhisattva level is "a change for the better" because it offers a means of practice superior to those that precede it. T26.1522, 167c16–21.

free from vexation. They conform to and practice *vīrya-pāramitā* (the perfection of vigorous exertion) because they know that the dharma nature is devoid of the characteristics of body and mind and free from laziness. They conform to and practice *dhyāna-pāramitā* (the perfection of meditative absorption) because they know that the dharma nature is constant and fixed and intrinsically devoid of confusion. They conform to and practice *prajñā-pāramitā* (the perfection of wisdom) because they know that the dharma nature is intrinsically awakened and free from ignorance.

3.3 Aspiration to Awakening through Realizing the Way

With the aspiration to awakening through realizing [the Way], what perceptual field is realized from the level of pure mind up to the final bodhisattva level? It is suchness. It is explained as a perceptual field based on the operating consciousness. With this realization, however, there are no perceptual fields; there is only cognition of suchness, which is called the dharma body.[194] [**581b**] These bodhisattvas are able to reach all realms of the ten directions without exception in a single thought-moment. They make offerings to buddhas and request that they turn the wheel of Dharma solely to guide and bring benefit to sentient beings, all without recourse to words. Some show how one may skip over the levels and rapidly accomplish true awakening, because they act for the benefit of timid sentient beings.[195] Some explain how even they themselves will accomplish the way of

---

194. The euphemism "suchness" here means that one simply sees everything just as it is: an omniscient, pervasive cognition replaces the fields of discrete perceptions. Bodhiruci's translation of the *Laṅkāvatāra-sūtra* also refers to "cognition of suchness" (*zhenru zhi* 眞如智). T16.671, 569a4–7.
195. The phrase "timid sentient beings" (*qieruo zhongsheng* 怯弱眾生) occurs only three times in extant texts before the *Treatise*, all translations attributed to Bodhiruci: the *Dilun*, T.26.1522, 190a4; the *Laṅkāvatāra-sūtra*, T16.671, 560c5; and the *Jin'gangxian lun*, T25.1512, 800b8–9.

a buddha only after countless *asaṃkhyeya-kalpa* (incalculable eons), because they are acting for the benefit of complacent sentient beings. Their ability to teach such countless skillful means is inconceivable, but in reality the capacities of those in the bodhisattva lineage are equal, their aspirations to awakening are equal, and what they realize is also equal. There is [in fact] no method for skipping over [the levels] because all bodhisattvas take three *asaṃkhyeya-kalpa* (incalculable eons) [to accomplish true awakening]. It is just that there are dissimilarities in what sentient beings see and hear, and in the nature of their capacities and desires, following differences between their worlds. As a result, there are also distinctions in what [the bodhisattvas] teach them to practice.

In addition, with this aspiration to awakening by bodhisattvas there are three subtle characteristics of mind. What are they?

The first is [the characteristic of] the true mind, because it is free from discrimination.

The second is [the characteristic of] the mind of skillful means, because it spontaneously operates everywhere and benefits sentient beings.

The third is [the characteristic of] the mind of karmic consciousness, because it subtly arises and ceases.[196]

In addition, these bodhisattvas, who have perfected their merit in the Ultimate Realm of Form, display the greatest, tallest bodies of all the mundane realms.[197] In other words, ignorance is suddenly

196. Wonhyo (T44.1844, 220c7–12) and Fazang (T44.1846, 280c12–20) comment that the first of these three kinds of mind refers to non-conceptual cognition (*nirvikalpa*); the second refers to subsequent cognition (*pṛṣṭhalabdha-jñāna*), which is the way awakened beings cognize after they have achieved awakening in the eighth bodhisattva level; the third supports the first two kinds of mind but, unlike them, does not form part of the pure qualities of buddhas, since it remains subject to arising and ceasing. Their glosses are questionable, however. For example, their gloss of the second mind offers an idiosyncratic interpretation of subsequent cognition.

197. The Ultimate Realm of Form (*Akaniṣṭha*) is the highest level of the last of the four meditation heavens in the realm of form. Huiyuan identifies "the greatest, tallest bodies of all the mundane realms" as recompense bodies. T44.1843, 200a28–29.

extinguished since they accord with insight in a single thought-moment. This is called "omniscience."[198] Endowed as a matter of course with inconceivable karmic action, they are able to appear in the ten directions and benefit sentient beings.

Question: Because space is boundless, worlds are boundless. Because worlds are boundless, sentient beings are boundless.[199] Because sentient beings are boundless, differentiations in mental activities are also boundless. So perceptual fields cannot be bounded, which makes them difficult to comprehend and to explain. If ignorance is eliminated, however, there is no conceptualizing, and so how is it possible for there to be a [mental] discernment [of unbounded perceptual fields] called "omniscience"?

Answer: All perceptual fields have always been the One Mind and are free from conceptualizing and conceiving. The minds of sentient beings have boundaries because they falsely perceive perceptual fields. They are incapable of discerning the dharma nature definitively because they falsely give rise to conceptualizing and conceiving and fail to correspond with it. Free from perceiving and conceptualizing, [the cognition of] buddhas—*tathāgatas*—is all-pervasive. [What they cognize] is precisely the nature of dharmas because their minds are true and real. Their minds' own intrinsic reality reveals and illuminates all false dharmas. With the function of great wisdom and countless skillful means, they are all able to elucidate the meaning of all kinds of dharma in accordance with what sentient beings ought to be capable of understanding. Therefore, it can be called "omniscience."[200]

198. The idea that omniscience (*yiqie zhongzhi* 一切種智) "accords with insight in a single thought-moment" appears several times, with identical phrasing, in Kumārajīva's translation of the *Dazhidu lun*. See, for example, T8.223, 378b20–22.

199. The same claim, in similar phrasing, appears in Dharmakṣema's early fifth-century translation of the *Upāsakaśīla-sūtra*, titled *Youposai jie jing* 優婆塞戒經 (Sutra on the Precepts for Laymen). T24.1488, 1037c26–27.

200. For Fazang, the attainment of omniscience is the natural result of eliminating all false concepts. T44.1846, 281a4–9. For Yinshun, the idea of omniscience developed in this

Another question: Given that buddhas benefit sentient beings by having [cognition of how] karmic action operates as a matter of course and by being capable of appearing everywhere, all sentient beings would obtain that benefit without exception if they were to perceive the bodies [of buddhas], to look at their divine transformations, or to hear their preaching. [581c] How is it, then, that most in the mundane world are unable to perceive [the bodies of buddhas]?

Answer: It is because the dharma body of buddhas—*tathāgatas*—pervades everywhere uniformly, without there being anything on which [sentient beings] might focus.[201] As a result, it is said to operate as a matter of course, yet it only actually appears on the basis of the minds of sentient beings. The minds of sentient beings can be likened to mirrors. If mirrors are sullied, images of forms do not appear. In the same way, if the minds of sentient beings are sullied, the dharma body does not appear.

PART 4: CULTIVATION OF THE COMMITMENT TO FAITH

Having explained the "elucidation," I will next explain the "cultivation of the commitment to faith."

Here I will explain cultivation of the commitment to faith because I am concerned with sentient beings who have not yet entered the group certain to achieve awakening. What is the commitment to faith and how is it cultivated?

---

passage of the *Treatise* has two senses. The first is the realization that all deluded dharmas are not apart from suchness. The second is the capacity of buddhas to save sentient beings by explaining dharmas in a way that accords with different individual capacities. In so doing, buddhas themselves remain aware that deluded dharmas are no different from ultimate truth, or dharma nature. *Dasheng qixin lun jiangji*, pp. 223–224.

201. What is ubiquitous cannot offer a point of focus precisely because it is ubiquitous—like a fish unable to know that it is in water.

SECTION 1: FOUR KINDS OF COMMITMENT TO FAITH

Briefly stated, there are four kinds of commitment to faith. What are they?

The first is faith in what is fundamental, which is because one takes pleasure in being mindful of the dharma of suchness.

The second is faith that the Buddha has countless qualities. This is because one is constantly mindful of drawing close to him, of making offerings to him, of venerating him, of initiating virtuous roots, and of vowing to seek omniscience.

The third is faith that the Dharma has great benefits. This is because one is constantly mindful of cultivating the *pāramitās* (perfections).

The fourth is faith that the Monastic Community is able to practice correctly what benefits itself and others. This is because one constantly takes pleasure in drawing close to the assembly of bodhisattvas and in seeking instruction in practices that accord with what is real.[202]

SECTION 2: FIVE GATEWAYS OF PRACTICE

There are five gateways of practice by which one is able to accomplish these commitments to faith. What are they?

The first is the gateway of giving.

The second is the gateway of moral discipline.

The third is the gateway of forbearance.

---

202. Following fundamental faith, the next three kinds of commitment to faith are versions of the three refuges with which the text began and which serve as the foundation for Buddhist thought and practice.

The fourth is the gateway of vigorous exertion.

The fifth is the gateway of calming and discernment.[203]

(dana) Why does one practice the gateway of giving? If one sees anyone coming in search of alms, one will give them one's possessions and wealth according to one's capacity, so divesting oneself of greed and making them happy. Or if one sees someone in hardship, fear, or adversity, one will give them courage to the best of one's ability. Or if there are sentient beings who come in search of the Dharma, one will explain it for them with skillful means to the best of one's understanding. All this is because one ought not to crave or seek fame, profit, or veneration; instead, one should be mindful only of benefitting oneself and others and of being dedicated to *bodhi* (awakening).

(sila) Why does one practice the gateway of moral discipline? Because it means that one does not kill, steal, engage in sexual misconduct, speak duplicitously, speak ill of others, speak falsely, or exaggerate; and one keeps avarice and envy, deceit, flattery, malice, and wrong views at a far remove. Also, because one leaves the home life to subdue the afflictions, one ought to keep hustle and bustle at a far remove, and always remain in calm and solitude, cultivating such practices as having few desires, satiety, and *dhūta* (austerity) until one even reaches the point of feeling trepidation, shame, and repentance over minor transgressions and cannot take lightly any of the prohibitions instituted by the Tathāgata. And one should guard against making disparaging remarks and prevent sentient beings from making the mistake of committing errors and transgressions.

(kesanti) Why does one practice the gateway of forbearance? Because it means that one ought to endure vexations caused by other people without harboring feelings of revenge; and that one should also endure such things as profit and loss, [582a] insults and praise, honor and slander, or pain and pleasure.

203. As discussed in the introduction, this list covers the first five of the six *pāramitās*.

Why does one practice the gateway of vigorous exertion? It means *(vīrya)* that one's mind does not slacken or give up when doing good deeds, and one resolves to be firm and strong, keeping timidity at a far remove. One should be mindful that one has experienced in vain great sufferings of body and mind for a long time past, without any benefit. Therefore, one ought to be diligent in cultivating merits, benefitting oneself and others, and keeping the many kinds of suffering at a far remove.[204]

Moreover, people may be plagued by *māra* demons despite cultivating a commitment to faith. This is because they are hindered by many evil karmic actions due to grave transgressions from past lives. Some may become entangled in various kinds of mundane affairs. Some may be afflicted by the suffering of illness. There is a multitude of such impediments. Therefore, they should be courageous and diligent, and they should worship buddhas, repent to them with a sincere mind, implore them, rejoice in them, and aim for *bodhi* (awakening) at all hours of the day and night. This is because, if they never give up, they will manage to escape the impediments and their virtuous roots will increase.

Why does one practice the gateway of calming and discernment?

"Calming" means stopping the characteristics of all perceptual fields because one conforms to the doctrine of *śamatha* meditation.[205]

"Discernment" means discriminating the characteristics of the causes and conditions of arising and ceasing because one conforms to the doctrine of *vipaśyanā* meditation.

204. Reading *yuan li* 遠離 for *su li* 速離 ("rapidly freeing oneself from [the many kinds of suffering]"), based on the recurrence of this phrase elsewhere in the text.

205. The phrase "in conformity with *śamatha*" appears in the *Saṃdhinirmocana-sūtra* made by Bodhiruci in 514, under the title *Jie shenmi jing* 解深密經 (Sutra Explaining the Profound and Esoteric Doctrine). T16.675, 674c11–12.

Why should one conform to them? Because these two will be experienced together only by cultivating them gradually, without separating one from the other.[206]

[calming] When cultivating calming, one stays in a quiet place, sits upright, and sets one's thinking straight without dwelling on the breath, on shapes or forms, on space, on earth, water, fire, or wind, until one even reaches a point where one does not dwell on sensory or cognitive awareness. One removes all concepts in the thought-moment that they arise. Indeed, one rejects the concept of removing [concepts]. Since all dharmas have always been without characteristics, they neither arise in successive thought-moments nor cease in successive thought-moments. Indeed, one will not follow the mind in conceiving of perceptual fields as external or subsequently [attempt to] remove the mind with the mind.[207] If the mind races away, one should rein it back in immediately and stay in correct mindfulness. With this correct mindfulness, one should know that there is only mind; there are no external perceptual fields. That is, moreover, this mind certainly has no characteristics of its own and is imperceptible in successive thought-moments. If at all times, in whatever one does—whether sitting or standing, coming or going, moving forward or staying put—one remains constantly mindful of skillful means and conforms to [the practices of calming and discernment] when carrying out investigations, and if one practices these for a long time until fully proficient, then one's mind will manage to stay focused. Because one's mind stays focused, one conforms to [these practices] with increasing fervor, readily obtaining entry to *samādhi* (meditative absorption) on suchness. One thoroughly subdues the afflictions,

---

206. This echoes phrasing that Bodhiruci uses in his translation of the *Dilun*, where he writes that "the two practices of *śamatha* and *vipaśyanā* are experienced together in a single thought-moment." T26.1522, 175b21–22. See the introduction for a discussion of *śamatha* and *vipaśyanā* meditation practices.

207. This is because the mind cannot self-reflexively conceive of itself.

one's commitment to faith increases, and one quickly attains non-regression. The only exceptions are doubters, disbelievers, slanderers, those with serious wrongs or karmic hindrances, the conceited, or the lazy: no such person will be able to enter.

[582b] Moreover, based on this *samādhi*, one knows the unitary characteristic of the dharma realm. That is, the dharma body of all buddhas and the bodies of sentient beings are uniform and non-dual, so it is called the *samādhi* of unifying practice.[208] One should know that suchness is the root of this *samādhi*. If people practice, they will eventually be capable of producing countless *samādhis*.[209] [By contrast,] if there are some sentient beings who lack the power of virtuous roots, they will be deluded and confused by *māras*, non-Buddhists, ghosts, and spirits. The *māras* and the others may even strike terror into them if the *māras* manifest themselves in physical form while such sentient beings are sitting [in meditation]. Some *māras* may appear with the characteristics of a righteous man or woman, but [these sentient beings] should be mindful that these are only the perceptual fields of the mind and, once they have ceased, [these sentient beings] will never again be bothered by them. Some *māras* may manifest themselves as the image of a god or of a bodhisattva, or even of a buddha replete with the major and minor physical characteristics.[210]

---

208. In the *Jin'gangxian lun* the buddha-natures of both the buddhas and sentient beings are said to be "of a unitary body, uniform, non-dual, and without differentiation." T25.1512, 804c5–8. There is a similar statement in the *Saptaśatikā-prajñāpāramitā-sūtra*, translated by *Mandra 曼陀羅仙 (fl. 503) in the early sixth century as *Wenshushili suoshuo Mohe bore boluomi jing* 文殊師利所說摩訶般若波羅蜜經 (The Large Prajñāpāramitā Sutra as Explained by Mañjuśrī): "With the unitary characteristic of the dharma realm, one takes the dharma realm as an object of contemplation. This is called the *samādhi* of unifying practice." T8.232, 731a26–27. In his commentary on the *Treatise*, Wonhyo draws attention to this similarity. T44.1844, 233b14–19.

209. Wonhyo understands the focus of this practice to be suchness. T44.1844, 233b24–25.

210. Buddhas are endowed with the physical characteristics of a great man (*mahāpuruṣa-lakṣaṇa*), such as a cranial lump (*uṣṇīṣa*) and a *cakra* design on their palms and the soles of their feet. They have thirty-two "major characteristics" and eighty "minor characteristics," which uniquely attest to their attainment of buddhahood. For a discussion of this

Some may teach[211] *dhāraṇīs* (spells), or some may teach giving, discipline, forbearance, vigorous exertion, meditative absorption, and wisdom.[212] Some may teach that true nirvana is undifferentiated, empty, devoid of characteristics, wishes, aversion, attachment, cause or effect, and ultimately empty and tranquil. Some may cause people to know things from past lives and even from the future, or to attain insights into others' minds or irrefutable eloquence.[213] They may be capable of causing sentient beings to yearn for, and grow attached to, matters of fame and profit in the mundane world. In addition, they may cause people's natures to vacillate with recurring feelings of hate or joy. Some of these people will become too compassionate, too sleepy, or too sick, or their minds will grow lazy. Some will have a sudden burst of vigorous exertion only to give up later and, having brought about a lack of faith, they will be riddled with doubts and anxiety. Some people will abandon their original superior practices and instead cultivate random karmic actions. If they grow attached to worldly affairs, then all kinds of entanglement will bind them. *Māras* may also be capable of making people attain a part or a semblance of a *samādhi*, although none of these will be a true *samādhi* but rather is of the kind attained by non-Buddhists. Some *māras* will also make

---

idea, see John Powers, *A Bull of a Man: Images of Masculinity, Sex, and the Body in Indian Buddhism* (Cambridge, MA: Harvard University Press, 2009), pp. 1–66.

211. Following the variant *huo shuo* 或說, for *ruo shuo* 若說, which appears in the versions of the text in several editions of the Tripiṭaka, and also in the 754 manuscript edition preserved in Kyōto's Kanchi in 觀智院. The same variant appears in the following phrase. See T32.1666, 582b8; Ui Hakuju 宇井伯寿 and Takasaki Jikido 高崎直道, trans. and eds., *Daijō kishin ron* 大乗起信論 (Treatise on Awakening Mahāyāna Faith) (Tokyo: Iwanami shoten, rpt. 2013), p. 98; Frédéric Girard, trans., *Traité sur l'acte de foi dans le Grand Véhicule*, p. 148.

212. These are the six *pāramitās* set out earlier in the *Treatise* under a discussion of "the aspiration to awakening through understanding and practicing the Way" [581a].

213. Huiyuan comments that these are all supernatural powers that may create confusion. T44.1843, 201a20–21.

people stay in [meditative] absorption for one, two, three, or even seven days, in which they will obtain delicious food and drink that appears spontaneously. These people will become satisfied in body and mind, without hunger or thirst, which will make them develop cravings and attachments. Some *māras* may also make people eat without moderation, either too much or too little, so that their appearance will change.

For these reasons, practitioners always ought to investigate wisely and not allow their minds to fall into the net of wrong doctrines. They should strive for correct mindfulness, neither grasping nor clinging, and then they will be capable of keeping these various hindrances of karmic action at a far remove. One ought to know that none of the *samādhi*s possessed by non-Buddhists is free from the mentalities of wrong views, cravings, or conceit. This is because they desire and are attached to fame, profit, and veneration in the mundane world. With the *samādhi* of suchness, [practitioners] do not stay focused on the characteristics of what is to be perceived or grasped. So even when they emerge from absorption, they will still have no indolence or conceit, and whatever afflictions they may have will gradually diminish.[214] Under no circumstances will ordinary beings obtain entry to the lineage of the *tathāgata*s unless they practice this method (dharma) of *samādhi*. By practicing mundane meditations and *samādhi*s, they will mostly give rise to appetites and cravings. Based on the view of self, they will become enmeshed in the three realms along with non-Buddhists. [582c] This is because they will give rise to non-Buddhist views if they become separated from the protection of good teachers.[215]

---

214. The final phrase of this sentence echoes Bodhiruci's translation of the *Mile pusa suowen jinglun* 彌勒菩薩所問經論 (Treatise on the Sutra of the Questions Asked by Maitreya), a commentarial treatise on the **Maitreya-paripṛcchōpadeśa-sūtra*. T26.1525, 238c11–13.

215. "Good teachers" (*shan zhishi* 善知識) is a technical term, equivalent to the Sanskrit *kalyāṇa-mitra*. It refers to people who provide help and advice on the path and who also bolster practitioners' enthusiasm and commitment.

Moreover, those who apply themselves single-mindedly to cultivating and learning this *samādhi* will obtain ten kinds of benefit in this world. What are they?

First, they will always be protected and cared for by the buddhas and bodhisattvas of the ten directions.

Second, they will be incapable of being terrified by *māras* and evil ghosts.

Third, they will not be deluded or confused by the ninety-five kinds of non-Buddhists or by ghosts and spirits.

Fourth, they will keep any denigration of the extremely profound Dharma at a far remove, and their serious wrongs and karmic hindrances will eventually diminish.

Fifth, they will eliminate all doubts and any detrimental investigation and analysis.

Sixth, their faith in the realm of *tathāgatas* will manage to increase.

Seventh, they will set sorrow and regret at a far remove, and they will be courageous and undaunted amid [the cycle of] birth and death.

Eighth, their minds will be gentle, they will abandon arrogance and haughtiness, and they will not be annoyed by others.

Ninth, they will be capable of decreasing their afflictions and not taking pleasure in the mundane world even if they have not yet attained [meditative] absorption at all times and in all perceptual fields.

Tenth, they will not be alarmed by external conditions or by any sounds if they attain *samādhi*.

Moreover, people's minds will sink into [inattention] or give rise to laziness if they cultivate only calming. They will not take pleasure in manifold virtues and will set great compassion at a far remove. They will therefore [also need to] cultivate discernment.

[discernment] When cultivating and practicing discernment, one should discern that no conditioned dharma of the mundane world manages

to remain stable for long, but all change and perish in an instant; *anicca*
and that all mental activities arise and cease in successive thought- *dukkha*
moments. It is because of this that people suffer. One ought to
discern that dharmas remembered from the past are vague, like a
dream. One ought to discern that dharmas conceived in the present *annatta*
are just like flashes of lightning. One ought to discern that dharmas
conceived in the future will be just like [formations] that suddenly
arise in clouds. One ought to discern that all things with bodies *impurity*
in the mundane world are impure, and that no kind of impurity is
pleasurable.

So one should be mindful that the mind is made to arise and *paticca-*
cease because all sentient beings have been habituated by ignorance *samut-*
from beginningless time. Having already experienced all the great *pada.*
sufferings of body and mind, they now face countless torments in *karma.*
the present, and their sufferings will also be unbounded in the future. *ignorance*
Yet they fail to be aware of this, finding it difficult to abandon or free ↓
themselves from [these sufferings]. What a great pity it is that sen- *suffering*
tient beings are like this!

Having reflected on this, then one ought to make the great
vow with courage: "I will cultivate all good merits throughout the *prani-*
ten directions because I vow to free my mind from constructing *dauna*
distinctions. I will save all suffering sentient beings in perpetuity
through countless skillful means, enabling them to attain the supreme
pleasure of nirvana." Because one will have initiated such a vow,
[583a] one's many virtues will, as far as one is able, prevent one from
abandoning cultivation and learning, and one's mind will not grow
lazy at any time or in any place. The sole exception is sitting in meditation, when one should concentrate on being mindful of calming. In
all other circumstances, one should investigate what ought and ought
not to be done. One ought to practice both calming and discernment
whether walking or standing, lying down or getting up. That is, even
when one is mindful that the self-nature of dharmas does not arise,

one is also mindful of the combination of causes and conditions, of good and bad karmic action, of the recompense of pain and pleasure, and of how they neither are lost nor perish.²¹⁶ And even when one is mindful of causes and conditions, of good and bad karmic actions, and of their recompense, one is also mindful that their nature cannot be apprehended.

Cultivating calming is an antidote to ordinary people's abiding attachments to the mundane world.²¹⁷ [With it,] one is able to abandon the timid views of the Two Vehicles. Cultivating discernment is an antidote to the Two Vehicles' faults of not giving rise to great compassion and narrow-mindedness.²¹⁸ [With it,] one sets oneself at a far remove from ordinary people, who do not cultivate virtuous roots. For this reason, each of the two gateways of calming and discernment helps the other to develop, without one being separated from the other. One would be unable to enter the way of *bodhi* (awakening) without full possession of both calming and discernment.

216. It is a basic Buddhist tenet that all karmic actions will come to fruition sometime in the future, without any loss of karmic consequences between the time of the initial action and its eventual maturation. Ōtake Susumu identifies in the phrasing of this passage an echo of Kumārajīva's translation of the *Vimalakīrti-nirdeśa-sūtra*; see Ōtake Susumu, "*Daijō kishin ron* no inyō bunken," p. 63. For the parallel in Kumārajīva's original work, see T14.475, 537c15–16.

217. This relates to the sixth reason given for composing the treatise: "... to show how to practice calming and discernment, which are antidotes to the mental faults of ordinary people and adherents of the Two Vehicles" [575c].

218. In this account, practitioners of the Lesser Vehicle feel that the path of the bodhisattva, who vows to save all sentient beings, is too difficult and so opt for the easier path of personal salvation. For Fazang, *śamatha* meditation counteracts ordinary beings' indulgence in worldly pleasures based on their belief that things have an intrinsic nature. It also counteracts the fear that adherents of the Two Vehicles feel because they witness suffering—their main obstacle to great compassion. T44.1846, 286b10–13.

SECTION 3: BEING MINDFUL OF AND VISUALIZING AMITĀBHA

Moreover, the minds of sentient beings are timid when they are still in the early stages of studying this Dharma and desire to have correct faith. Since they reside in this Sahā realm, they fear that they will be unable to encounter buddhas all the time, or to serve and make offerings to them.[219] Those who, filled with fear, think that a commitment to faith is difficult to accomplish and that their commitment will likely regress should know that *tathāgatas* have excellent skillful means for protecting the commitment to faith. This means that those sentient beings attain rebirth in other buddha lands in accordance with their vows by concentrating on the causes and conditions for being mindful of buddhas. They will eternally be free from the bad paths [of rebirth] by constantly perceiving buddhas.[220] As a sutra states: "If one concentrates on being mindful of Amitābha— the buddha of the western paradise—the virtuous roots that one cultivates will be directed to one's vow to be born in his realm, and then one will attain rebirth there. Because one constantly perceives the buddha, in the end there will be no regression."[221] If one visualizes

219. The Sahā realm refers to our world. Since Śākyamuni died, buddhas do not occupy our world. The next buddha, Maitreya, is not due to arrive for a long time. As a result, it is impossible to fulfil the stipulation of meeting a buddha. The solution of being mindful of buddhas was a crucial Mahāyāna innovation.
220. As noted above, the "bad paths" of rebirth are those of animals, hungry ghosts, and hell beings.
221. At the time of the *Treatise's* composition, the practice of "being mindful of buddhas" (*buddha-anusmṛti*) mainly comprised elaborate visualizations of buddhas and their realms, sometimes accompanied by recitations for the buddhas and physical actions. This passage is a truncated version of earlier visualization sutras that elaborate how and why one engages in such visualizations. Amitābha is the buddha of the western paradise, Sukhāvatī. According to later East Asian Pure Land traditions, one cultivates the karmic conditions for being reborn there by constantly reciting his name. See the introduction for an outline of these practices and their development. Ōtake Susumu identifies the source of this scriptural quotation as Saṃghavarman's third-century translation of the

this buddha's dharma body of suchness and constantly strives to cultivate and practice, then one will ultimately attain rebirth and stay in correct meditative absorption.

PART 5: EXHORTATION TO PRACTICE AND TO REAP THE BENEFITS

Having explained the "cultivation of the commitment to faith," I will next explain "exhortation to practice and to reap the benefits."

So I have now provided a general explanation of Mahāyāna, the recondite treasury of the buddhas. If there are sentient beings who wish to arouse correct faith in the extremely profound realms of *tathāgatas*, and to set denigration of the Great Vehicle at a far remove and instead enter into it, then they should uphold this treatise, reflect on it, and cultivate it, until they are ultimately able to arrive at the unsurpassed Way. If a person does not become timid after hearing this Dharma, one should know that this person will definitely carry on the buddha lineage and will inevitably be given a prediction of awakening by the buddhas. Even if there were a person able to convert the sentient beings who fill the great trichiliocosm realm and to cause them to practice the ten kinds of wholesome behavior, this person would not be equal to someone who thinks truly of this dharma for just one mealtime.[222] [583b] It is impossible to convey how far the latter's merit surpasses that of the former.

Sukhāvatīvyūha-sūtra, titled *Wuliang shou jing* 無量壽經 (Sutra of Limitless Life); see Ōtake Susumu, "*Daijō kishin ron* no inyō bunken," p. 62. The *locus classicus* is T12.360, 272b11–13.

222. A great trichiliocosm realm denotes the whole domain of the Buddha. In ancient Indian cosmology, it also serves figuratively to indicate the vastness of the universe. As Ōtake Susumu notes, this content and phrasing find parallels in the *Sarvadharmapravṛttinirdeśa-sūtra*, translated by Kumārajīva in 401 under the title *Zhufa wuxing jing* 諸法無行經

Moreover, if someone retains, investigates, and practices this treatise, if only for just one day and night, then their merits will be countless, limitless, and inexpressible. And even if this person's merits were extolled by each of the buddhas of the ten directions for countless, boundless *asaṃkhyeya-kalpa*s (incalculable eons), that would still be unable to do the person full justice. Why? Because the merits of the dharma nature are inexhaustible and, in the same way, this person's merits would also be boundless.

When there are sentient beings who slander what is in this treatise and lack faith in it, the retribution for their sin will be great suffering for countless *kalpa*s (eons). Sentient beings therefore simply ought to revere and have faith in it. They ought not to denigrate it; to do so would profoundly harm themselves and others, and would sever all of the lineages of the Three Jewels. This is because all *tathāgata*s attain nirvana on the basis of this Dharma, and because all bodhisattvas depend on it to cultivate practice and enter into buddha wisdom.

One should know that bodhisattvas of the past have managed to accomplish pure faith on the basis of this Dharma; bodhisattvas of the present now manage to accomplish pure faith on the basis of this Dharma; and bodhisattvas of the future will also manage to accomplish pure faith on the basis of this Dharma. Sentient beings therefore ought to strive to cultivate and learn it.

Now, to the best of my ability, I have provided a summary account for retention

Of the extensive and great import of the buddhas, so extremely profound and vast.

(Sutra Denying Practice in Various Methods); see Ōtake Susumu, "*Daijō kishin ron* no inyō bunken," p. 64. The *locus classicus* is T15.650, 753b19–22.

I transfer the merits from this, in accordance with the dharma nature,

For the universal benefit of all realms of sentient beings.

Treatise on Awakening Mahāyāna Faith, in One Fascicle.

ENGLISH-TO-CHINESE GLOSSARY

accommodate: *sui* 隨.

accord with: *sui* 隨.

adapt to conditions: *sui yuan* 隨緣.

adapt to: *sui* 隨.

ālaya consciousness: *aliye shi* 阿梨耶識 (Skt. *ālayavijñāna*).

arising-and-ceasing: *shengmie* 生滅.

arouse the aspiration (for awakening): *faxin* 發心 (Skt. *bodhicitta* or *cittotpāda*).

associated: *xiangying* 相應.

awakening (to have an unobstructed mind that pervades everything): *jue* 覺.

awakening: *puti* 菩提 (Skt. *bodhi*).

awareness: *jue* 覺.

bodhisattva (being that pursues awakening): *pusa* 菩薩.

boundary: *fenqi* 分齊.

a buddha, the Buddha (Tathāgata): *rulai* 如來 (Skt. *tathāgata*).

Buddhist doctrine: *fa* 法 (Skt. Dharma).

the basic factors of experience: *fa* 法 (Skt. dharma)

calming: *zhi* 止 (Skt. *śamatha*).

characteristics: *xiang* 相.

cognition, cognitive: *zhi* 智.

combine: *hehe* 和合.

commitment to faith: *xinxin* 信心.

conceive: *nian* 念.

conceptual and sensory fields: *chen* 塵.

conceptualize: *xiang* 想.

conditioned dharmas: *youwei fa* 有為法.

consciousness: *shi* 識 (some early commentators also used the term to refer to the first six consciousnesses).

constantly abiding: *chang zhu* 常住 (Skt. *nitya*).

continuing consciousness, one of the five names for mentation (*yi* 意): *xiangxu shi* 相續識.

correct mindfulness: *zheng nian* 正念.

dependent arising: *yuanqi* 緣起.

dharma body: *fashen* 法身 (Skt. *dharmakāya*).

dharma nature (the true nature of reality; suchness): *faxing* 法性.

dharma realm (the full range of experiential fields): *fajie* 法界 (Skt. *dharmadhātu*).

differentiate: *chabie* 差別.

discern: *zhi* 智.

discerning consciousness: *zhi shi* 智識.

discernment: *guan* 觀 (Skt. *vipaśyanā*).

discriminate, discrimination: *fenbie* 分別.

dissociated: *bu xingying* 不相應.

distinctions: *chabie* 差別.

eighth consciousness: *alaiye shi* 阿賴耶識 (Skt. *ālayavijñāna*).

faith: *xin* 信 (Skt. *śraddhā*).

false thoughts: *wang nian* 妄念.

final awakening: *jiujing jue* 究竟覺.

free from: *li* 離.

good qualities: *fa* 法 (Skt. *dharma*).

Great Vehicle: *dasheng* 大乘 (Skt. Mahāyāna).

habituation: *xunxi* 熏習 (Skt. *vāsanā*).

hindrance: *zhang* 障.

ignorance: *wuming* 無明.

incalculable eons: *asengqi jie* 阿僧祇劫 (Skt. *asaṃkhyeya-kalpa*).

inherent awakening: *ben jue* 本覺.

initial awakening: *shi jue* 始覺.

intrinsic characteristics: *zixiang* 自相.

intrinsic nature: *tixing* 體性.

intrinsic reality (the quality of something being so of itself, without relying on anything more fundamental to be what it is): *ti* 體.

itself: *ti* 體.

karmic consciousness, one of the five names for mentation (*yi* 意): *ye shi* 業識.

laws: *fa* 法 (Skt. *dharma*).

level of practice: *di* 地 (Skt. *bhūmi*).

Mahāyāna: *moheyan* 摩訶衍.

meditative absorption: *sanmei* 三昧 (Skt. *samādhi*).

memory: *nian* 念.

mental and physical constituents: *fa* 法 (Skt. *dharma*).

mental consciousness; the sixth consciousness (*manovijñāna*): *yi shi* 意識.

mental perceptions: *xinyuan* 心緣.

mentation: *yi* 意 (*manas*).

merit: *gongde* 功德 (Skt. *puṇya*).

mind: *xin* 心 (some early commentators also used the term to refer to the seventh consciousness).

mindfulness: *nian* 念.

mundane: *shijian* 世間.

nature of the mind: *xinxing* 心性.

non-awakening: *bu jue* 不覺.

non-dual: *wu'er* 無二.

operating consciousness, one of the five names for mentation (*yi* 意): *zhuan shi* 轉識.

own intrinsic reality: *ziti* 自體.

perceptual fields: *jingjie* 境界.

perfections (practices that deliver one to the other shore of enlightenment or buddhahood): *boluomi* 波羅蜜 (Skt. *pāramitā*).

permeation: *xunxi* 熏習 (Skt. *vāsanā*).

the potential for awakening (buddhahood): *rulaizang* 如來藏 (Skt. *tathāgatagarbha*).

presenting consciousness, one of the five names for mentation (*yi* 意): *xian shi* 現識.

principles: *fa* 法 (Skt. dharma).

qualities: *gongde* 功德 (Skt. *guṇa*).

recompense body or bodies: *baoshen* 報身 (Skt. *saṃbhogakāya*).

relapse: *tui* 退.

response body or bodies: *yingshen* 應身 (Skt. *nirmāṇakāya*).

rules: *fa* 法 (Skt. dharma).

sensory and conceptual fields: *chen* 塵.

separate from: *li* 離.

set at a distance: *yuan li* 遠離.

skillful means: *fangbian* 方便.

sovereign: *zizai* 自在.

store consciousness: *alaiye shi* 阿賴耶識 (Skt. *ālayavijñāna*).

store: *zang* 藏.

suchness (reality as it truly is without any conceptual overlay): *zhenru* 真如 (Skt. *tathatā*).

supramundane: *chu shijian* 出世間.

sutra/s: *xiuduoluo* 修多羅 (Skt. *sūtra*).

thought-moment: *nian* 念.

trust: *xin* 信 (Skt. *śraddhā*).

Two Gateways (the two aspects of the One Mind): *er men* 二門.

unconditioned dharmas: *wuwei fa* 無為法.

understanding: *jie* 解.
uniform: *pingdeng* 平等.
untainted: *wulou* 無漏.
ways of understanding reality: *fa* 法 (Skt. Dharma/dharma).
wisdom: *zhi* 智.

CHINESE-TO-ENGLISH GLOSSARY

alaiye shi 阿賴耶識 (Skt. *ālayavijñāna*): store consciousness; the eighth consciousness.

aliye shi 阿梨耶識: *ālaya* consciousness (= *ālayavijñāna*).

asengqi jie 阿僧祇劫 (Skt. *asaṃkhyeya-kalpa*): incalculable eons.

baoshen 報身 (Skt. *saṃbhogakāya*): recompense body or bodies.

ben jue 本覺: inherent awakening.

boluomi 波羅蜜 (Skt. *pāramitā*): perfections (practices that deliver one to the other shore of enlightenment or buddhahood).

bu jue 不覺: non-awakening.

bu xingying 不相應: dissociated.

chabie 差別: distinctions; differentiate.

chang zhu 常住 (Skt. *nitya*): constantly abiding.

chen 塵: sensory and conceptual fields.

chu shijian 出世間: supramundane.

dasheng 大乘: Great Vehicle (Skt. Mahāyāna).

di 地 (Skt. *bhūmi*): level of practice.

er men 二門: Two Gateways (the two aspects of the One Mind).

fa 法 (Skt. Dharma/dharma): 1. Buddhist doctrine. 2. the basic factors of experience, mental and physical constituents. 3. good qualities, principles, rules or laws, practices. 4. ways of understanding reality, truth.

fajie 法界: (Skt. *dharmadhātu*): dharma realm (the full range of experiential fields).

fangbian 方便: skillful means.

fashen 法身 (Skt. *dharmakāya*): dharma body.

faxin 發心 (Skt. *bodhicitta* or *cittotpāda*): arouse the aspiration (for awakening).

faxing 法性: dharma nature (the true nature of reality; suchness).

fenbie 分別: discriminate; discrimination.

fenqi 分齊: 1. boundary, bounded. 2. in moderation.

gongde 功德: 1. merit (Skt. *puṇya*). 2. qualities (Skt. *guṇa*).

guan 觀 (Skt. *vipaśyanā*): discernment.

hehe 和合: combine.

jie 解: understanding.

jingjie 境界: perceptual fields.

jiujing jue 究竟覺: final awakening.

jue 覺: awakening, awareness (to have an unobstructed mind that pervades everything).

li 離: free of/from; separate (from).

moheyan 摩訶衍: Mahāyāna.

nian 念: 1. mindfulness or memory. 2. thought-moment. 3. conceive, conceiving.

pingdeng 平等: uniform, uniformity.

pusa 菩薩: bodhisattva (being that pursues awakening).

puti 菩提: *bodhi* (awakening).

rulai 如來 (Skt. *tathāgata*): a buddha; the Buddha (Tathāgata).

rulaizang 如來藏 (Skt. *tathāgatagarbha*): the potential for awakening (buddhahood).

sanmei 三昧 (Skt. *samādhi*): meditative absorption.

shengmie 生滅: arising-and-ceasing.

shi 識: consciousness (some early commentators also used the term to refer to the first six consciousnesses).

shijian 世間: mundane.

shi jue 始覺: initial awakening.

sui 隨: to accord with; to accommodate; to follow; to respond to; to adapt to.

sui yuan 隨緣: adapt to conditions.

ti 體: 1. intrinsic reality: the quality of something being so of itself, without relying on anything more fundamental to be what it is. (Alternative translations: substance, essence). 2. itself.

tixing 體性: intrinsic nature.

tui 退: relapse.

wang nian 妄念: false thoughts.

wu'er 無二: non-dual.

wulou 無漏: untainted.

wuming 無明: ignorance.

wuwei fa 無為法: unconditioned dharmas.

ye shi 業識: karmic consciousness, one of the five names for mentation (*yi* 意).

youwei fa 有為法: conditioned dharmas.

yuan li 遠離: set at a distance; far removed from.

xiang 相: characteristics.

xiang 想: conceptualize.

xian shi 現識: presenting consciousness, one of the five names for mentation (*yi* 意).

xiangxu shi 相續識: continuing consciousness, one of the five names for mentation (*yi* 意).

xiangying 相應: associated.

xin 心: the mind (some early commentators also used the term to refer to the seventh consciousness).

xin 信 (Skt. *śraddhā*): faith, trust.

xinyuan 心緣: mental perceptions.

xinxin 信心: commitment to faith.

xinxing 心性: the nature of the mind.

xiuduoluo 修多羅 (Skt. *sūtra*): sutra/s.

xunxi 熏習 (Skt. *vāsanā*): habituation, permeation.

yi 意 (*manas*): 1. mentation. 2. the continuity- and ego-positing consciousness.

yingshen 應身 (Skt. *nirmāṇakāya*): response body or bodies.

yi shi 意識: mental consciousness; the sixth consciousness (*manovijñāna*).

yuanqi 緣起: dependent arising.

zang 藏: store.

zhang 障: hindrance.

zhenru 真如 (Skt. *tathatā*): suchness (reality as it truly is without any conceptual overlay).

zheng nian 正念: correct mindfulness.

zhi 止 (Skt. *śamatha*): calming.

zhi 智: 1. wisdom. 2. cognition, cognitive. 3. discern.

zhi shi 智識: discerning consciousness.

zhuan shi 轉識: operating consciousness, one of the five names for mentation (*yi* 意).

ziti 自體: own intrinsic reality.

zixiang 自相: intrinsic characteristics.

zizai 自在: sovereign.

BIBLIOGRAPHY

Aṅgulimālīya-sūtra (*Yangjuemoluo jing* 央掘魔羅經; Sutra of Aṅgulimāla), trans. Guṇabhadra (394–468), T2.120.

Aoki Takashi 青木隆, "Tonkō shahon ni miru Jiron kyōgaku no keisei" 敦煌写本にみる地論教学の形成 (The Formation of the Doctrines of the Dilun School as Seen in Dunhuang Manuscripts), in Geumgang Daehak bulgyo munhwa yeon'guso, comp., *Jiron shisō no keisei to hen'yō.*

Asaṅga (fourth century CE), *Mahāyānasaṃgraha-śāstra* (*She dasheng lun* 攝大乘論; Compendium of the Great Vehicle), trans. Buddhaśanta (fl. 525–539), T31.1592.

Asaṅga (attrib.), *Mahāyānasaṃgraha-śāstra* (*She dasheng lun* 攝大乘論; Compendium of the Great Vehicle), trans. Paramārtha. T31.1593.

Avataṃsaka-sūtra (*Dafangguangfo huayan jing* 大方廣佛華嚴經; Flower Garland Sutra), trans. Buddhabhadra (358–429), T9.278.

Bodhisattvabhūmi-sūtra (*Pusa dichi jing* 菩薩地持經; Bodhisattva Levels Sutra), trans. Dharmakṣema (385–433), T30.1581.

Chinkai 珍海 (1092–1152), *Sanron genso bungi yō* 三論玄疏文義要 (Essentials of the Meaning of the *Profound Commentary on the Three Treatises*), T70.2299.

Clower, Jason, "The Awakening of Faith," in Richard K. Payne, ed., *Oxford Bibliographies in Buddhism* (New York: Oxford University Press, 2013).

Daoxuan 道宣 (596–667), *Xu Gaoseng zhuan* 續高僧傳 (Supplementary Biographies of Eminent Monks), T50.2060.

Daoxuan, comp., *Da Tang neidian lu* 大唐內典錄 (Record of Buddhist Scriptures in the Great Tang), T55.2149.

Daśabhūmika-sūtra (*Jianbei yiqie zhide jing* 漸備一切智德經; Sutra on Gradually Obtaining the Virtue of Omniscience), trans. Dharmarakṣa (c. 230–316), T10.285.

Dasheng qixin lun 大乘起信論 (Treatise on Awakening Mahāyāna Faith). (1) trans. attributed to Paramārtha (499–569), T32.1666; (2) trans. Śikṣānanda (fl. 700), T32.1667.

Eichō 永超 (1014–1095), *Tōiki dentō mokuroku* 東域傳燈目錄 (Record of the Transmission of the Lamp to the Eastern Regions), T55.2183.

Enchō 圓超 (fl. early tenth century), *Kegonshū shōsho narabini inmyō roku* 華嚴宗章疏并因明錄 (A Record of Commentaries and Logic Texts of the Huayan School), T55.2177.

Fajing 法經 (fl. 594) et al., *Zhongjing mulu* 衆經目錄 (Catalogue of Scriptures), T55.2146.

Fazang 法藏 (643–712), *Dasheng qixinlun yiji* 大乘起信論義記 (Notes on the Meaning of the *Treatise on Awakening Mahāyāna Faith*), T44.1846.

Fazang, *Huayan yisheng jiaoyi fenqi zhang* 華嚴一乘教義分齊章 (Essay on the Classified Meaning of the Teaching of the One Vehicle of the *Avataṃsaka*), T45.1866.

Funayama Tōru 船山徹, "Shintai sanzō no katsudō to chosaku no kihonteki tokuchō" 真諦三蔵の活動と著作の基本的特徴 (Fundamental Characteristics of the Activities and Works of Paramārtha), in Funayama Tōru, ed., *Shintai sanzō kenkyū ronshū* 真諦三蔵研究論集 (Studies of the Works and Influence of Paramārtha) (Kyoto: Kyōto daigaku jinbunkagaku kenkyūshō, 2012).

Gayāśīrṣa-sūtra (*Jiaye shanding jing* 伽耶山頂經; Summit of Mt. Gaja Sutra), trans. Bodhiruci (d. ca. 535), T14.467.

Geumgang Daehak bulgyo munhwa yeon'guso 金剛大学佛教文化研究所 comp., *Jiron shisō no keisei to hen'yō* 地論思想の形成と変容 (The Formation and Transformation of Dilun Thought) (Tokyo: Kokusho kankōkai, 2010).

Geumgang Daehak bulgyo munhwa yeon'guso, comp., *Jironshū no kenkyū* 地論宗の研究 (Studies of the Dilun School) (Tokyo: Kokusho kankōkai, 2017).

Gimello, Robert Michael, "Chih-yen and the Foundation of Hua-yen Buddhism," PhD diss., Columbia University, 1976.

Girard, Frédéric, trans., *Traité sur l'acte de foi dans le Grand Véhicule* (Tokyo: Keio University Press, 2004).

Hanshan Deqing 憨山德清 (1546–1623), *Qixin lun zhijie* 起信論直解 (Direct Interpretation of the *Treatise on Awakening Mahāyāna Faith*), X45.766.

Huiyuan 慧遠 (523–592), *Dasheng qixin lun yishu* 大乘起信論義疏 (Elucidation of the Meaning of the *Treatise on Awakening Mahāyāna Faith*), T44.1843.

Hyegyun 慧均 (fl. 570s), *Daseung saron hyeonui gi* 大乘四論玄義記 (Record of the Profound Meanings of the Four Treatises of Mahāyāna), cited in Chinkai, *Sanron genso bungi yō*.

Ibuki Atsushi 伊吹敦, "Jironshū Hokudōha no shinshikisetsu ni tsuite" 地論宗北道派の心識説について (On the Mind and Consciousness Theory of the Northern Faction of the Dilun School), *Bukkyōgaku* 佛教学 40 (1999): pp. 86–92.

Ikeda Masanori 池田將則 (이케다 마사노리), "Kyō'u shōku shozō Tonkō bunken *Daijō kishin ron sho* (gidai, *Hane 333V*) ni tsuite" 杏雨書屋所藏敦煌文獻大乘起信論疏 (擬題, 羽333V) について (On the Dunhuang Manuscript *Dasheng qixin lun shu* Held in the Kyō'u Library [provisional title *Hane 333 Verso*]), *Bulgyohak ribyu* 불교학리뷰 (Critical Review for Buddhist Studies) 12 (2012): pp. 45–167.

Ishii Kōsei 石井公成, "Jironshū kenkyū no genjō to kadai" 地論宗研究の現状と課題 (The Present Situation and Issues of Dilun School Studies) in Geumgang Daehak bulgyo munhwa yeon'guso, comp., *Jiron shisō no keisei to hen'yō*.

Ishii Kōsei, *Kegon shisō no kenkyū* 華厳思想の研究 (Studies on Huayan Thought) (Tokyo: Shunjūsha, 1996).

Jin'gangxian lun 金剛仙論 (Treatise of *Vajrarṣi), trans. attrib. Bodhiruci (d. ca. 535), T25.1512.

Kashiwagi Hiroo 柏木弘雄, *Daijō kishin ron no kenkyū: Daijō kishin ron no seiritsu ni kansuru shiryōronteki kenkyū* 大乘起信論の研究 : 大乘起信論の成立に関する資料論的研究 (Studies on the *Treatise on Awakening Mahāyāna Faith*: Document-based Studies on the Dating of the *Treatise on Awakening Mahāyāna Faith*) (Tokyo: Shunjūsha, 1981).

Keng Ching, "Yogācāra Buddhism Transmitted or Transformed? Paramārtha (499–569) and His Chinese Interpreters," PhD diss., Harvard University, 2009.

Laṅkāvatāra-sūtra. (1) *Lengqie abaduoluo baojing* 楞伽阿跋多羅寶經, trans. Guṇabhadra (394–468), T16.670; (2) *Ru Lengqie jing* 入楞伽經, trans. Bodhiruci (d. ca. 535), T16.671.

Lilley, Mary E., ed., *The Apadāna of the Khuddaka Nikāya* (London: Pali Text Society, 1925).

Lü Cheng 呂澂, "Chanxue shuyuan" 禪學述源 (Tracing the Origins of Chan Learning), in *Lü Cheng Foxue lunzhu xuanji* 呂澂佛學論著選集 (Lü Cheng on Buddhism: Selected Works) 5 vols. (Jinan: Qilu shushe, 1991), vol. 1.

Lü Cheng, "Qixin yu Chan—duiyu *Dasheng qixin lun* laili de tantao" 起信與禪—對於大乘起信論來歷的探討 (Awakening Faith and Chan: An Investigation into the Historical Origins of the *Treatise on Awakening Mahāyāna Faith*), reprinted in *Xiandai Fojiao xueshu congkan* 現代佛教學術叢刊 (Modern Buddhist Scholarship Series), vol. 35, Zhang Mantao 張曼濤, ed. (Taipei: Dasheng wenhua chubanshe, 1978).

Lü Cheng, *Zhongguo Foxue yuanliu lüejiang* 中國佛學源流略講 (Brief Lectures on the Origin and Development of Chinese Buddhism) (Beijing: Zhonghua shuju, rpt. 1979).

Mahāparinirvāṇa-sūtra (*Da banniepan jing* 大般涅槃經; Nirvana Sutra), T12.374.

Makeham, John, ed., *Transforming Consciousness: Yogācāra Thought in Modern China* (New York: Oxford University Press, 2014).

Makransky, John J., *Buddhahood Embodied: Sources of Controversy in India and Tibet* (Albany: State University of New York Press, 1997).

Mile pusa suowen jinglun 彌勒菩薩所問經論 (Treatise on the Sutra of the Questions Asked by Maitreya), trans. Bodhiruci (d. ca. 535), T 26.1525.

Mochizuki Shinkō 望月信亨, *Kōjutsu Daijō kishin ron* 講述大乘起信論 (An Account of the *Treatise on Awakening Mahāyāna Faith*) (Tokyo: Fuzambō, 1938).

Nagao, Gadjin M., *Mādhyamika and Yogācāra: A Study of Mahāyana Philosophies*, trans. and ed. Leslie S. Kawamura (Albany: State University of New York Press, 1991).

Nāgārjuna (344–413) (attrib.), *Mahāprajñāpāramitā-śāstra* (*Dazhidu lun* 大智度論; Treatise on the Great Perfection of Wisdom), trans. Kumārajīva (344–413), T25.1509.

Nattier, Jan, *Once Upon a Future Time: Studies in a Buddhist Prophecy of Decline* (Berkeley, CA: Asian Humanities Press, 1991).

Okamoto Ippei 岡本一平, "Jōyō ji Eon no chosaku no zengo kankei ni kansuru shiron" 淨影寺慧遠の著作の前後関係に関する試論 (On the Chronological Relationship of Writings by Huiyuan of Jingying Monastery), in Geumgang Daehak bulgyo munhwa yeon'guso, comp., *Jiron shisō no keisei to hen'yō*.

Okamoto Ippei, "Jōyō ji Eon ni okeru shoki no shikiron" 淨影寺慧遠における初期の識論 (Early Theories of the Consciousnesses by Huiyuan of Jingying Monastery) in Geumgang Daehak bulgyo munhwa yeon'guso, comp., *Jironshū no kenkyū*.

Ōtake Susumu 大竹晋, "*Daijō kishin ron* no inyō bunken" 大乘起信論の引用文献 (Sources Cited in the *Treatise on Awakening Mahāyāna Faith*), *Tetsugaku shisō ronsō* 哲学・思想論叢 22 (2004): pp. 51–65.

Ōtake Susumu, "Jironshū no busshinsetsu" 地論宗の佛身説 (The Dilun Theory of the Buddha Bodies), in Geumgang Daehak bulgyo munhwa yeon'guso, comp., *Jironshū no kenkyū*.

Ōtake Susumu, "Yugagyōha bunken to *Daijō kishin ron*" 瑜伽行派文献と大乘起信論 (Yogācāra Documents and the *Treatise on Awakening Mahāyāna Faith*), *Tetsugaku shisō ronsō* 哲学・思想論叢 20 (2002): pp. 49–62.

Paul, Diana, *Philosophy of Mind in Sixth Century China: Paramārtha's "Evolution of Consciousness"* (Stanford, CA: Stanford University Press, 1984).

Powers, John, *A Bull of a Man: Images of Masculinity, Sex, and the Body in Indian Buddhism* (Cambridge, MA: Harvard University Press, 2009).

Powers, John, "Yogācāra: Indian Buddhist Origins," in John Makeham, ed., *Transforming Consciousness: Yogācāra Thought in Modern China.*

Pusa yingluo benye jing 菩薩瓔珞本業經 (Sutra on the Primary Activities that are the Necklaces of the Bodhisattvas), trad. attrib. to Zhu Fonian 竺佛念 (fourth century), T24.1485.

Radich, Michael, "Tathāgatagarbha Sūtras," in Jonathan Silk, Oskar von Hinüber, and Vincent Eltschinger, eds., *Brill's Encyclopedia of Buddhism*, Volume One: Literature and Languages (Leiden: Brill, 2015).

Ratnagotravibhāga-mahāyānottaratantra-śāstra (*Foxing fenbie dasheng jiujing yaoyi lun* 佛性分別大乘究竟要義論 or *Baoxing lun* 寶性論; Treatise on the Jewel Nature), trans. Ratnamati (fl. 508), T31.1611.

Saddharmasmṛtyupasthāna-sūtra (*Zhengfa nianchu jing* 正法念處經; Sutra on the Bases of Mindfulness of the True Dharma), trans. Gautama Prajñāruci (fl. 538–543), T17.721.

Saṃdhinirmocana-sūtra (*Jie shenmi jing* 解深密經; Sutra Explaining the Profound and Esoteric Doctrine), trans. Bodhiruci (d. ca. 535), T16.675.

Saptaśatikā-prajñāpāramitā-sūtra (*Wenshushili suoshuo Mohe bore boluomi jing* 文殊師利所說摩訶般若波羅蜜經; The Large Prajñāpāramitā Sutra as Explained by Mañjuśrī), trans. *Mandra 曼陀羅仙 (fl. 503), T8.232.

Sarvadharmapravṛttinirdeśa-sūtra (*Zhufa wuxing jing* 諸法無行經; Sutra Denying Practice in Various Methods), trans. Kumārajīva (344–413), T15.650.

Sinpyeon jejong gyojang chongnok 新編諸宗教藏總錄 (Newly Compiled Comprehensive Record of the Canonical Works of the Various Schools), Uicheon 義天 (1055–1101) ed., T55.2184.

Sukhāvatīvyūha-sūtra (*Wuliang shou jing* 無量壽經; Sutra of Limitless Life), trans. Saṃghavarman (third century CE), T12.360.

Sopa, Geshe, "Śamathavipaśyanāyudanaddha: The Two Leading Principles of Buddhist Meditation," in Minoru Kiyota, ed., *Mahāyāna Buddhist Meditation: Theory and Practice* (Honolulu: University of Hawaii Press, 1978).

Sponberg, Alan, "Meditation in Fa-hsiang Buddhism," in Peter N. Gregory, ed., *Traditions of Meditation in Chinese Buddhism* (Honolulu: University of Hawaii Press, 1986).

Śrīmālādevī-siṃhanāda-sūtra (*Shengman shizi hou yisheng da fangbian fangguang jing* 勝鬘師子吼一乘大方便方廣經; Sutra on the Lion's Roar of Queen Śrīmālā), trans. Guṇabhadra (394–468), T12.353.

Śuddhamati (d.u.), *Pratītyasamutpāda-śāstra* (*Shier yinyuan lun* 十二因緣論; Treatise on the Twelve Links of Dependent Arising), trans. Bodhiruci (d. ca. 535), T32.1651.

Takemura Makio 竹村牧男, *Kaiteiban Daijō kishin ron dokushaku* 改訂版大乘起信論読釈 (Revised Edition of An Interpretative Reading of the *Treatise on Awakening Mahāyāna Faith*) (Tokyo: Sankibō busshorin, 1993).

Tanaka, Kenneth K., *The Dawn of Chinese Pure Land Buddhist Doctrine: Ching-ying Hui-yuan's Commentary on the Visualization Sutra* (Albany: State University of New York Press, 1990).

Tanyan 曇延 (516–588), *Qixin lun yishu* 起信論義疏 (Elucidation of the Meaning of the *Treatise on Awakening* [*Mahāyāna*] *Faith*), X45.755.

Tipo pusa po Lengqie jingzhong waidao xiaosheng sizong lun 提婆菩薩破楞伽經中外道小乘四宗論 (The Critique of Deva Bodhisattva of the Four Tenets of the Non-Buddhists and Hīnayānists in the *Laṅkāvatāra-sūtra*), trans. Bodhiruci (d. ca. 535), T32.1639.

Ui Hakuju 宇井伯寿, and Takasaki Jikido 高崎直道, trans. and eds., *Daijō kishin ron* 大乘起信論 (Treatise on Awakening Mahāyāna Faith) (Tokyo: Iwanami shoten, rpt. 2013).

Upāsakāśīla-sūtra (*Youposai jie jing* 優婆塞戒經; Sutra on the Precepts for Laymen), trans. Dharmakṣema (385–433), T24.1488.

Vasubandhu (fourth century), *Daśabhūmi-vyākhyāna/Daśabhūmika-sūtra-śāstra* (*Shidi jing lun* 十地經論; Commentary on the Discourse on the Ten Stages [of the Bodhisattva Path]), trans. Bodhiruci (d. ca. 535), T26.1522.

Vasubandhu, **Mahāyānasaṃgraha-bhāṣya* (*She dasheng lun shi* 攝大乘論釋; Commentary on the *Compendium of the Great Vehicle*), trans. Paramārtha (499–569), T31.1595.

Vasubandhu (attrib.), *Saddharmapuṇḍarīkopadeśa* (*Miaofa lianhua jing youbotishe* 妙法蓮華經憂波提舍; Commentary on the *Lotus Sutra*), trans. Bodhiruci (d. ca. 535), T26.1519.

Vasubandhu, **Sukhāvatīvyūhōpadeśa* (*Wuliang shou jing youbotishe* 無量壽經優波提舍; Commentary on the Sutras of Limitless Life), trans. Bodhiruci (d. ca. 535), T26.1524.

Vasubandhu, *Viśeṣacintābrahmapariprcchā-śāstra* (*Sheng siwei fantian suowen jinglun* 勝思惟梵天所問經論; Treatise on the Sutra of the Questions of Viśeṣacintābrahma), T26.1532.

Vimalakīrti-nirdeśa-sūtra (*Weimojie suoshuo jing* 維摩詰所說經; The Sutra Preached by Vimalakīrti), trans. Kumārajīva (344–413), T14.475.

Wonhyo 元曉 (617–686), *Gisil lon so* 起信論疏 (Explanation of the *Treatise on Awakening* [*Mahāyāna*] *Faith*), T44.1844.

Wonhyo, *Daeseung gisil lon byeolgi* 大乘起信論別記 (Further Notes on the *Treatise on Awakening Mahāyāna Faith*), T44.1845.

Xuanzang 玄奘 (602–604), *Cheng weishi lun* 成唯識論 (Demonstration of Nothing but Consciousness), T341.1585.

Yang Weizhong 楊維中, *Zhongguo Weishizong tongshi* 中國唯識宗通史 (General History of the Chinese Vijñānavāda School) (Nanjing: Fenghuang chubanshe, 2008), 2 vols.

Yinshun 印順 (1906–2005), *Dasheng qixin lun jiangji* 大乘起信論講記 (Lecture Notes on the *Treatise on Awakening Mahāyāna Faith*) (Beijing: Zhonghua shuju, 2010).

Yoshihide Yoshizu 吉津宜英, "Eon *Daijō kishin ron gisho* no kenkyū" 慧遠『大乘起信論義疏』の研究 (A Study of Huiyuan's *Elucidation of the Meaning of the Treatise on Awakening Mahāyāna Faith*), *Komazawa daigaku Bukkyō gakubu ronshū kenkyū kiyō* 駒沢大学仏教学部研究紀要 34 (1976): pp. 151-173.

Yoshihide Yoshizu, "Hōzō no *Daijō kishin ron gigi* no seiritsu to tenkai" 法蔵の「大乗起信論義記」の成立と展開 (Date and Development of Fazang's *Notes on the Meaning of the Treatise on Awakening Mahāyāna Faith*) in Hirakawa Akira 平川彰, ed., *Nyoraizō to Daijō kishin ron* 如来蔵と大乗起信論 (*Tathāgatagarbha* and the *Treatise on Awakening Mahāyāna Faith*) (Tokyo: Shunjūsha, 1990).

Young, Stuart H., *Conceiving the Indian Buddhist Patriarchs in China* (Honolulu: University of Hawaii Press, 2015).

Zhanran 湛然 (711-782), *Fahua xuanyi shiqian* 法華玄義釋籤 (Comments on the *Profound Meaning of the Lotus Sutra*), T33.1717.

Zhiyi 智顗 (538-597), *Mohe zhiguan* 摩訶止觀 (The Great Calming and Discernment), T46.1911.

Zimmermann, Michael, "The Process of Awakening in Early Texts on Buddha-Nature in India," in Chen-kuo Lin and Michael Radich, eds., *A Distant Mirror: Articulating Indic Ideas in Sixth and Seventh Century Chinese Buddhism* (Hamburg: Hamburg University Press, 2014).

Zürcher, Eric, *The Buddhist Conquest of China: The Spread and Adaption of Buddhism in Early Medieval China* (Leiden: Brill, 1959).

INDEX

For the benefit of digital users, indexed terms that span two pages (e.g., 52–53) may, on occasion, appear on only one of those pages.

and awakening, 77–78n62

and characteristics (*xiang*) and function (*yong*), 66

of suchness (*zhenru; tathatā*), 102–3

of *tathāgatagarbha*, 111–12

jewel (*maṇi*), 117, 125n202

karmic action

coming to fruition of, 134n216

giving rise to, 81

of ignorance, 97n125

illusion of, 88n97

inconceivable, 77, 81–82n76

residual effects of, 118–20, 119n190

suffering through bondage of, 81

karmic consciousness, 84, 106–7

Kashiwagi Hiroo, 37–38

Kumārajīva, translator, 80n69

Laṅkāvatāra-sūtra

on analogy of ocean and wind, 19–21, 21n42

and characteristic of perceptual fields, 80–81n72

in commentary by Huiyuan, 40–41

on discriminating good and bad dharmas, 87

influence of, 16–18, 69n40, 74n55

on kinds of consciousness, 80–81n72

Lesser Vehicle, 2–3n2, 2–3

Liang state, sixth-century China, 8, 9–10

Lokakṣema, translator, 2–3n2

Lü Cheng, 17–18

Magadha, India, 58n9

Mahāyāna, and the meaning of dharma, 66–67n34, 66

See also Great Vehicle (*dasheng; Mahāyāna*)

Mahāyānasaṃgraha-bhāṣya, 37–38

Mahāyānasaṃgraha-śāstra (Asaṅga), 52–53

Mahāyāna teachings

introduction of, 2–3n2

on methods of Buddhist practice, 2–3

revelation of, 26

Makio Takemura, 111n170, 112n171

maṇi (jewel). *See* jewel

māra

definition of, 62n24

manifestation of, 127, 129–31

meditative absorption (*zhi; samādhi*)

attainment of, 23–24, 128–29

and discernment (*guan; vipaśyanā*), 23–24

forms of, 116n181

and suchness, 101n138, 129–31

and perceiving buddhas, 100–1

See also calming

mental consciousness, 83, 86n89

habituation by, 101

as name of the continuously flowing consciousness, 85–86

mentation

five names for, 33–34, 83–84

habituation by, 96

See also seventh consciousness *and* consciousnesses

methods

of Mahāyāna practice, 2

for winning people over (*saṃgraha-vastu*), 99–100n133, 99–100

mind (*xin*)

as arising and ceasing, 71–72n46, 71–72

and awakening, 72–79n65, 72–79, 116–17

characteristics of, 122n196, 122

and consciousnesses, 102–3, 107–8

and continuous flow, 91–92

directly focused mind, 116

kinds of, 116n182, 116, 122n196, 122

nature of, 38n59, 104n144, 104

non-awakened mind, 79–80, 84, 89, 93–94

purified mind, 77–78n62

six types of defiled mind, 33–34

as suchness, 68–69

See also seventh consciousness

moral discipline, 126

names, devising, 81

nescience, 118n186, 118